D0930770

Financing
Your Small Business

Techniques for Planning, Acquiring & Managing Debt

By Art DeThomas

Edited by Vickie Reierson

The Oasis Press® / PSI Research
Grants Pass, Oregon

92

Published by The Oasis Press

Financing Your Small Business:
Techniques for Planning, Acquiring & Managing Debt

Editor: Vickie Reierson
Formatting: Scott Crawford and Jan Olsson
Typographic Assistance: Melody Joachims and Constance C. Dickinson

Please direct any comments, questions, or suggestions regarding this book to
The Oasis Press, Editorial Department, at the address below.

The Oasis Press offers PSI Successful Business Software for sale.
For information, contact:

     PSI Research
     300 North Valley Drive
     Grants Pass, OR 97526
     (503) 479-9464

The Oasis Press is a Registered Trademark of Publishing Services, Inc.,
an Oregon corporation doing business as PSI Research.

Library of Congress Catalog Card Number: 92-50147
ISBN 1-55571-160-X (paperback)

Printed in the United States of America
First edition 10 9 8 7 6 5 4 3 2 1   Revision Code: 92

 Printed on recycled paper when available.

Table of Contents

About the Author   vi

Preface   vii

Section I   Financial Fundamentals

Chapter 1:   Financial Information for Decision Making   **1**

Sources of Financial Information   1

Interpreting Financial Statements with Ratios   10

The Cash Conversion Cycle and Financing Needs   16

Chapter 2:   Financing Fundamentals   **19**

General Characteristics of Financial Methods   19

Debt Financing and the Magic of Financial Leverage   27

Other Factors Influencing the Financing Decision   33

Calculating the Cost of Debt Financing   36

Chapter 3:   Planning Your Financing Mix   **45**

Factors Influencing Your Financing Mix   45

Tools for Estimating Financial Risk   48

Cash-Flow Analysis   54

A Final Word on Risk   57

Chapter 4:   Planning Your Firm's Financing Needs   **59**

Planning Short-Term Financing Needs   59

Planning Long-Term Financing Needs   72

A Bonus from the Financial Planning Process   78

About the Author

Arthur R. DeThomas

Dr. Arthur R. DeThomas currently serves as professor of finance at Valdosta State College's School of Business Administration in Valdosta, Georgia, where he brings more than 20 years of teaching and business experience to his students. He is also a business consultant specializing in small business finance, and he has worked with the U.S. Small Business Administration, the Georgia Small Business Development Center, and many small business clients over the past 15 years. His numerous management training and business workshops specialize in small business issues and topics, and he serves on the editorial review boards of several publications, including *Entrepreneurship: Theory and Practice* and *Journal of Economics and Finance*.

Dr. DeThomas is a member of the Financial Management Association and the Southern Academy of Economics and Finance. His educational background includes a Bachelors degree from Indiana University, a Masters of Business Administration from the University of Arizona, and a Ph.D. from Mississippi State University. He has published more than 30 articles and publications, including *Financial Management Techniques for Small Business*, which is another helpful guide for any entrepreneur. Dr. DeThomas has also co-developed a financial analysis and planning software program that is designed for and is a companion to *Financial Management Techniques for Small Business*. This sophisticated software program is extremely user-friendly, and anyone with a limited financial background will find it easy-to-use and very helpful in generating financial statements. Sold under the product name, FAST, this powerful software program is available through PSI Research/The Oasis Press.

Preface

Operating a small business can provide you with numerous tangible and intangible benefits. For instance, the profits created by your business flow directly into your pocket, and because you are the decision maker, those profits can be used in whatever manner you deem appropriate. Of equal importance is your ability to make and implement decisions quickly without the need for approval from other administrative levels. Possibly the most important benefit of all, however, is the personal satisfaction you gain from your individual effort and accomplishment.

Unfortunately, there is a down side. Small size often means limited opportunities for meeting your firm's financing needs. In the eyes of many creditors and equity investors, providing financing to small businesses entails too much risk. All too often, small businesses have narrow product lines, restricted markets, insufficient resources, and limited capacity to withstand adversity. Given these shortcomings, ownership capital is generally limited to the personal investment of the firm's principals and the funds generated by operations. The opportunity to sell common stock outside the business or attract a new investing partner is many times virtually nonexistent. Faced with these realities, debt financing is your only practical option for additional funding.

Thus, while *Financing Your Small Business* discusses various available financing methods for your small business, the book's main emphasis is mostly on debt financing. You will see that debt can be both an invaluable ally and a formidable enemy. Like working with a sharp, two-edged sword, it can cut for you as well as against you.

For example, debt financing can provide the funds needed to conduct your firm's operations, to meet its growing needs, and to boost the rate of return on the owner's invested capital; however, your possible failure to accurately assess your firm's capacity for using debt can also spell financial disaster. Along with its benefits, debt financing also creates an unavoidable risk — that is, creditors have prior, contractual claims on your firm's cash flows, profits, and assets. Failure to meet the agreed interest and principal payments allows creditors to sue for breach of contract. This can mean bankruptcy and the loss of the business.

To acquire and use debt successfully requires that you know how to identify your firm's needs, seek appropriate sources and types of financing, and prepare and present an effective financing proposal. What's more, to gain the full benefits from debt financing, while at the same time minimizing its risk, you must carefully apply sound financial management principles. Meeting these objectives is the purpose of this book, which offers a concise guide to evaluating, acquiring, and managing debt financing for the business layperson. In doing so, this book dispels some of the most common and potentially destructive myths surrounding debt financing. Some of these myths include:

Common Financing Myths

- Lenders are lined up and eager to provide money to small businesses.
- The U.S. Small Business Administration has cheap, readily available financing for small firms.
- Banks are willing sources of financing for start-up businesses.
- Loans are obtained by talking the lender out of the funds.
- When it comes to seeking money, the company speaks for itself.
- A bank, is a bank, is a bank, and all banks are cold, impersonal institutions.
- Banks, especially large ones, do not need and really do not want the business of a small firm.

To replace these myths with information on practical, effective financial skills, *Financing Your Small Business* is divided into three sections. Combined, these sections take you through the initial decision-making process; show you how to acquire the right type of debt financing for your business; and explain what you can do if your business experiences rapid growth.

Financial Fundamentals

Section I, Financial Fundamentals, contains the background information you need to analyze, evaluate, and plan for your firm's financing needs. This section focuses on:

- Learning the sources of financial information;
- Using financial information in the financing decision process;
- Understanding the nature and characteristics of debt financing;
- Determining the appropriate amount of debt for your firm; and
- Planning for your firm's short- and long-term financing needs.

Section II, Acquiring Debt Financing, takes you a step further by examining the various types and sources of debt financing available to a small business; explaining a banker's perspective and your banking relationship; and discussing how to prepare a business plan and financing proposal.

Acquiring Debt Financing

Section III, Financing for the Rapidly Growing Firm, focuses on financing alternatives for those fortunate small businesses with substantial growth potential. This section contains a chapter on venture capital financing and another on going public with a common stock issue.

Financing for the Rapidly Growing Firm

You do not have to be a financial wizard to understand the material in this book. Once some of the mysteries surrounding financial management are stripped away, you will easily grasp the principles and master the techniques.

The various financing topics discussed in *Financing Your Small Business* are built on the fundamental principles of financial management; however, planning for and acquiring financing are only parts of a broader system of small firm financial management. All too often, small business managers focus only on acquiring funds and ignore other equally important aspects of finance, such as financial management. This is a costly mistake. The absence of elementary financial management skills is a major reason for the high failure rate among small businesses. Hopefully, as you become comfortable with the financial principles discussed in this book, you will expand your investigation into debt financing and financial management. If you would like further details on financial sources of information and related financing fundamentals, you may wish to obtain the book, *Financial Management Techniques for Small Business*, a related resource published by PSI Research/The Oasis Press.

A Word for the Future

Financial Fundamentals

Chapter 1:
Financial Information for Decision Making

Chapter 2:
Financing Fundamentals

Chapter 3:
Planning Your Financing Mix

Chapter 4:
Planning Your Firm's Financing Needs

Chapter 1

Financial Information for Decision Making

This book's primary goal is to provide you with the information necessary to successfully plan for, obtain, and manage the financing needed to support your firm's operation. To accomplish this, one of the first financial fundamentals you will need to know is what information to have and evaluate. Financial information is the raw material of decision making and understanding this information is a prerequisite to sound debt management.

Your firm's financial statements — the balance sheet, income statement, and cash-flow statement — are an important source of financial information. These statements serve a number of uses, such as measuring the profits and cash flows earned by the business, identifying potential problem areas, or securing a bank loan; therefore, as a small business manager, you should be familiar with the essentials of these statements.

Sources of Financial Information

The balance sheet is one of three basic financial statements that summarize a firm's business transactions during a given accounting period. When interpreted properly, this statement offers an overview of a firm's sources and amounts of financing and how these funds have been used. This perspective of a business is important for many business decisions, including those associated with debt financing.

The Balance Sheet

To learn what information this statement provides, take a close look at Table 1.1, which reflects the 19X1 and 19X2 balance sheets for The Ideal Leverage Company, a hypothetical sales and service business. The business has been incorporated and is owned by a small group of stockholders all of which are actively involved in management.

Assets

The first set of figures shown on the balance sheet reflect the accountant's valuation of the assets or physical resources owned and used by the business. Note that they are separated into two major categories:

- Current assets, consisting primarily of cash, accounts receivable, and inventory; and
- Fixed assets, consisting of land, building, equipment, and vehicles.

Current assets, hopefully liquid items, are expected to be converted into cash within what is referred to as the normal cash cycle or working capital cycle. For accounting purposes, this cycle is arbitrarily defined as one year. Since the current assets are assumed to be relatively short-term items, they represent that portion of the firm's financing that has been invested in or committed to short-term uses. In Ideal's case, this investment totals $200,000 in 19X1 and $250,000 in 19X2.

The fixed asset section of the balance sheet contains a listing of the long-term or more permanent assets used in the business. As shown on Ideal's balance sheet, these include investments by the business in such resources as land, buildings, equipment, and vehicles. This group of investments, which for Ideal totals $140,000 in 19X1 and $150,000 in 19X2, have these common characteristics:

- Each has been purchased for use in the business as opposed to intended conversion into cash. For example, a building is purchased to house the firm's operations, and not for resale.
- With the exception of land, the original cost of these investments is being gradually written off or expensed as a cost of doing business each period. This write-off appears on the firm's income statement as depreciation expense.
- The dollar value of fixed assets shown on the balance sheet is the original or historical cost of the item at the time of purchase. The book value of fixed assets (net asset value) is the original cost of the asset less the total amount of the depreciation expense that has been taken to that date. Total depreciation expense appears under the account title, accumulated depreciation.

Care must be exercised when evaluating fixed asset amounts shown on the balance sheet. The book value figure does not represent either the current market value of the asset, its replacement cost or value, or the price for which it could be sold (liquidation value). Book value means nothing more than original cost less accumulated depreciation.

Table 1.1

THE IDEAL LEVERAGE COMPANY

Annual Balance Sheets

For the Periods Ending December 31, 19X1 and 19X2

ASSETS	19X1	19X2
Current Assets		
Cash	$ 20,000	$ 10,000
Accounts Receivable	80,000	110,000
Inventory	100,000	130,000
Total Current Assets	$200,000	$250,000
Fixed Assets		
Land & Building	$120,000	$120,000
Equipment & Vehicles	45,000	60,000
Less Accumulated Depreciation	(25,000)	(30,000)
Total Net Fixed Assets	$140,000	$150,000
TOTAL ASSETS	$340,000	$400,000
LIABILITIES & OWNER'S EQUITY		
Current Liabilities		
Notes Payable	$ 30,000	$ 40,000
Accounts Payable	80,000	110,000
Accrued Expenses	10,000	10,000
Total Current Liabilities	$120,000	$160,000
Long-Term Liabilities		
Mortgage Payable	75,000	70,000
Total Long-Term Liabilities	$ 75,000	$ 70,000
TOTAL LIABILITIES	$195,000	$230,000
Owner's Equity		
Capital Stock	$ 50,000	$ 50,000
Retained Earnings	95,000	120,000
Total Owner's Equity	$145,000	$170,000
TOTAL LIABILITIES & OWNER'S EQUITY	$340,000	$400,000

Liabilities

While the various assets shown on the balance sheet indicate how funds have been invested by Ideal's management, the liabilities and owner's equity amounts reveal the sources of these funds. The total liability figure represents the portion of the firm's financing provided by its various creditors. Current liabilities, which total $120,000 in 19X1 and $160,000 in 19X2, reflect obligations that would normally be paid within one year. These consist of:

- **Notes payable.** Notes payable represent short-term borrowings from financial institutions, such as a bank or commercial finance company. The note itself evidences a legally binding, contractual financial obligation.
- **Accounts payable.** Accounts payable represent the amount owed for inventory purchased on credit from the firm's trade suppliers. In finance, accounts payable are often referred to as trade credit.
- **Accrued expenses.** Accrued expenses are wage and tax amounts owed to employees and taxing authorities that were not paid at the close of that accounting period.

Long-term liabilities are debt obligations that will mature or come due beyond the one-year period. They consist of such items as term loans, which are installment-type loans ranging in maturity from 2 to 10 years or, as in Ideal's case, a mortgage obligation for financing on its land and building. The total liability figure, $195,000 in 19X1 and $230,000 in 19X2, is the sum of current and long-term liabilities.

Owner's Equity

The owner's equity section of the balance sheet reveals the amount invested by the owner(s) of the business, and the amount of earnings from past accounting periods that have not been withdrawn or paid out in the form of dividends. For an incorporated business such as Ideal, the owner's paid-in-capital is represented as the par or stated value of the outstanding shares of common stock. Past earnings that have been retained or plowed back into the business — not withdrawn or paid as dividends — are shown in the account as retained earnings.

It is important to note that the total liabilities and equity figure in a given year, $340,000 in 19X1 and $400,000 in 19X2, equals the total asset figure in that year. This is correct. The balance sheet provides a picture of how funds have been used in the business (invested in assets), and the liability and equity sources that have provided those funds. Logically, the total amount of funds used in a given time period must equal the total amount that was available.

The Income Statement

The income statement is a summary of the sales revenues earned in a given period and the expenses that were incurred in earning that revenue. The net sales revenue figures of $444,000 in 19X1 and $500,000 in 19X2 shown on Table 1.2 represent the cash and credit sales that have been generated by selling Ideal's products and rendering service to its customers.

The percent of sales figures shown beside the dollar values on the statement provide important information on profit margins and cost ratios.

The expenses incurred in normal operations of the business appear on the income statement as cost of sales and operating expenses. Cost of sales, $275,000 in 19X1 and $300,000 in 19X2, are those expenses that are directly related to generating sales revenue. For Ideal, they include the cost of product sold (finished goods inventory) and the cost of any inventory used in rendering service. If Ideal were a manufacturing firm, cost of sales would reflect the cost of purchased raw materials and the direct and overhead costs associated with converting the raw materials into finished goods. From the percent of sales column, you can see that Ideal maintained gross profit margins of 38.1% ($169,000 divided by $444,000 multiplied by 100) in 19X1 and 40% ($200,000 divided by $500,000 multiplied by 100) in 19X2. The gross profit margin or percentage is a critical figure for a retailing firm such as Ideal. It is the principal indicator of the firm's ability to maintain its markup over cost, which is the markup attached to the cost of goods to arrive at the selling price.

Operating expenses — $114,000 in 19X1 and $122,000 in 19X2 on Table 1.2 — represent the expenses associated with conducting the selling and administrative activities that are normal to a business. The difference between the dollar amounts of gross profit and total operating expense is net operating income. The net operating income figure is another important indicator of financial performance because it reveals the amount of profit a firm is able to generate from normal operations. That is, sales revenue less the cost associated with selling and operating the business. The net operating income margin or percentage, 12.4% in 19X1 and 15.6% in 19X2, indicates the profitability of operations relative to sales. The larger this percentage (margin), the more profit remaining from normal operations after the costs of operations have been deducted from each sales dollar.

On Table 1.2, the interest expense figure shown below net operating income represents the interest paid on the firm's indebtedness. For an incorporated business such as Ideal, the subsequent net taxable income figure is the basis for the firm's tax liability. Since Ideal is in the corporate tax bracket of 34%, its income tax liability figure is calculated as .34 times net taxable income.

The remaining net income figure, $34,000 in 19X1 and $50,000 in 19X2, is the residual amount that has been earned on behalf of the firm's ownership. In accounting terms, net income is the amount which can either be plowed back into the business (retained earnings) or paid out in dividends (owner's withdrawals). The net income percentage, 7.7% in 19X1 and 10% in 19X2, reveals the percentage of each sales dollar that remains after all expenses and taxes have been paid. It is also an important indicator of financial performance. All other things being equal, the larger the net income margin, the more profitable the business.

Table 1.2

THE IDEAL LEVERAGE COMPANY

Annual Income Statements

For the Periods Ending December 31, 19X1 and 19X2

	19X1		19X2	
	Dollars	% of Sales	Dollars	% of Sales
Net Sales	$444,000	100.0%	$500,000	100.0%
Cost of Sales	275,000	61.9	300,000	60.0
Gross Profit	$169,000	38.1%	$200,000	40.0%
Operating Expenses:				
Wages & Salaries	$ 63,000	14.2%	$ 69,000	13.8%
Payroll Taxes	7,000	16.0	8,000	1.6
Lease Payments	8,000	1.8	8,000	1.6
Utilities	4,000	0.9	5,000	1.0
Insurance	9,000	2.0	9,000	1.8
Selling & Advertising	5,000	1.1	5,000	1.0
Maintenance & Repairs	6,000	1.4	6,000	1.2
Supplies Expense	4,000	0.9	4,000	0.8
Accounting & Legal	3,000	0.7	3,000	0.6
Depreciation	5,000	1.1	5,000	1.0
Total Operating Expenses	$114,000	25.7%	$122,000	24.4%
Net Operating Income	$ 55,000	12.4	$ 78,000	15.6
Less: Interest Expense	3,000	0.7	2,000	0.4
Net Taxable Income	$ 52,000	11.7%	$ 76,000	15.2%
Less: Income Taxes	18,000	4.0	26,000	5.2
Net Income	$ 34,000	7.7%	$ 50,000	10.0%

Schedule of 19X2 Retained Earnings

Retained Earnings – 19X1	$ 95,000
Plus: Net Income – 19X2	50,000
Minus: Dividends Paid – 19X2	(25,000)
Retained Earnings – 19X2	$120,000

To depict how the 19X2 retained earnings figure of $120,000 on Table 1.1 was derived, a schedule of 19X2 retaining earning is included on the income statements, Table 1.2. This schedule calculates the retained earnings for 19X2 by taking the retained earnings for 19X1 ($95,000) from Table 1.1 and adding it to the 19X2 net income ($50,000) from Table 1.2. The dividends paid for 19X2 ($25,000), which is taken from Table 1.3, is then subtracted from this total. As seen later in this chapter, dividend payments (owner's withdrawals) represent an important use of cash. When dividends are paid, those dollar amounts are not available for internal financing. The smaller the amount of internal financing available, the larger the amount of external financing that must be raised to meet the firm's needs.

Schedule of Retained Earnings

The balance sheet and income statement provide some, but not all, of the information you need for planning and decision making. While net profit is a good long-term indicator of financial performance, it is the cash generated by a firm's normal operations that determines its ability to meet obligations and conduct business. In short, unless a business is able to consistently generate a satisfactory level of cash flow from operations, it will not be in business to earn a profit.

The Cash-Flow Statement

The cash-flow statement measures the cash impact of a firm's operating, investing, and financing activities over a given time period. This statement effectively combines balance sheet and income statement data to provide a summary of the sources of cash available to a business and how this cash was used. These variables are by far the most important indicators of a firm's financial health, and a close look at Ideal's 19X2 cash-flow statement on page 8 illustrates this point.

The first and most important section of the cash-flow statement is cash flow from operations (CFFO). Through time, cash flow from operations is the primary determinant of a firm's ability to maintain normal operations, invest in new assets, grow, and obtain outside financing. As shown on Table 1.3, Ideal's normal operating activities during 19X2 produced a positive cash flow of $25,000. It is useful to understand how the various factors that constitute CFFO influence the net result. These factors represent the reasons why cash was either provided or drained by a firm's day-to-day activities. The determination of cash flow from operations starts with the net income figure from the income statement. Recall that net income is what remains after cost of sales, operating expenses, and taxes have been deducted from the volume of sales revenue generated during a given period. Since the purpose of the cash-flow statement is to measure the cash from operations rather than profit from operations, the net income figure is adjusted for any expenses that were deducted from sales revenue that do not use cash, such as depreciation expense. The remaining calculations reflect changes in those items directly related to operations that either trap or release cash.

Cash Flow from Operations

Table 1.3

THE IDEAL LEVERAGE COMPANY

Cash-Flow Statement

For the Period Ending December 31, 19X2

Cash Flow from Operations:

Net Income	$ 50,000
Plus: Depreciation	5,000
Minus: Increase in Accounts Receivables	(30,000)
Minus: Increase in Inventory	(30,000)
Plus: Increase in Accounts Payable	30,000
Plus: Change in Accrued Expenses	0
Cash Flow from Operations	$ 25,000

Cash Flow from Investing Activities:

Minus: Increase in Fixed Assets	(15,000)
Cash Flow from Investing Activities	$(15,000)

Cash Flow from Financing Activities:

Plus: Increase in Notes Payable	10,000
Minus: Decrease in Mortgage Payable	(5,000)
Minus: Dividends Paid	(25,000)
Cash Flow from Financing Activities	$(20,000)
Net Cash Flow	$(10,000)

Reconciliation:

Change in Cash Account 19X1 to 19X2	$(10,000)
Net Cash Flow	(10,000)
Difference	$0

The first of these expenses on Ideal's cash-flow statement is the $30,000 increase in accounts receivable. As shown on its balance sheets, Ideal's accounts receivable increased by this amount between 19X1 and 19X2 ($110,000 minus $80,000). This increase represents additional dollars of credit sales that were not collected and a sizable drain on CFFO. In effect, cash was used to finance the activities required to produce sales, but as yet this cash has not been recouped. Since these dollars are literally tied up in uncollected accounts, they cannot be used to meet other needs of the firm. On the other hand, had accounts receivable declined between the two statement dates, the decrease would have produced CFFO.

Table 1.1's $30,000 increase in inventory between 19X1 and 19X2 ($130,000 minus $100,000) also caused a drain on CFFO. The build up represents additional dollars that were invested in inventory but not recaptured through additional sales. Conversely, the increase in accounts payable of $30,000 between 19X1 and 19X2 ($110,000 minus $80,000) relieved some of the strain on CFFO caused by the expansion of receivables and inventory. To the extent that Ideal was able to obtain credit from its suppliers (an accounts payable), the outflow of cash for payment of inventory purchases was delayed. This delay represents an important source of financing for most small businesses.

As suggested by Ideal's statements, monitoring the behavior of accounts receivable, inventory, and accounts payable is an important activity. Needless build up in these assets because of poor credit and collection policy or sloppy inventory controls have led to the demise of many small businesses.

Cash Flow from Investing and Financing Activities

The investment and financing portions of a cash-flow statement provide information on changes that occurred in a firm's nonoperating cash activities between accounting periods. For Ideal, changes occurred in fixed assets, notes payable, long-term liabilities, and equity items. Table 1.3's $15,000 increase in fixed assets between 19X1 and 19X2 ($60,000 minus $45,000) resulted from an investment in additional fixed assets. This purchase used cash and is treated as an outflow of funds on the statement. The financing section of the statement indicates that Ideal's management raised $10,000 of short-term financing in the form of notes payable. This cash inflow was more than offset by the payments made to reduce the balance on the long-term mortgage loan by $5,000 and to pay $25,000 in dividends. The net effect of these financing activities is a $20,000 cash outflow.

Net Cash Flow

The net result of combining the $25,000 of cash inflow from operations, the $15,000 outflow caused by Ideal's investment in new fixed assets, and the $20,000 outflow from financing activities is the net cash outflow of $10,000. Net cash flow is simply a summary of the impact of all of the firm's transactions on its cash account during the period. If the cash-flow statement is prepared properly, the net cash flow figure will be equal to the change in the cash account between the two balance sheet dates. For example, from Ideal's balance sheets for 19X1 and 19X2 — Table 1.1 — cash decreased by $10,000, which is equal to the net cash flow figure of $10,000 for 19X2 on Table 1.3. The total sources of financing for the period, $25,000 from operations and $10,000 drawn from the cash account, must equal total uses of financing for the period, the negative $15,000 invested in fixed assets and the negative $20,000 from financing and dividend activities.

Table 1.4			
Summary			
Sources of Cash			
From Operations	$25,000	Fixed Asset Purchases	$(15,000)
Reduction in		Debt Reduction and	
Cash Account	$10,000	Dividend Payment	(20,000)
Total Sources (Uses)	$35,000		$(35,000)

Interpreting Financial Statements with Ratios

Because financial statements reflect dollar amounts, much of the important information for planning and decision making is hidden. In fact, without some method for making comparisons between these various dollar amounts, financial statements are confusing even to the most gifted financial analyst. Fortunately, there is a simple financial technique that eliminates this confusion and makes financial statement data useful for planning and decision making. This tool is known as ratio analysis.

Ratio analysis is the process of comparing one selected financial statement value to another. This is accomplished by making a simple fraction of the items being considered. The fraction may contain a balance sheet or income statement value in the numerator, and another balance sheet or income statement value in the denominator. The result produced by dividing numerator by denominator is a meaningful percentage or index number.

For example, the gross profit figures of $169,000 in 19X1 and $200,000 in 19X2 from Ideal's income statement, Table 1.1 on page 3, have little meaning when viewed as absolute dollar amounts. When these figures are converted, however, to simple financial ratios by dividing them by sales — this was done to produce the percent of sales values on Ideal's income statement — the resulting gross profit margins of 38.1% and

40% become useful information. These values are easily compared to some meaningful standard such as a historical trend of gross profit figures for Ideal or the average gross profit margin figures for other businesses in the retail industry.

While a large number of descriptive ratios can be calculated from a given set of financial statements, only a few are needed to provide the information necessary for sound debt management. To learn how easy it is to calculate and interpret these key measures, study the explanations following Table 1.5, which uses data from Ideal's financial statements for 19X1 and 19X2.

Selected Ratio Results

Table 1.5

THE IDEAL LEVERAGE COMPANY
Selected Ratio Results
For 19X1 and 19X2

Ratio	19X1	19X2
Average Collection Period	66 days	80 days
Inventory Turnover	2.75 times	2.3 times
Average Payment Period	35 days	42 days
Debt to Total Capital	57.4%	57.5%
Financial Burden Coverage	N/A	2.5 times
Return on Investment	16.2%	19.5%
Return on Owner's Equity	23.4%	29.4%

The average collection period (ACP) ratio, which is sometimes referred to as the average days credit sales outstanding, measures the average number of days that credit sales remain on the books as uncollected receivables. It is a useful tool for indicating the extent to which you are controlling credit and collections. The ratio is calculated by multiplying the ending accounts receivable figure from the balance sheet by 365 and then dividing the result by the net sales from the income statement.

Average Collection Period Ratio

$$\text{Average Collection Period (in days)} = \frac{\text{Accounts Receivable} \times 365}{\text{Net Sales}}$$

Table 1.5 shows the ACP for Ideal was 66 days in 19X1 ($80,000 multiplied by 365 divided by $444,000) and 80 days in 19X2, ($110,000 multiplied by 365 divided by $500,000). Given Ideal's credit terms of net 45 days, these results indicate an existing collection problem that appears to be growing worse.

In general, the lower the ACP or number of days, the shorter the time period scarce cash is locked into receivables. Conversely, a rising trend of ACP values is a clear warning signal of eventual liquidity problems. ACP values that exceed a firm's normal credit terms reflect poor credit and financial management. For example, if your business extends credit terms of 30 days but has an ACP of 50 days, then financing must be arranged for both the normal credit period of 30 days and the collection lag of 20 days. This results in unnecessary financing cost, and needlessly uses a portion of your firm's valuable debt capacity.

Inventory Turnover Ratio

The inventory turnover ratio measures the average number of times per period that the dollars invested in inventory are converted into sales. This ratio indicates how well you are controlling your investment in inventory. The ratio is calculated as cost of sales from the income statement divided by ending inventory from the balance sheet.

$$\text{Inventory Turnover} = \frac{\text{Cost of Sales}}{\text{Ending Inventory}}$$

The inventory turnover rate for Ideal on Table 1.5 was 2.75 times per year in 19X1 ($275,000 divided by $100,000), and 2.3 times per year in 19X2 ($300,000 divided by $110,000). These annual turnover rates can be converted to days by dividing the turnover figure into 365. For Ideal, the turnover rates translate to 133 days in 19X1 (365 divided by 2.75) and 159 days in 19X2 (365 divided by 2.3). The days of inventory values indicate the length of time an item is in inventory before it is liquidated through sales.

All other things being equal, the higher the annual inventory turnover rate, or the lower the number of days of inventory:

- The more liquid a business since dollars of inventory are recaptured more rapidly;
- The more profitable a firm since less dollars on average are invested in assets; and
- The lower the amount of outside financing required since average inventory balances are lower.

The benefits gained from rapid inventory turnover become readily apparent if inventory is thought of as dollars tied up in working capital. Each time a dollar invested in inventory is sold, one step in a firm's normal cash cycle or working capital cycle is completed. This cycle is nothing more than the length of time required to move from the purchase of inventory — or purchase and production of inventory if a business is a manufacturing business — to sales and from accounts receivable back to cash. When a dollar of invested inventory is returned to cash, it is accompanied by a firm's pennies of profit margin. The more times the cash cycle is completed (the higher the inventory turnover ratio), the larger the amount of cash flow and profit that is returned. Also, since rapid turnover allows a smaller average investment in inventory, less financing is required to support a firm's working capital needs.

The average payment period (APP) ratio is the counterpart to the ACP ratio. The APP ratio measures the average number of days that accounts payable are on the books before payment is made to trade suppliers. If a business is following sound payment practices, the APP should be roughly equivalent to the terms offered by its trade creditors. For example, if your business receives terms of net 30 days, then your APP should be about 30 days.

Average Payment Period Ratio

A rising trend value for the APP means a firm's payment rate has slowed. Late payments suggest poor payment practices, a liquidity problem, or both. Any of these possibilities present a danger signal for creditors. These are signals that the cash-hungry small business cannot afford to send.

The APP is calculated by multiplying accounts receivable by 365 and then dividing the result by the dollar amount of inventory purchases.

$$\text{Average Payment Period} = \frac{\text{Accounts Payable} \times 365}{\text{Purchases}}$$

The dollar amount of purchases are found on the income statement, if the statement reveals the detail accounts that comprise cost of sales. Otherwise, the value for purchases must be obtained from a firm's accounting records. In Ideal's case, the firm's purchases journal indicated inventory purchases totaled $834,000 in 19X1 and $956,000 in 19X2. This resulted in an APP of 35 days in 19X1 ($80,000 multiplied by 365 divided by $834,000) and 42 days in 19X2 ($110,000 multiplied by 365 divided by $956,000). Since Ideal is offered net 30 days terms by its trade creditors, these APP values indicate a lagging payment pattern that Ideal management should investigate. As is true with all retailers, Ideal cannot risk jeopardizing relations with its trade creditors. Trade credit is an important form of financing for most small businesses and to be put on a cash-only status or have the firm's credit rating lowered because of poor payment practices is begging for disaster.

The debt-to-total capital ratio, often referred to as the debt ratio, is calculated by dividing the total liabilities from the balance sheet by either the total liabilities and equity figure or the total asset figure also from the balance sheet.

Debt-to-Total Capital Ratio or Debt Ratio

$$\text{Debt-to-Total Capital} = \frac{\text{Total Debt}}{\text{Total Assets or Total Capital}}$$

The resulting ratio value indicates the percentage of a firm's assets that have been financed by creditors as opposed to that of the owner(s). Large debt ratio values spell too much risk. The higher the proportion of debt financing used (larger debt ratio value), the larger the amount of interest and principal that must be repaid, and the greater the risk that cash will not be available to meet these obligations. This subject of financial risk will receive a great deal of attention throughout the remainder of this book.

The debt ratio for Ideal was 57.4% in 19X1 ($195,000 divided by $340,000 multiplied by 100) and 57.5% in 19X2 ($230,000 divided by $400,000 multiplied by 100). On the surface, these values are not alarmingly high, but they do warrant further investigation.

Financial Burden Coverage Ratio

In financial parlance, fixed contractual obligations, such as the interest and principal payments on debt financing and lease payments, are referred to as financial burden. The financial burden coverage ratio represents mandatory payments that must be met regardless of a firm's level of cash flow or profits. The larger the level of mandatory payments — such as debt financing or leasing — the greater the risk of insolvency.

The amount of operating cash flow available to meet existing financial burden is critical to a firm's ability to meet its obligations to creditors. The larger the amount of cash flow from operations generated by a business relative to the dollars of contractual obligations that must be paid, the greater the likelihood that a firm will remain solvent. Or stated another way, the lower the financial burden relative to cash flow from operations, the lower a firm's financial risk.

The financial burden coverage ratio is calculated as cash flow from operations (CFFO) from the cash-flow statement divided by total financial burden. Financial burden consists of any contractual debt payments you must meet to avoid legal ramifications. For Ideal, this financial burden would also include lease payments.

$$\text{Financial Burden Coverage} = \frac{\text{CFFO}}{\text{Financial Burden}}$$

Lease obligations appear on the income statement under operating expenses and interest expense below net operating income. The principal portion of debt obligations does not appear on the income statement because principal repayment is considered a return of capital not an expense of doing business. This figure must be obtained from a firm's records.

Ideal had total debt payments in 19X2 of $2,000 and lease payments of $8,000. Its financial burden coverage ratio for 19X2 was $2.50 ($25,000 divided by $10,000). This means that Ideal was able to generate $2.50 of CFFO for every dollar of contractual obligations; or, stated alternatively, CFFO could decline by $2.50 before Ideal's ability to meet debt obligations would be in jeopardy. On the surface, this cushion appears to be comfortable, but judgment should be reserved until all debt financing considerations have been examined.

The financial burden coverage ratio for 19X1 is not listed because a cash-flow statement could not be calculated for 19X1 since the 19X0 balance sheet is not available.

The return on investment (ROI) ratio and the return on owner's equity ratio are two important long-term measures of a firm's financial performance. They measure a firm's financial productivity by revealing how efficiently the financing supplied to the business, as well as invested in its assets, has been used. The more efficiently the financing invested in assets is used, the higher the ROI and the larger the amount of sales, cash flow, and profit a business generates per dollar of invested capital.

Return on Investment Ratio

The ROI ratio measures the return a business is able to earn on the total financing or total assets used. This ratio is calculated by dividing the net operating income from the income statement by the total assets (or total liabilities and owner's equity) from the balance sheet.

$$\text{Return on Investment} = \frac{\text{Net Operating Income}}{\text{Total Assets or Total Capital}}$$

Table 1.5 indicates the ROI for Ideal was 16.2% in 19X1 ($55,000 divided by $340,000 multiplied by 100), and 19.5% in 19X2 ($78,000 divided by $400,000 multiplied by 100). In general, small businesses able to generate ROI values in the 20% range or better are performing above average. With this information, you may notice that Ideal is approaching this rough benchmark.

The return on owner's equity (ROE) ratio measures the dollars of net income earned relative to an owner's invested capital and, as such, reflects the efficiency with which an owner's financing has been employed. Generating a satisfactory return is the primary reason why you or any other entrepreneur risk time, effort, and capital. If a firm does not produce a compensatory return for its owner(s), then there is no economic justification for its existence.

Return on Owner's Equity Ratio

The ROE ratio is calculated as net income from the income statement divided by the owner's equity from the balance sheet.

$$\text{Return on Owner's Equity} = \frac{\text{Net Income}}{\text{Owner's Equity}}$$

By referring back to Table 1.5, you can see that Ideal was able to earn a return of 23.4% for its owners in 19X1 ($34,000 divided by $145,000 multiplied by 100) and 29.4% in 19X2 ($50,000 divided by $170,000 multiplied by 100). The next chapter deals with how and why ROE can exceed ROI. It is known as the "magic of favorable financial leverage."

The Cash Conversion Cycle and Financing Needs

The most pressing need for financing in most small businesses is the demands of day-to-day operations. Funds must be available to support inventory and accounts receivable, to meet payroll, and to make timely payment on debt obligations. These ongoing commitments are known as working capital needs, and the financing used to support them is usually referred to as a working capital loan.

In general, the amount of financing necessary to support working capital as well as the time period for which this financing is required are determined by:

- The type of business a firm conducts and the volume of its sales;
- The efficiency with which management conducts operations;
- The credit terms extended to a firm's customers;
- The credit terms extended a business by its trade suppliers; and
- The seasonal influences affecting normal operations.

For example, firms in the retail or wholesale business will have larger inventory requirements and, therefore, larger working capital needs than service businesses. Likewise, firms with products requiring long manufacturing cycles or liberal credit terms will have long working capital cycles and greater working capital needs.

A full service department store is a striking example of the impact that highly seasonal activity has on working capital needs. To accommodate the anticipated Christmas holiday sales bulge, a typical department store makes large inventory purchases during the summer. As holiday sales materialize, accounts receivable swell and because of the increased level of transactions during the period, larger than normal cash balances must be maintained. At the end of the peak period, sales levels decline and the funds invested in working capital are recaptured: inventory is sold down; receivables are collected; excess cash balances are reduced. During the time of the seasonal build up, however, financing is required to support this increased activity. It is management's job to estimate the amount and the time period for which these funds are needed.

Calculating the Cash Conversion Cycle

A rough estimate of a firm's working capital needs can be obtained using an estimate of its average cash expenditures per day and a simple calculation known as the cash conversion cycle (CCC). The CCC is the average length of time required for a business to turnover its inventory — purchase and/or produce and sell inventory — and collect its receivables.

This time period can be estimated using the inventory turnover ratio converted to days and the average collection period (ACP) ratio. For example, assume your business has an inventory turnover rate of 4 times per year. This means that funds are tied up in inventory approximately 91 days (365 divided by 4). Assume further that its average collection period is 45 days. The combined value of 136 days (91 plus 45) represents the length of time cash is committed to working capital and for which financing is needed.

If your business, however, has an established credit relationship with its inventory supplier(s), some of its working capital financing is provided by accounts payable. Remember, if your business can purchase inventory and delay payment, it is using the trade creditor's funds for the period of the credit terms. The value of the average payment period (APP) ratio indicates the number of days for which trade creditors are supplying working capital needs. If the APP for your business is 35 days, then the CCC or working capital cycle that must be financed from sources other than accounts payable is 101 days. This is calculated as:

Cash Conversion Cycle = (Inventory Turnover in Days + ACP) – APP
$$= (365 \div 4) + 45 - 35$$
$$= (91 + 45) - 35$$
$$= 136 - 35$$
$$= 101 \text{ days}$$

Once the CCC calculation is made, all that is needed to generate a rough estimate of the required amount of working capital financing is an estimate of the average amount spent each day to meet cash expenses. Simply stated, working capital needs are a function of the number of days in the cash cycle times the average amount that your firm must spend each day. The logic for this calculation is straightforward: If your business has average operating expenditures of $100 per day and the CCC is 101 days, then roughly $10,100 of financing is required to support this 101-day working capital cycle. This is calculated as:

Required Financing = CCC x Average Cash Expenditures per Day
$$= 101 \text{ days x } \$100 \text{ per day}$$
$$= \$10,100 \text{ of working capital financing}$$

To obtain a working estimate of your firm's average daily cash expenditures (ADE), either one of two simple techniques can be used. First, actual cash payments for the year can be obtained by examination of your firm's cash payments journal or its check register. The total is divided by 365 to obtain the average daily expenditure estimate. Or more simply, total relevant expenses as shown on your firm's income statement can be used as a proxy for cash expenditures. As used here, relevant expenses refer to amounts shown for cost of sales plus operating expenses minus any non-cash expense item, such as the depreciation expense. This amount is then divided by 365 to obtain the ADE estimate.

$$\text{Average Daily Cash Expenditure} = \frac{\text{Cost of Sales + Operating Expenses} - \text{Depreciation}}{365}$$

Chapter 3 discusses the problem of estimating working capital needs; however, before leaving this discussion, one important point should be emphasized, and that is, the CCC calculation is also a useful tool for depicting the effects of changes in the rate of inventory turnover, receivables collection, or the payment pattern of accounts payable on a firm's cash position and financing needs. For example, in the above illustration, if the ACP increases from 45 to 60 days, the CCC increases to 116 days and required financing jumps to $11,600. This is whopping 14.8% increase in the amount that must be borrowed to support operations for the 116-day working capital cycle. The message is clear: Sound debt management begins with sound financial management and planning.

Chapter 2

Financing Fundamentals

A continuous supply of capital is the lifeblood of any business. Whether your intention is to start a new firm, meet seasonal working capital requirements for a going business, replace aging assets, or expand into new markets, adequate financing is essential. Without it, your business is doomed to stagnate or even perish.

Thus, locating and attracting reliable sources of capital is an essential goal for your small firm. Yet, before this formidable task is undertaken, you must learn how to approach those who supply the capital. You must know why and when to seek financing, how much to seek, and how to repay it. To do so requires a clear understanding of the characteristics as well as the advantages and disadvantages of the two basic sources of financing: debt and equity. Debt and equity are the building blocks of financing your small business.

General Characteristics of Financing Methods

Technically, there are two basic sources of funds for your small business: internal and external financing.

Internal financing consists of funds invested by you, the existing owner, and internally generated cash flow from operations. For many small firms, these sources are the primary means of financing the business, be

Internal Sources of Small Firm Financing

it voluntarily or involuntarily. Yet, both forms of internal financing are limited. Your investment is limited by the depth of your pockets, and internally generated cash flow is limited by the size and profitability of your firm's operations.

External Sources of Small Firm Financing

Theoretically, there is no limit to the amount of money that can be raised from sources outside your business. As long as outside investors can be convinced that funds invested in your firm will earn an acceptable rate of return for the risk involved, you should find willing takers. In practice, however, convincing investors of the desirability of financing your small business is a difficult task. Experienced financiers perceive the small business as an extremely risky investment, and either refuse to provide financing or provide it only at a very high cost. Despite this difficulty, external financing is a must for small firms with financing requirements that exceed the limits of internal sources. Success in doing so is more likely if you are capable of identifying and planning your firm's financing needs, finding the right sources for these funds, making an effective presentation of these needs, and efficiently managing available financing.

External financing may be obtained from creditors in the form of debt capital or from equity investors through the sale of additional ownership interests in the business. While both sources are raised outside the business, any similarity between the two stops there. They differ in legal status, maturity, tax considerations, and impact on a firm's financial position.

Debt Capital Characteristics

Debt financing represents the funds provided by creditors under a legally binding, contractual agreement. The contract obligates the borrower (debtor) to repay the money or credit advanced, plus stipulated interest, at some designated future date(s) and to honor all other specified provisions or restrictions. Although the debt agreement gives the creditor a legally enforceable, prior claim on a firm's cash flows and assets, it also limits the creditor's relationship with a firm. Creditors have no voice in the management of the business; they do not share in a firm's earnings beyond the agreed repayments; and their ties to a business are limited to the duration of the debt agreement.

Equity Capital Characteristics

Equity capital represents the ownership interest in the business. In contrast to debt financing, equity claims are residual and are assumed to continue for the life of the business unless otherwise agreed. As residual claimants, the ownership interest in a firm is entitled to all cash flows and asset values remaining after all other claims, including those of creditors, employees, and taxing authorities have been satisfied. In short, ownership interest in a business means taking most of the risk, but also reaping most of the rewards.

External equity financing is raised by selling a portion of a firm's ownership interest to an outsider. If a small business is incorporated, the new ownership interest is represented by a proportionate number of shares of a firm's outstanding common stock. For example, assume the original owner of a business has 100,000 shares of stock but sells 20,000 shares to an outside investor to raise capital. The new owner would have a 20% interest in the company (20,000 shares divided by 80,000 plus 20,000 shares multiplied by 100). This interest entitles the new owner to 20% of the firm's residual cash flows and asset values and to a voice in management equal to the votes represented by 20,000 shares of stock.

If a business is not incorporated, a new equity investment is represented by a partnership interest. A partner shares in the value of a business in proportion to what is agreed upon and specified in the partnership agreement. The partnership interest can take the form of a general partner, which has a voice in management, or a limited partner, which does not.

As will be discussed in chapters 9 and 10, raising external equity capital is difficult, if not impossible, unless a small firm presents an investment opportunity promising exceptional growth. Unfortunately, even when this potential exists, external equity financing can be prohibitively expensive. This means that the financing opportunities for many small businesses are limited in number and, when possible, limited to debt financing.

Legal Status of Debt and Equity Financing

The most distinguishing feature of debt financing relative to equity is mandatory repayment. If contractual debt repayments are not made on time and in the proper amounts, a creditor can take a variety of legally enforceable actions to collect. Depending on the terms of the agreement, a creditor may take claim to some of a firm's assets, prevent salary or dividend payments to the owner, obtain a voice in management, or force a firm out of business through bankruptcy proceedings.

Creditors also have a prior claim on a firm's earnings and assets. Legally, interest payments, which come from a firm's cash flows before taxes, must be paid before owner's withdrawals are made. Failure to pay interest is a breach of contract which allows creditors to enforce their legal rights. There is, however, no legal requirements to pay dividends to the owner (allow withdrawals) of a business.

Creditors' claims also rank ahead of those of the owner in the event operations are voluntarily or involuntarily (bankruptcy) dissolved. If the assets of the business are sold, creditors have prior claim on the proceeds to the extent of the principal and interest owed by the business. For example, assume a business is liquidated and all of the assets are sold for $1 million. If the principal and interest owed to creditors on borrowed funds totaled $1 million or more, the owner(s) would receive nothing from the liquidation.

In return for the reduced risk and increased safety associated with prior claims on income and assets, creditors' payments are limited exclusively to the amount specified in the debt agreement. They do not share in a firm's earnings beyond what is owed to them. Conversely, while there are no legal guarantees associated with equity claims, an owner is entitled to whatever earnings success the business enjoys. All cash flows remaining after the limited claims of creditors are satisfied belong to the owner.

For example, if a firm's income statement shows earnings before interest and taxes of $50,000 and interest expense is $20,000, the owner receives before-tax earnings of $30,000. If interest expense is $60,000, the owner incurs a loss of $10,000 before taxes. Conversely, if earnings before interest and taxes are $500,000, the creditors receive only the agreed amount of interest, but the owner receives $480,000 of before tax income. In the language of finance, the claims of owners and creditors are contrasted in terms of their risk/return tradeoff: creditors receive limited return for limited risk and owners receive larger potential returns for increased risk exposure.

Collateral Requirements

In making loans to small businesses, creditors often require additional security in the form of collateral. The collateral may take the form of a claim on a firm's current or fixed assets or the personal assets of its owner, or both. A pledge of collateral provides creditors with a security interest in the asset(s) and a legal claim (lien) to their title in the event of borrower default. In essence, this means a creditor has the right to repossess and sell the secured asset(s) to satisfy the amount of the owed debt. Collateral requirements, while often a necessary evil for a business, restrict management's discretionary authority over the pledged assets, limit financial flexibility, and increase the risk exposure.

Restrictive Covenants

In addition to collateral requirements, a creditor will often place contractual restrictions on the borrower. These restrictions are designed to maintain the borrower's financial condition and/or to prohibit the borrower from engaging in activities that would increase the likelihood of the creditor's loss on the loan. If the borrower violates a restrictive covenant, the creditor has the right to call for full payment of the loan. Some of the more commonly used covenants include restrictions on:

- **Working capital requirements.** These requirements specify a minimum liquidity position a business must maintain.
- **Salaries and dividends (owner's withdrawals).** These withdrawals limit management's right to increase salaries or make dividend payments without prior lender approval.
- **Additional borrowing.** This type of borrowing places limits on a firm's right to use additional debt financing, including leasing, without prior approval from the lender.
- **Use of assets.** This use limits the right of a firm's management to sell existing fixed assets or acquire additional fixed assets without prior approval from the lender.
- **Financial reporting.** This type of reporting requires the borrower to supply financial statements and other information on the business to the lender on a regular basis. As is the case with collateral requirements, restrictive covenants limit management's discretionary

authority and increase the risk associated with debt financing. Collateral requirements are discussed in Chapter 6.

Maturity Differences Between Debt and Equity Financing

The ownership interest in a business is permanent. Legally, an owner's proportionate claim on a firm is assumed to continue forever unless otherwise specified by contract. For example, a partnership agreement can provide for the termination of a partner's interest, or a preferred stock contract for an incorporated business can provide for retirement of the stock at some specified date. Therefore, with exception of these possibilities, an ownership interest in a business is assumed to continue as long as the business is in existence.

Conversely, a creditor's claim on a firm's income and assets is limited to the time period of the debt contract. Assuming all terms of the agreement are met, the creditor's interest in a business is terminated at maturity. Chapters 5 and 6 discuss the maturity of a debt agreement can be short- or extended-term. Short-term debt is usually defined as obligations that have maturities of one year or less. Extended-term financing involves maturities of intermediate length, usually 1 to 10 years, and long-term duration of beyond 10 years.

Tax Status of Debt and Equity Financing

One important advantage that debt financing provides over equity is the tax deductibility of interest payments. This means that the Internal Revenue Service (IRS) allows the interest portion (not the principal portion) of a loan payment to be deducted from sales revenue on a firm's income statement. Such a deduction lowers a firm's taxable income and, as a result, lowers its tax bill. The effect of this tax savings is to lower the true cost of debt financing and to improve cash flow.

Assume The Ideal Leverage Company, which is in the corporate tax bracket of 34%, has the two abbreviated income statements shown on Table 2.1 on the following page. The first statement reflects the assumption that Ideal uses no debt financing. In this case, there is no interest expense, and there are no loan payments. The other statement reflects the assumption that Ideal has borrowed $100,000 at a 10% interest rate and pays annual interest of $10,000 ($100,000 multiplied by .10). With the exception of interest expense and tax liability, the two statements are identical. They show the same sales revenue, operating expenses, and depreciation expense.

The tax effects of Ideal's interest expense are reflected in the net income before taxes and income tax figures on the two statements. Because of the $10,000 of interest expense shown on Statement 2, Ideal's taxable income is $10,000 lower than that on Statement 1. As a result, the amount of taxes owed where debt financing exists is $17,000 as opposed to the $20,400 that would be due if the interest expense did not exist. The effect of the $10,000 interest charge is to save Ideal $3,400 ($20,400 minus $17,000) in income taxes.

Table 2.1

THE IDEAL LEVERAGE COMPANY
Hypothetical Income Statements

		Statement 1 without Interest Cost	Statement 2 with Interest Cost
Sales Revenue		$200,000	$200,000
Less:	Cost of Sales	60,000	60,000
	Operating Expenses	60,000	60,000
	Depreciation Expense	20,000	20,000
	Interest Expense	0	10,000
Net Income Before Taxes		$ 60,000	$ 50,000
Less:	Income Tax (@ 34%)	20,400	17,000
Net Income		$ 39,600	$ 33,000

In financial terms, interest expense is referred to as a tax shield. A tax shield is simply a tax-deductible expense that produces tax savings. Since any business must pay its taxes in cash, the tax savings from a tax shield results in an important cash flow. In Ideal's case, because of the tax shield, the company saved $3,400 that would have otherwise gone to the Internal Revenue Service (IRS).

Calculating the Tax Shield

The tax savings produced by a tax shield can be quickly calculated by multiplying the amount of the tax shield by a firm's tax rate. Applying this relationship to the illustration below, the $3,400 in tax savings created by the $10,000 of interest expense is calculated as:

Tax Savings = Amount of Tax Shield x Tax Rate
$$= \$10,000 \times .34$$
$$= \$3,400$$

The concept of the tax shield and resulting tax savings applies to any tax-deductible expense. Its impact is most dramatic, however, when viewed in terms of a noncash expense item, such as depreciation. Recall in Chapter 1 that depreciation is an expense which appears on the income statement but does not require a cash outlay. For example, Ideal does not have to write a check in payment of the $20,000 of depreciation expense shown on Table 2.1. This expense is simply an income statement write-off of the past cost of an asset. Since depreciation is a tax-deductible expense, its existence also lowers Ideal's taxable income. For example, without the $20,000 of depreciation expense net income before taxes would be $80,000 ($200,000 minus $60,000 minus $60,000) in Statement 1, and $70,000 ($200,000 minus $60,000 minus $60,000 minus $10,000) in

Statement 2, as opposed to the $60,000 and $50,000 respectively that exists with the depreciation write-off. This reduction also lowers Ideal's tax bill. The tax savings created by the $20,000 of depreciation expense is $6,800. This is calculated as:

Tax Savings = Amount of Tax Shield x Tax Rate
$$= \$20,000 \times .34$$
$$= \$6,800$$

Significant differences exist between the effect of debt and equity financing on a firm's cash flows, its capital structure — the mix of debt and equity financing used — and its ability to service debt.

The most dramatic effect of debt financing on your firm's financial position is the reduction in its discretionary or free cash flow. These cash flows are the funds you have available for the normal replacement of assets, expansion, and for dividend payments (owner's withdrawals). To illustrate this effect, use Ideal's hypothetical income statements on Table 2.1 to include a rough approximation of cash flow from operations (CFFO).

To do this, assume for now that Ideal operates its business on a strict cash basis, and the business does not experience any change in the level of inventory from period to period. Under these extreme hypothetical conditions, Ideal would have no accounts receivable or accounts payable. Also, all sales would be cash sales, and all expenses, except depreciation which is a noncash charge, would be paid in cash. By using the tax liability figures calculated from the first and second income statements on Table 2.1, $20,400 and $17,000, CFFO can be approximated by excluding the noncash depreciation charge from these statements.

Impact of Debt and Equity Financing

Debt Financing and Free Cash Flow

Table 2.2

THE IDEAL LEVERAGE COMPANY
Modified CFFO Statements

	Statement 1 without Interest Cost	Statement 2 with Interest Cost
Sales Revenue	$200,000	$200,000
Less: Cost of Sales	60,000	60,000
Operating Expenses	60,000	60,000
Income Tax	20,400	17,000
Interest Expense	0	10,000
Cash Flow from Operations	$ 59,600	$ 53,000
Less: Debt Principal Paid	2,000	11,000
Discretionary Cash Flow	$ 57,600	$ 42,000

Discretionary cash flow is CFFO minus the principal portion of each loan payment. If the principal portion of existing loan payments is $2,000, and if the principal payment on the $100,000 of additional debt financing is $9,000, Ideal's total loan-principal payment would be $2,000 without the new debt financing and $11,000 ($9,000 plus $2,000) with the new loan. The modified CFFO statements for Ideal are shown on Table 2.2 on the previous page.

The impact of debt repayment on Ideal's liquidity position is reflected in the discretionary or free cash flow figures. The interest and principal payments drastically reduce free cash flow from $57,600 to $42,000. Had Ideal used equity financing to meet its needs, the $11,000 of new interest and principal payments would not exist, and management would have an additional $15,600 of free cash flow at its disposal.

Debt Financing and the Capital Structure

Capital structure refers to the percentages of debt and equity financing used to fund a firm's asset base. These proportions were discussed in Chapter 1 as the debt-to-total capital ratio or debt ratio. The debt ratio is simply the percentage of total financing provided by creditors as opposed to that of the owner(s). As previously indicated, the debt ratio is a measure of the financial risk to which a business is exposed. The higher the percentage of debt financing used, the larger the debt payments that must be made, and the greater the risk that cash flow will not be available to meet debt payments.

While the concept of financial risk and the capital structure is the subject of the next chapter, a brief discussion on potential debt financing and its effect on Ideal's capital structure is worthwhile. Ideal's current debt ratio was calculated in Chapter 1 as 57.5%. (See discussion on pages 13 and 14.)

Debt Ratio = Total Debt ÷ Total Assets (or Total Capital)
= $230,000 ÷ $400,000 x 100
= 57.5%

If Ideal's management raises $100,000 of capital through debt financing, e.g., borrowing the funds, it not only raises the $100,000 of capital, but it also incurs $100,000 of contractual debt obligations. Therefore, Ideal's debt ratio in this circumstance would increase to a disturbing 66%.

Debt Ratio = Total Debt ÷ Total Assets (or Total Capital)
= $330,000 ÷ $500,000 x 100
= 66%

It is apparent that a debt ratio this large is alarming. In fact, Ideal's management would probably have a difficult time convincing a prospective creditor that the firm deserves consideration for such a loan. Recall from the discussion on the debt rates that when debt is added, the business increases its contractual obligations and the risk that these payments cannot be made. Creditors will not simply accept unreasonable financial risk.

If, on the other hand, Ideal has the capability to raise $100,000 of capital through the sale of an additional equity interest in the firm, the debt ratio would decline to 46%, because $100,000 of debt would not be incurred.

Debt Ratio = Total Debt ÷ Total Assets (or Total Capital)
$$= \$230,000 \div \$500,000 \times 100$$
$$= 46\%$$

All other things being equal, most creditors would consider a debt ratio of this size an acceptable level of risk. In general, creditors often use a debt ratio of 50% as a rough percentage of the upper limit for this measure of risk. It is important to note, however, that an acceptable debt ratio depends on the circumstances in which it is measured.

Debt Financing and Burden Coverage

Another ratio often used to measure financial risk is burden coverage. This measure serves as an indicator of a firm's ability to meet all mandatory payments associated with debt financing. These include such contractual obligations as rental, lease, principal, and interest payments. The larger the obligatory payments (financial burden) relative to cash flow from operations, the larger the degree of risk associated with debt financing. Recall that burden coverage is calculated as cash flow from operations divided by financial burden. (See discussion on page 14.)

Debt Financing and the Magic of Financial Leverage

Debt has been defined as a two-edged sword that cuts favorably as well as unfavorably. This means that the use of debt holds the potential for magically boosting the return on owner's equity (ROE) but, at the same time, adds a dangerous element of risk exposure for a business. The power to magnify both potential return and risk is known as financial leverage.

The magnification effects of leverage are caused by the fact that interest expense on any given amount of debt financing is a fixed cost. While a firm's sales and operating income fluctuate, interest costs do not change. So, as long as a business can earn a rate of return on its investment in assets that is greater than the cost of debt, an owner benefits through greater ROE. Unfortunately, if a firm earns a return that is less than the cost of borrowed funds, an owner suffers.

Financial Leverage and the Perplexed Company

Assume that another hypothetical business, the Perplexed Company, is considering three different financing strategies.

- The first consists of financing the firm's $100,000 of assets entirely with owner's capital (equity).
- The second alternative, a more risky combination, consists of one-half debt financing ($50,000) and one-half equity financing ($50,000).

- The third, an extremely risky possibility, consists of three-fourths debt financing ($75,000) and one-fourth equity financing ($25,000).

If either of the debt financing alternatives are used, Perplexed estimates that the funds can be raised at an interest cost of 10%. Under these assumptions, the capital structure choices appear on the simplified balance sheet below.

Table 2.3

PERPLEXED COMPANY
Simplified Balance Sheet
Alternative Capital Structures Choices

	100% Equity	50% Debt	75% Debt
Total Debt	$ 0	$ 50,000	$ 75,000
Total Equity	100,000	50,000	25,000
Total Capital	$100,000	$100,000	$100,000

Assume further that Perplexed, based on its sales forecast and cost projections, estimates the business should earn a net operating income of $20,000. If Perplexed is in the 50% tax bracket — using this unrealistic tax rate simplifies the calculations — the abbreviated income statement for each financing strategy is on Table 2.4.

These simplified income statements provide a great deal of information about the magic of financial leverage. Note first that the firm's operating income, $20,000, is not affected by the type of financing used. Operating

Table 2.4

PERPLEXED COMPANY
Abbreviated Income Statement
Alternative Capital Structures Choices

	100% Equity	50% Debt	75% Debt
Net Operating Income	$20,000	$20,000	$20,000
Interest Expense	0	5,000	7,500
Taxable Income	$20,000	$15,000	$12,500
Income Tax @ 50%	10,000	7,500	6,250
Net Income	$10,000	$ 7,500	$ 6,250
ROE	10%	15%	25%

income is determined by the sales revenue generated and the cost of operating the business. These variables are a function of the economic, market, and competitive factors which influence the business and not by the method with which it is financed.

The amount of interest expense that is charged against operating income is determined by the amount of debt financing used and the interest rate paid. For example, the interest expense of $5,000 under the 50% debt alternative results from using $50,000 of debt financing and an interest rate of 10%.

Interest Expense = Amount of Debt Financing x Interest Rate
$$= \$50,000 \times .10$$
$$= \$5,000$$

Likewise, the $7,500 of interest expense under the 75% debt financing alternative is determined by multiplying the $75,000 of debt financing by the 10% interest rate. Compared to the 100% equity strategy, the interest expense that would be paid if debt financing is used provides a tax savings of $2,500 under the 50% debt alternative ($5,000 multiplied by 50%), and $3,750 under the 75% debt alternative ($7,500 multiplied by 50%). Remember the tax savings provided by a tax shield is calculated by multiplying the amount of the shield by the tax rate.

While net income is lower under the debt alternatives, the return available to the firm's owner is considerably higher. ROE is 10% ($10,000 of net income divided by $100,000 of equity investment) under the 100% equity alternative; 15% ($7,500 divided by $50,000) when 50% debt financing is used; and 25% ($6,250 divided by $25,000) under the 75% debt alternative. The larger the percentage of debt financing used, the larger the owner's return. Thus, while the method of financing used by the business does not affect net operating income, it does impact owner's return, because an owner does not have to invest as many dollars out of his or her pocket to finance the firm's assets. Creditors are carrying some of the burden of financing assets by providing nonownership, fixed-cost financing. This phenomenon of boosting the return available to the firm's owner(s) is referred to as favorable financial leverage. There are two reasons for its existence, and it is important that you understand both.

Components of Favorable Financial Leverage

As illustrated in the Perplexed example, one reason that debt financing can magnify the rate of return on equity is a smaller proportion of invested capital by the owner. When the business uses debt, creditors are financing some portion of the asset base in return for a fixed interest return. For each dollar creditors supply a firm, an owner is able to avoid investing a dollar. The smaller equity base provides the potential for increasing the percentage return for the owner, and as indicated in the example, the larger the percentage of financing supplied by creditors, the greater the potential leverage effect.

Favorable financial leverage is also the result of the difference between the rate of return earned on assets (ROI) and the cost of debt financing. If a business is able to earn an ROI that is greater than the cost of its debt financing, the difference literally flows into an owner's pocket. For example, on Table 2.4, Perplexed is generating an ROI of 20% using the 100% equity alternative ($20,000 of operating income divided by $100,000 of total capital or total assets). The cost of debt financing is, however, only 10%. This difference between what is earned and the cost of financing, 10% (20% minus 10%), flows to the owner and boosts ROE over what would be if only equity capital is used. As the proportion of debt financing increases, the advantage provided by leverage also increases. Note again that ROE under the 75% debt strategy is 25%, 15% under the 50% debt alternative, and 10% with 100% equity financing.

The Magnification Effect of Favorable Financial Leverage

The benefits produced by favorable leverage are magnified when a business is able to increase operating income. When leverage is favorable, a given percentage increase in net operating income will cause a larger percentage increase in ROE. For example, use the abbreviated income statement format to examine the percentage change in ROE when net operating income is increased by 50% from $20,000 to $30,000. Perplexed is still considering the same three financing alternatives for its $100,000 asset base.

Table 2.5

PERPLEXED COMPANY
Abbreviated Income Statements for Alternative Capital Structure Choices
(increased net operating income)

	100% Equity	50% Debt	75% Debt
Net Operating Income	$30,000	$30,000	$30,000
Interest Expense	0	5,000	7,500
Taxable Income	$30,000	$25,000	$22,500
Income Tax @ 50%	15,000	12,500	11,250
Net Income	$15,000	$12,500	$11,250
ROE	15.0%	25.0%	45.0%
% Change in ROE	50.0%	66.7%	80.0%

From these statements, you notice that while net operating income increases by 50% to $30,000, interest expense remains the same. Interest cost is a contractual, fixed expense, and the amount of debt financing being considered has not been changed. As a result, net income and ROE both increase with the increase in net operating income. There are, however, important differences in the rate of increase in ROE.

Under the 100% equity alternative, ROE increases from 10% when net operating income is $20,000 to 15% when operating income is $30,000. This is an increase of 50%; the same percentage increase as that of net operating income. An increase in ROE identical to that in net operating income is correct. If debt financing is not used, there is no leverage or magnification effect. Owner's return benefits only from the increase in net operating income.

This, however, is not the case when debt financing is used. Under the debt alternatives, the percentage increase in ROE is greater than the percentage increase in net operating income. What's more, the larger the amount of debt financing used, the greater the percentage increase in ROE. For example, under the 50% debt alternative, ROE increased by 66.7% (25% minus 15% divided by 15%) when operating net income increased by 50%, and by 80% (45% minus 25% divided by 25%) when 75% debt was used.

The reason behind the magnification of ROE is the inflexibility of interest expense. Interest expense for a given level of debt is a contractual obligation and remains fixed regardless of the fluctuation in net operating income. As a result, the percentage increase in ROE is greater than the percentage increase in net operating income.

Unfortunately, when operating income declines, interest cost still remains a fixed, contractual obligation. When this happens, debt financing results in unfavorable leverage. Unfavorable leverage is as detrimental to the owner's position as favorable leverage is beneficial.

The Down Side of Leverage

Unfavorable financial leverage is exactly the opposite case of favorable leverage. It occurs when a firm earns a rate of return on its asset base or invested capital that is less than the cost of debt financing. When leverage is favorable, the positive differential between what is earned and the cost of debt financing accrues to the owner and boosts ROE. Leverage, however, cuts both ways. If a firm's ROI is less than the interest rate on debt, the owner must, in effect, make up the difference. ROE is penalized. By contractual agreement, creditors must be paid regardless of whether a business is profitable or the owner feels that ROE is adequate.

To illustrate the damaging effect on ROE, assume the same asset base and financing strategies for the Perplexed Company, but include a decline in net operating income sufficient to cause an ROI below 10%. At any ROI less than 10%, Perplexed is earning less on invested capital than the 10% cost of debt financing. For example, assume that Perplexed suffers a sales decline that reduces net operating income to $8,000. This is a percentage decrease of 73.3% from the previous level of $30,000 ($30,000 minus $8,000 divided by $30,000). The abbreviated income statements for the three financing alternatives now would appear as shown in Table 2.6 on the following page.

At an operating income level of $8,000, Perplexed is generating an ROI of only 8% ($8,000 of net operating income divided by $100,000 of assets).

Since this is lower than the 10% cost of debt financing, the owner's position is penalized when debt is used. Notice that ROE is lower under the debt strategies than under the 100% equity alternative. The reason is straightforward: Since creditors have been promised a 10% interest return regardless of the firm's earnings success, the owner must make up the difference between what is earned, 8% in this example, and what is paid to creditors, 10%.

Table 2.6

PERPLEXED COMPANY
Abbreviated Income Statements for Alternative Capital Structure Choices
(decreased net operating income)

	All Equity	50% Debt	75% Debt
Net Operating Income	$ 8,000	$ 8,000	$8,000
Interest Expense	0	5,000	7,500
Taxable Income	$ 8,000	$ 3,000	$ 500
Income Tax @ 50%	4,000	1,500	250
Net Income	$ 4,000	$ 1,500	$ 250
ROE	4.0%	3.0%	1.0%
% Change in ROE	-73.3%	-80.0%	-97.8%

If the net operating income in this example had dropped below $7,500, the 75% debt alternative would have produced a loss. For example, if net operating income were $6,000, Perplexed would suffer a loss of $1,500 ($6,000 minus $7,500) with 75% debt financing. If operating income were $4,000, the 50% debt alternative would result in a $1,000 loss ($4,000 minus $5,000), and the 75% debt alternative a loss of $3,500 ($4,000 minus $7,500).

The point is clear: Debt financing works well when leverage is favorable, but it is dangerous to a firm's existence when the possibility of unfavorable leverage exists. If the probability is high that net operating income will decline to the point of unfavorable leverage, there is considerable risk in using excessive amounts of debt financing.

It is your job to find the level of debt financing that balances the risk and potential benefits from the use of debt financing. This task is the essence of the financing decision. To help you better understand the factors and concerns in making your financing decision, follow the discussions throughout the remainder of this chapter. Each section explains important areas you should consider in the decision-making process as well as provides insight into some helpful calculations.

Other Factors Influencing the Financing Decision

At the heart of any financing decision is the ever-present threat that something will go wrong and creditors cannot be paid. To improve your chances of making a sound financing decision, you can identify and evaluate the various types of risk to which your business is exposed. Not surprisingly, both creditors and equity investors are also concerned about your firm's risk exposure. Because they have provided financing, both groups have an important stake in the business. Since they can only be compensated if your business is successful, they are effectively exposed to the same risks.

Debt Financing and Risk

Risk can be defined as uncertainty about future events or the possibility that a less than desirable outcome can occur. It is present whenever future events, such as the amount of sales or cash flow your firm will generate, are not completely predictable. The risks you face can be grouped into two categories — business risk and financial risk.

What Is Risk?

Business risk is the underlying uncertainty to which any business firm is exposed, regardless of how it is financed. It consists of the unpredictable fluctuations in sales and operating cash flows that result from changes in the general level of business and economic activity, conditions within a particular market, and the degree of competition. The more sensitive your firm's sales, costs, and prices are to these influences, the greater the degree of business risk and the greater the uncertainty over the ability to generate sales and cash flows that will fully compensate you and your creditors. For example, sales, prices, and cash flows of an automobile dealership are extremely sensitive to such influences as recessions, the general level of disposal income, rising interest rates, the price of gasoline, and competition. Unfavorable movements in any or all of these factors can adversely effect a firm's sales and cash flow. On the other hand, a public utility which is a state regulated monopoly is far less affected by external factors such as these.

Business Risk

The degree of business risk faced by your small firm, while substantial, is increased by the absence of product and market diversification and by limited financial resources. Large firms often have multiple product lines which are sold in a wide array of markets. This diversification offers a measure of protection against total devastation when a particular product or market is unfavorably effected. Moreover, large firms tend to have the financial resources to weather the storm when such difficulties are encountered.

Conversely, small businesses tend to have all of their eggs in one basket. They typically operate with a limited product line in narrowly defined markets. The absence of diversification makes them vulnerable to even small economic disturbances, and limited financial resources reduce the ability to withstand such adversity.

Financial Risk

Additional risk, known as financial risk, is created when debt financing is used by your firm. The legal obligation to repay creditors is not offset by a guarantee that sufficient cash flow will be available to make payment. Uncertain cash flows coupled with contractual payments increases your firm's risk exposure and the possibility of financial disaster. As was indicated above, the greater the degree of business risk, the greater the fluctuation in your firm's sales and cash flow and the greater the dangers of using excessive debt financing.

If you are involved in a financing decision, two important points on risk should be kept in mind.

First, there is no financial risk associated with equity financing because there are no mandatory payments associated with its use. In fact, the use of equity financing reduces some of the impact of business risk because there are no compulsory financial payments that threaten insolvency.

Second, firms with large amounts of debt are exposed to considerable financial risk, and it is extremely hazardous to heap this additional risk on a high degree of business risk. Substantial business risk means large fluctuations in sales and cash flow, and a greater likelihood that fixed financial obligations cannot be paid. As will be discussed in the next chapter, financial risk is minimized by using a level of debt financing that your business can reasonably expect to service.

Financing Availability

Because of risk, available sources of financing for your firm are often limited. Unless there is the potential for exceptional sales and earnings growth, the opportunity for equity financing is limited to internally generated cash flow, additional investment from existing owners, or the sale of a partnership interest. This reality often leaves debt capital financing as the only possible source of working capital and extended-term financing for many small businesses.

Financing Cost

The cost of debt financing is fixed and, when compared to the cost of raising new equity, usually a much cheaper form of financing. When new equity financing is used, the new owners have open-end participation in all profits, and the cost of attracting this type investor to a small business is often too high. On the other hand, the cost of debt financing is known in advance, and creditor's claims on a firm's cash flows are limited strictly to what has been agreed upon.

Cost Advantages of Debt Financing

As previously discussed, debt financing also offers a tax advantage. Since interest expense is tax deductible, the true cost of debt financing is lowered even further relative to that of equity capital. If, for instance, a firm's tax rate is 34%, the effective (after-tax) cost of debt to a business is approximately two-thirds the interest rate that must be paid. Each dollar of interest expense reduces taxable income and, at the 34% tax rate, saves a firm $0.34 (34 cents) in tax payments; therefore, the effective, after-tax cost of the $1.00 of interest expense is only $0.66 (66 cents).

The after-tax cost of debt can be quickly calculated by multiplying the interest rate on the debt by (1 minus tax rate). For example, going back to Ideal, if the company is able to borrow through an extended-term loan at a 14% interest rate, the after-tax cost of debt to the business is 9.24%.

After-Tax Cost of Debt = Borrowing Rate of Interest x (1 – Tax Rate)

$$= 14\% \times (1 - .34)$$
$$= .14 \times .66 \times 100$$
$$= 9.24\%$$

On the other hand, equity financing provides no tax subsidy for any firm. Distributions to a firm's owner in the form of dividends or withdrawals are not tax deductible and, therefore, must be paid out of after-tax dollars. This makes such payments considerably more expense than interest payments. For example, at a 34% tax rate, Ideal must generate $1.52 in before-tax cash flow in order to make a $1.00 dividend payment. This is calculated as follows:

Required Amount Before Taxes = After-Tax Payment ÷ (1 – Tax Rate)

$$= \$1.00 \div (1 - .34)$$
$$= \$1.00 \div .66$$
$$= \$1.52$$

Further enhancing the attractiveness of debt financing over equity is the possibility that in an inflationary economy, debt may be paid back with effectively cheaper dollars. For example, the principal on a long-term loan obligation due in 10 years may be repaid with dollars whose purchasing power may have shrunk in value by 50% to 60%. Presumably, lenders charge higher interest rates during inflationary periods to compensate for the loss of purchasing power, but this is not always the case.

Cost Disadvantages of Debt Financing

Lenders often impose restrictive provisions in debt contracts with small businesses. Such restrictions limit management's activities or its freedom to make decisions. These covenants take a variety of forms, such as limits on the firm's use of future debt financing, on its ability to buy or sell fixed assets, or its discretion to pay dividends or raise salaries. The effect of restrictive covenants is that of an implicit cost. While an implicit cost does not represent out-of-pocket dollars, it is a burden that management must bear. As such, restrictive covenants raise the true cost of debt financing.

Capital Structure Considerations

In theory there is no limit to the amount of equity financing that a business can use. There are, however, very real limits on the amount of debt financing that can be employed at any one time. As larger amounts of debt financing are used, lenders recognize the increase in financial risk and will restrict credit availability. When financial risk measures, such as the debt ratio and burden coverage, are perceived by creditors to be at unacceptable levels, they will not make loans.

Control Issues

While creditors have specific legal rights to income and assets, they do not have a proportionate share of the profits or a voice in management. In short, creditors are not owners, and the use of debt financing does not dilute the owner's interest in the business. On the other hand, new equity financing requires the existing ownership to relinquish a share of the controlling interest in a firm. Since equity financing is costly for small firms, the percentage of ownership that must be relinquished may be quite large. Such a concession may defeat a primary objective of many entrepreneurs: total ownership and operation of the business.

Calculating the Cost of Debt Financing

Financing has a cost. It is your job as a manager or owner to raise required funds in the proper amounts and at the proper time, but to do so at the least possible cost. Unfortunately, the true cost of debt financing is not always readily apparent. Lenders often use different methods to calculate the proceeds of a loan, the interest on the loan, and the amount and timing of the repayment schedule. These inconsistencies may result in a significant difference between the loan's stated or nominal rate of interest and the true cost to the borrower. The true cost of debt financing, referred to as the effective rate of interest or the annual percentage rate (APR), depends on:

- The amount of the loan proceeds the borrower has available for use,
- The length of time these funds are used; and
- The amount and timing of the repayments made by the borrower.

True cost is often the most important consideration when borrowing money, and unless this value is known, alternative loans cannot be realistically compared and evaluated.

Working through the following material may not make you an instant expert on interest rate calculations, but it will give you a basic understanding of the implications of assuming one type of interest obligation as opposed to another. Equally as important, this background will give you the insight to ask the right questions about a proposed set of loan conditions and to bargain these conditions more effectively. To help you investigate and better understand the more important fundamentals of calculating interest cost, follow the formulas discussed below.

Calculating the Dollar Cost of Interest

For many types of loans, the procedure used to calculate the effective rate of interest relies on nothing more than the most elementary interest rate relationships. The first of these is:

Interest = Principal x Rate x Time

Interest represents the dollar amount paid by the borrower for the use of the principal or amount borrowed from the lender. Interest is paid as long as the borrower has use of the funds. For example, if The Ideal Leverage Company borrows $1,000 (the principal) for one year at an annual interest rate of 12%, the dollar amount of interest paid on the loan is $120. Using the interest rate relationship, this is calculated as:

Interest = Principal x Rate x Time

$$= \$1,000 \times .12 \times 1$$
$$= \$120$$

If the $1,000 is borrowed for six months, the time variable in the basic interest relationship must reflect that portion of the year. This is easily accomplished by expressing time as either 6 months divided by 12 months or 180 days divided by 360 days. The interest cost in this situation is $60.

Interest = Principal x Rate x Time

$$= \$1,000 \times .12 \times \frac{180}{360} \qquad \text{or} \qquad = \$1,000 \times .12 \times \frac{6}{12}$$
$$= \$1,000 \times .12 \times .5 \qquad \qquad \quad = \$1,000 \times .12 \times .5$$
$$= \$60 \qquad \qquad \qquad \qquad \quad = \$60$$

Simple Interest Cost in Short-Term Financing

As a small business borrower, you are usually confronted with the problem of calculating the effective rate of interest when the principal, the stated rate of interest, and the time are known. This is easily accomplished by using another version of the basic interest rate relationship.

Rate = (Interest ÷ Available Amount) x Annualized Equivalent Time

In this case, rate is the effective annual interest rate (compounding is ignored); interest is the dollar amount of interest paid; available amount is the amount of loan proceeds you actually have available for use; and annualized equivalent time is the portion converted to an annual period. Often, the available amount is the same as the principal, but occasionally this is not the case. When there is a difference between the two, the difference has a major impact on the true cost of borrowing.

In order to gain a feel for calculating the effective rate of interest, assume Ideal borrows $1,000 from Friendly Bank for one year at a 12% stated (nominal) rate of interest. If Friendly Bank uses the simple-interest method to calculate Ideal's interest charge, the true cost of the loan is the same as the stated rate of 12%. Using the simple-interest method, the bank applies the 12% interest rate to the the amount of principal actually available to Ideal ($1,000 in this case), and the interest is paid along with the principal at the end of the loan period (one year).

The reason the stated and effective rate of interest are identical is straightforward. The entire principal is available to Ideal for the entire period of the loan, and interest is paid only on what was actually used. The following illustration, using the basic interest rate relationship and the effective-rate version of this relationship, makes this important point more clear.

Step 1: Calculate the dollar amount of interest.

Interest = Principal x Rate x Time

$$= \$1,000 \times .12 \times \frac{360}{360}$$

$$= \$1,000 \times .12 \times 1$$

$$= \$120$$

Step 2: Calculate the effective rate of interest.

Rate = (Interest ÷ Available Amount) x Annualized Equivalent Time

$$= (\$120 \div \$1,000) \times \frac{360}{360}$$

$$= .12 \times 1 \times 100$$

$$= 12\%$$

If the loan had been for three months rather than a year, the effective rate of interest (again ignoring compounding) is calculated by following the same procedure as outlined above.

Step 1: Calculate the dollar amount of interest.

Interest = Principal x Rate x Time

$$= \$1,000 \times .12 \times \frac{90}{360}$$

$$= \$1,000 \times .12 \times .25$$

$$= \$30$$

Step 2: Calculate the effective rate of interest.

Rate = (Interest ÷ Available Amount) x Annualized Equivalent Time

$$= (\$30 \div \$1,000) \times \frac{360}{90}$$

$$= .03 \times 4 \times 100$$

$$= 12\%$$

The effective rate is also 12% because the amount of interest paid is adjusted for the time period (three months) the loan proceeds are used by The Ideal Leverage Company.

Discounted Interest Cost in Short-Term Financing

Instead of calculating interest charges using the simple-interest method, banks often discount the interest on the loan. Calculating interest charges using the discounted-interest method involves these steps:

- The stated rate of interest is applied to the full amount of the principal to determine the dollar interest cost.
- The dollar amount of interest is deducted from the principal to determine the proceeds to the borrower.

As an aid to understanding a discounted loan, it is useful to think of it as one in which the borrower:

- Receives the full amount of the principal;
- Immediately pays the lender interest on the full amount of principal; but
- Repays the full amount of the principal at maturity just as if the full amount of the principal had been received.

The amount received at the time the loan is made, the discounted proceeds, is what you, as the borrower, have available for use. Since you pay interest on the full amount of the principal, but only has the discounted proceeds available for use, the effective rate of interest on a discounted loan is substantially higher than the stated rate. Again, ignoring the effects of compounding, assume Ideal now borrows $1,000 for one year at the stated rate of 12%, but the loan is discounted. Since interest is charged on the full amount borrowed (principal), the dollar amount of interest on the loan is calculated in the usual manner.

Step 1: Calculate the dollar amount of interest.

Interest = Principal x Rate x Time

$$= \$1,000 \times .12 \times \tfrac{360}{360}$$
$$= \$120$$

The effective rate calculation must, however, reflect the discounted proceeds. In this case, the $120 of interest is first deducted from the principal and Ideal receives only $880. It is important to note in the following calculation how discounted interest influences the effective rate of interest.

Step 2: Calculate the effective rate of interest.

Rate = (Interest ÷ Available Amount) x Annualized Equivalent Time

$$= (\$120 \div \$880) \times \tfrac{360}{360}$$
$$= .136 \times 1 \times 100$$
$$= 13.6\%$$

Because Ideal paid interest on the entire $1,000 but only had $880 available to use, the effective rate of interest on the discounted loan rose to 13.6%. Unfortunately, when the loan is repaid in one year, Ideal must pay the full amount of the principal, $1,000.

If Ideal's borrowing needs were actually $1,000 rather than the $880 proceeds, the company would have to borrow $1,000, plus an additional amount to pay the discount interest. In this case, Ideal would have to borrow $1,136.36. This calculation is made using this formula:

Amount Borrowed = Amount Needed ÷ (1 – Stated Interest Rate)

$$= \$1,000 \div (1 - .12)$$
$$= \$1,000 \div .88$$
$$= \$1,136.36$$

To show that this is the correct amount when the stated rate of interest is 12%, you can follow the same procedure the lender would use to determine the interest charge and the loan proceeds. This involves nothing more than calculating the dollar interest charge and deducting this amount from $1,136.36. The remainder should be the required amount, $1,000.

Step 1: Calculate the dollar amount of interest.

Interest = Principal x Rate x Time

$$= \$1,000 \times .12 \times \tfrac{360}{360}$$

$$= \$136.36$$

Step 2: Determine the proceeds of the discounted loan.

Loan Proceeds = Amount Borrowed (Principal) – Interest

$$= \$1,136.36 - \$136.36$$

$$= \$1,000$$

Extended-Term Financing

Extended-term financing refers to loans that have a maturity longer than one year. Most often, this type of loan takes the form of an installment contract which requires the periodic repayment of interest and principal over the life of the loan. There are three basic types of interest on such a loan: interest on the unpaid balance, discounted interest, and add-on interest. Each interest has its own method of being calculated.

Interest on the Unpaid Balance Methods

When interest is calculated on the unpaid balance, the lender has the option of using either the simple-interest method or the full-amortization method. In either case, the interest portion of each installment payment is calculated only on the amount of principal outstanding since the last payment.

With this type of installment loan, each loan payment has two components: 1) interest on the unpaid balance; and 2) a reduction of the outstanding balance. This means that the loan payments provide for the gradual reduction of the loan principal (amount borrowed) over the life of the loan. Because interest charges are determined in this manner, interest is paid only on the amount of the outstanding principal and only for the time period for which it is used.

Simple-Interest Method

For example, assume Ideal borrows $50,000 at 14% simple interest to be repaid in 60 monthly installments. The first monthly payment would be $1,416.66. This payment is calculated in two steps.

First, the portion of each loan payment applied to the principal is determined. Under the simple-interest method, this amount is constant over the life of the loan and is calculated as follows:

Step 1: Determine the amount applied to principal.

Principal Portion of Payment = Principal ÷ Number of Payments

$$= \$50,000 \div 60$$

$$= \$833.33$$

Second, the interest portion of each payment is calculated on the amount of principal outstanding since the last payment. Since each monthly payment causes the principal to decline over the life of the loan, the amount of interest paid each period also declines. For example, when the first payment is made, the outstanding principal would be the full $50,000, and the interest charge is $583.33.

Step 2: Determine interest portion of payment.

Interest Portion of Payment   = Outstanding Principal x Rate x Time

$$= \$1,000 \times .12 \times \frac{1 \text{ month}}{12 \text{ months}}$$

$$= \$50,000 \times .14 \times \frac{1}{12}$$

$$= \$583.33$$

The total amount of the first payment is the sum of interest and principal or $1,416.66 ($833.33 plus $583.33). Each subsequent payment is calculated in the same manner. For example, the thirteenth payment is $1,300. This is the sum of the $833.33 principal payment and the interest charge of $466.67. To calculate the interest portion of the thirteenth payment, follow these steps:

Step 1: Determine the amount of principal reduced.

Principal Reduced   = Payments to Date x Principal Payment

$$= 12 \times \$833.33$$

$$= \$9,999.96$$

Step 2: Determine the outstanding balance.

Outstanding Balance   = Original Principal – Amount of Principal Reduced

$$= \$50,000 - \$9,999.96$$

$$= \$40,000.04$$

Step 3: Determine the interest portion of the payment.

Interest Portion of Payment   = Outstanding Principal x Rate x Time

$$= \$40,000.04 \times .14 \times \frac{1 \text{ month}}{12 \text{ months}}$$

$$= \$466.67$$

It is important to note that because the principal portion of each payment is constant under the simple-interest method, the amount of each monthly payment declines over the life of the loan.

Full-Amortization Method

If the more common full-amortization method is used by the lender, the loan payments are constant over the life of the loan. Each payment is divided between interest on the outstanding balance and the reduction of principal. Regardless of which method is used, the stated rate of interest is the same as the effective rate. This is so because the borrower pays interest only on the amount of principal and for the time period it has been used.

The mathematics required to calculate the effective interest rate using either method are beyond the scope of this book; however, you can take comfort in the fact that lenders are now required by law to provide you with these important details of a loan contract. Included in these details is the amount of a loan's annual percentage rate (APR). APR is what you look at when comparing borrowing alternatives.

Discounted Interest Method

The procedure used to determine the proceeds for a discounted extended-term installment loan is exactly the same as that used for a discounted short-term loan. The interest for the entire loan period is calculated, and this amount is deducted from the principal to determine your proceeds. While as the borrower, you repay the entire principal, there is less than this amount available for use. The result is an effective rate of interest that is substantially higher than the stated rate.

Add-On Interest Method

The add-on interest method of calculating interest is in direct contrast to the unpaid balance methods. The add-on interest method involves charging interest on the full amount of the principal throughout the life of the loan even though each periodic loan payment reduces the outstanding principal. Since interest is paid on the entire principal — even though a borrower does not have the entire principal available for use — the effective rate or APR is significantly higher than the stated rate of interest.

Assume Ideal borrows $1,000 under an installment-loan contract which calls for repayment over 36 months at a 14%, add-on interest rate. The monthly payments would be determined in this fashion:

Step 1: Determine interest for one year.

Interest for One Year = Principal x Rate x Time

$$= \$1,000 \times .14 \times 1$$
$$= \$140$$

Step 2: Determine total interest to be paid.

Total Interest = Interest for One Year x Number of Years

$$= \$140 \times 3 \text{ years}$$
$$= \$420$$

Step 3: Determine total amount to be repaid.

Total Repayment = Total Interest + Principal

$$= \$420 + \$1,000$$
$$= \$1,420$$

Step 4: Determine monthly payments.

Monthly Payment = Total Repayment ÷ Number of Months

$$= \$1,420 \div 36$$
$$= \$39.44$$

Since information on the true cost of the loan (APR) is provided by the lender, you need only be concerned with evaluating the loan using this figure.

A Final Thought

To complete the discussion on planning your firm's financing needs, you must address two basic questions.

- How much total debt financing can your small business afford to use?
- How do you identify the amounts of short- versus long-term debt financing needed?

The next chapter addresses the first of these two questions, and Chapter 4 considers the second.

Chapter 3

Planning Your Financing Mix

The term financing mix, or capital structure as it is referred to in finance, refers to the proportions of debt and equity capital used to finance a business' investment in assets. Small firms, by necessity, rely heavily on the use of debt to meet their needs. While debt financing offers a number of advantages over equity capital, its use does increase a business' risk of insolvency. In fact, the heavy dependence on debt financing is a major reason for the high failure rate among small businesses.

Nevertheless, a large majority of small businesses are perfectly capable of assuming a certain amount of financial risk. As a small business manager, you need be interested in employing a level of debt commensurate with your firm's capacity to assume risk if — and this is an important if — risk exposure is carefully controlled. This control can be accomplished through careful analysis of your firm's ability to service its debt.

Factors Influencing Your Financing Mix

Many business firms, whether small or large, go through four distinct phases in their developmental process. This sequence is referred to as the firm's life cycle, and each stage of this cycle is a major determinant of the type of financing available to management.

Life Cycle Stages

The Embryo Stage

This initial phase in your firm's life cycle consists of your conceptualization, planning, and organization of the business. During this start-up period, the financing available to your business is usually restricted to your personal wealth. This includes your equity investment in the firm and any borrowing secured by your personal assets.

The Formative Stage

During the early periods of your firm's development, you are concerned with building a customer base and gaining product acceptance. Without a proven record of compensatory cash flow and earnings, your firm has little capacity for raising debt, and available financing is again limited to your capital and internally generated cash flow. When and if your business obtains a consistent earning power, develops a solid asset base, and cultivates viable creditor relationships, limited debt capacity may become available. This debt capacity generally takes the form of credit terms offered by trade suppliers, short-term working capital loans from a bank or commercial finance company, and possibly some well-secured, extended-term financing.

The Rapid Growth Stage

If your business either enjoys or holds the promise for spectacular earnings success, both additional debt capacity and equity opportunities materialize. Not only will your firm have the latitude to choose from a wider assortment of creditors, but raising external equity capital through new ownership interest becomes a realistic prospect.

The Maturity Stage

When your firm's growth rate slows to a pace evidenced by stable cash flows and earnings, it has usually achieved the enviable status of having more debt capacity than is necessary. With the minor exceptions of borrowing to meet temporary working capital needs or using an occasional extended-term loan for fixed-asset replacement, firms of this stature are often able to meet the bulk of their financing requirements through internally generated cash flow.

Business Risk

The decision on financing mix is heavily influenced by the degree of business risk to which your firm is exposed. Recall that business risk is the extent to which a firm's sales and cash flow fluctuate in response to economic, market, and competitive conditions. The disadvantages of size increase this element of uncertainty in small businesses, and you must consider the impact of business risk when making your financing mix decision. It is certain that a prospective creditor will do so. The greater the degree of business risk to which your business is exposed, the higher the probability of insufficient cash flow, and the less debt financing the business can safely afford to use.

In short, financial prudence dictates that firms with a high degree of business risk do not compound the danger by adding excessive financial risk.

Lenders typically have firmly established, preconceived ideas of what constitutes an appropriate proportion of debt for a small firm in a given industry. Such notions are an important influence on the amount of debt financing creditors are willing to make available. For example, old-line bankers often use the 50% rule as a guideline for establishing the maximum percentage of a small firm's total financing that should be provided by creditors. Or, creditors may compare selected ratio values for a firm with those of other firms in the same industry. Despite the obvious weaknesses in these rule-of-thumb techniques, their use in determining the debt capacity of a small firm is firmly entrenched in American financial institutions.

Lender's Standards

A business' earnings record, combined with estimates of its future earnings potential, are widely used by prospective creditors as a guide to the amount of debt financing a business can safely afford. While earnings-based approaches can take a variety of forms, they all share the same underlying rationale: The business must evidence and offer promise of maintaining a level of accounting profit, usually operating income, that sufficiently covers the repayment obligations associated with a given amount of debt financing. As is the case with other financial ratios, creditors will often employ standards for these coverage ratios that are based on arbitrary rules-of-thumb.

Past and Future Earnings

You can effectively use earnings-based analysis — discussed later in this chapter — to estimate the amount of financial risk associated with a given level of debt financing. This approach has serious limitations, however, when used to decide the issue of an acceptable financing mix. Most important among these is the use of profits as an indicator of ability to pay. The ability to make payments is determined by your firm's cash position not its level of profit. Second, this approach leaves the critical question raised by the financing-mix decision unanswered: How much debt financing can your firm safely afford to use?

The major risk associated with debt financing is meeting the contractual burden that obligates your business. Interest and principal payments must be made on time to avoid the legal difficulties which creditors can impose. Your business must then generate operating cash flow at least equal in amount to that required to service a given level of debt. The greater or lower the level of debt, the greater or lower the amount of cash flow from operations required to service that debt.

Future Cash Flow

In the final analysis then, your business' debt capacity should be determined by the minimum amount of cash flow that operations are expected to produce. If the financial charges associated with a given level of debt exceed this minimum, your firm is unable to meet those obligations. Minimum cash flows typically occur during periods of adversity, such as a general business slowdown (economic recession), and any decision on your firm's financing mix should focus on these worst-case scenarios.

Tools for Estimating Financial Risk

The question of an appropriate proportion of debt financing has important financial consequences for you and your business. Mistakes caused by the unheeded, excessive use of debt can lead to your firm's insolvency and the ultimate loss of your investment of time, effort, ingenuity, and capital. Given this possibility, prudent financial management dictates a carefully analyzed and planned decision. The primary tools available for this purpose are debt and coverage ratios and cash-flow analysis.

Leverage Ratios

Debt and coverage ratios, or financial leverage ratios as they are often referred to in finance, are widely used by creditors as guidelines for identifying the upper limit of a firm's debt capacity. While these measures are often calculated differently by different analysts, all are designed to indicate either the amount of debt financing used, or the ability to meet the financial obligations associated with a given amount of debt. You can use leverage ratios to gain a feel for the risk associated with alternative debt levels and to gain insight into how a prospective creditor views your firm's financing mix. As will be discussed in Chapter 8, this latter information is often useful for preparing an effective financing proposal.

Debt Ratios

Traditional debt ratios focus on the right-hand side of the balance sheet by comparing the amount of debt financing to either total financing, total assets, or the amount of owner's investment (equity capital). The most common of the debt measures is known as the debt-to-total capital ratio or simply the debt ratio and is calculated as total debt divided by total liabilities and equity (or total assets). This ratio measures the proportion of total financing supplied by creditors. See Chapter 1 for an explanation of the debt ratio.

From a creditor's standpoint, the lower the percentage of debt financing, or alternatively the higher the percentage of equity capital, the better. Creditors regard ownership funds as a buffer protecting them from loss. If, for example, debt is only 10% of total financing (total assets), theoretically assets could, if they had to be repossessed and sold, shrink in value by up to 90% and still be sufficient to cover creditor's claims. On the other hand, if debt financing represented 90% of total capital, a shrinkage of more than 10% would leave creditors' claims unsatisfied.

Coverage Ratios

Coverage ratios are used to measure the extent to which a business is able to meet its fixed financial charges. This is accomplished by relating some measure of ability to pay, such as earnings or cash flow, in the numerator of the ratio to some aspect of financial obligation, such as interest or financial burden, in the denominator. While these ratios can also be calculated using different methods, the two most widely used forms are times interest earned (TIE) and burden coverage.

Chapter 1 explained that the burden coverage ratio is calculated as cash flow from operations divided by financial burden. Financial burden consists of all fixed financial payments such as interest and principal payments, and lease obligations. The ratio measures the dollars of cash flow that have been available to meet existing financial obligations. From a creditor's standpoint, the larger the amount of cash flow relative to financial burden, the lower the financial risk, and the more secure the creditor's position.

The coverage measure most widely used by creditors is the traditional times interest earned ratio. The TIE ratio is based on the same concept and is interpreted in the same manner as burden coverage: ability to pay. It compares two income statement items: operating income, which is the earnings of the firm before deductions for interest expense and taxes, to interest expense. It is calculated as net operating income divided by interest expense. The resulting ratio value is interpreted as the extent to which net operating income can decline before the business would have difficulty meeting interest payments. In general, the larger the TIE value, the more secure the creditor's position.

How to Use Leverage Ratios

Despite the popularity of leverage ratios among creditors, used alone they cannot provide an answer to the important question of what proportion of debt is appropriate. The reason is simple: There are no objective standards available that relate the value of a particular leverage ratio to what is generally considered an appropriate financing mix.

Creditors often use pet rules of thumb, such as a 50% debt ratio, a times interest earned value of at least five, or an industry average to determine whether a firm's debt level fits into a general pattern suited to the situation or to the character of the industry in which the business operates. These standards are arbitrary, however, and do not offer an objective measure of a firm's future ability to service debt. Whether a given ratio depicts a good or bad condition rests with a particular analyst's viewpoint, and the final choice must be left to individual judgment in each particular case.

Of what value, then, are leverage ratios to you when confronting the financing mix decision? Used appropriately and together with other tools, they offer insight into the degree of financial risk associated with a given level of debt financing.

The greatest threat to the use of debt is the extent to which a firm's sales and cash flows fluctuate. Unpredictable declines in these key variables may leave a business incapable of covering its financial obligations, and the greater the potential fluctuation in operations, the greater the risk of this happening. To obtain useful information from leverage ratios, you need to calculate these measures using realistic estimates of a reasonable range over which net operating income and cash flow from operations (CFFO) may fluctuate as business conditions change. To do so, answer this question: What amount of operating income and cash flow would your business generate under the worst possible conditions, under normal conditions, and under ideal conditions? By using a range of values for operating income and CFFO, you gain a feel for how changes in these variables affect the important indicators of financial risk.

Using the Times Interest Earned Ratio

To illustrate how leverage ratios can be used, return to the Perplexed Company example from Chapter 2 where Perplexed's management was evaluating the financial leverage effect of three capital structure choices. Since then, Perplexed has decided that another debt alternative should be considered: 25% debt financing.

Table 3.1

PERPLEXED COMPANY
Alternative Capital Structures

	100% Equity	25% Debt	50% Debt	75% Debt
Total Debt	$ 0	$ 25,000	$ 50,000	$ 75,000
Total Equity	100,000	75,000	50,000	25,000
Total Capital	$100,000	$100,000	$100,000	$100,000

To start the analysis, Perplexed's management carefully evaluates the firm's historical financial data to determine how earnings and cash flow behaved during different periods of business and economic activity. The resulting estimates for operating income — or earnings before interest expense and taxes (EBIT) as it is often referred to in finance — and CFFO under different economic conditions are shown on Table 3.2. Perplexed's management continues to anticipate an interest rate of 10% on any debt financing used and also expects that debt principal would be repaid in equal annual installments over a five-year period.

Table 3.2

PERPLEXED COMPANY
Expected EBIT and CFFO
Under Different Business Conditions

	Worst Case Economic Recession	Average Case Normal Conditions	Best Case Robust Conditions
EBIT	$ 8,000	$20,000	$30,000
CFFO	$12,000	$24,000	$34,000

Chapter 2 explained that financial leverage analysis provided some indication of the risk/return potential from debt financing. Large amounts of debt produced a boon for return on owner's equity (ROE) when return on investment (ROI) was above the cost of debt, but a negative influence occurred when ROI was below interest cost. This ever present element of financial risk from debt financing is made clear by the information provided on Table 3.3 shown below and Table 3.5 on page 53. The first table depicts times interest earned (TIE) values under the four capital structure choices using the estimated range of net operating income (EBIT) from Table 3.2. Table 3.5 contains burden coverage ratio values using the company management's CFFO estimates and the four capital structure choices.

Table 3.3

PERPLEXED COMPANY
Times Interest Earned Values
Using an Estimated Range of EBIT and Selected Capital Structures

EBIT	100% Equity	25% Debt	50% Debt	75% Debt
$ 8,000	N/A	3.2 times	1.6 times	1.1 times
$20,000	N/A	8.0 times	4.0 times	2.7 times
$30,000	N/A	12.0 times	6.0 times	4.0 times

At an interest rate of 10%, interest expense is calculated as .10 multiplied by the amount of debt financing used — see Table 3.1. For the three debt choices available to Perplexed, interest expense would be $2,500 ($25,000 multiplied by .10); $5,000 ($50,000 multiplied by .10); and $7,500 ($75,000 multiplied by .10). These values along with management's EBIT estimates were used to calculate the TIE ratio values shown on Table 3.3.

For example, the TIE value of 3.2 times for the EBIT estimate of $8,000 and 25% debt financing (interest expense of $2,500) is calculated by:

Times Interest Earned = EBIT ÷ Interest Expense
$$= \$8,000 \div \$2,500$$
$$= 3.2 \text{ times}$$

The remaining TIE values shown on Table 3.3 are calculated in the same manner.

Interpreting the TIE Results

An overview of the TIE values on Table 3.3 reveals the increased financial risk associated with increasing debt use. Notice first how the ratio values for a given level of operating income decline with larger percentages of debt financing. For example, with 25% debt and EBIT of $8,000, Perplexed is able to generate $3.20 of operating income for each $1.00 of interest expense. With 75% debt financing this figure drops to $1.10 of EBIT for each $1.00 of interest charges. In the former case, operating income could decline by slightly more than $2.00 ($3.20 minus $1.00) before interest payments would be jeopardized. With 75% debt financing, there is only a $0.10 (10 cents) ($1.10 minus $1.00) margin of safety between operating income and interest expense.

Notice also that the value of the coverage ratios under any financing alternative increases as the level of EBIT increases. For example, under the 25% debt financing alternative, TIE grows from 3.2 times to 12 times as expected EBIT increases. Interest charges for a given level of debt are fixed by contract and are, therefore, completely independent of fluctuations in operating income. As EBIT grows, interest costs become less of a drain on earnings.

Using the Burden Coverage Ratio

Another effective indicator of financial risk is the burden coverage ratio. This ratio is considered a better indicator than the TIE ratio.

Burden Coverage = CFFO ÷ Total Financial Burden

By substituting CFFO for EBIT and dividing it by the total financial burden rather than the interest (as done in the TIE ratio), these substitutions provide a more realistic measure of both ability to pay and financial risk. Recall from the discussion in Chapter 1 that the accounting concept of earnings is not a true measure of liquidity in any particular time period. This capacity is determined solely by available cash flow.

The burden coverage ratio also recognizes that interest expense is not the only obligation associated with the use of debt financing. Commitments, such as lease payments or the repayment of debt principal, must also be met in a timely fashion. Failure to do so is just as damaging to a firm's financial health as missing interest payments.

Table 3.4

PERPLEXED COMPANY
Total Financial Burden Values

	25% Debt	50% Debt	75% Debt
Annual Interest Payment	$ 2,500	$ 5,000	$ 7,500
Annual Principal Payment (Principal / 5 Years)	5,000	10,000	15,000
Total Financial Burden	$ 7,500	$15,000	$22,500

The mechanics of burden coverage analysis are the same as those used in evaluating TIE. First, estimates of a reasonable range for CFFO under various business and economic scenarios are made. Second, CFFO estimates are used to calculate burden coverage values under each capital structure choice. In the Perplexed example, it has been assumed that principal payments would be made in five equal annual installments. For example, if 50% debt financing is assumed, the principal of $50,000 would be repaid at the rate of $10,000 per year. Combining the interest expense and principal payments for each capital structure choice on Table 3.4 produces the total financial burden values.

The total financial burden values and management's CFFO estimates are used to produce the burden coverage ratio values shown on Table 3.5. For example, the coverage value of .8 times under the 50% debt alternative is calculated as:

Burden Coverage = CFFO ÷ Total Financial Burden

$$= \$12{,}000 \div \$15{,}000$$
$$= .8 \text{ times}$$

Table 3.5

PERPLEXED COMPANY
Burden Coverage Ratio Values
Using an Estimated Range of CFFO and Selected Capital Structures

CFFO	100% Equity	25% Debt	50% Debt	75% Debt
$12,000	N/A	1.6 times	0.8 times	0.5 times
$24,000	N/A	3.2 times	1.6 times	1.1 times
$34,000	N/A	4.5 times	2.3 times	1.5 times

Interpreting the Burden Coverage Results

Burden coverage ratios are interpreted in the same manner as TIE ratios. A given ratio value indicates the dollars of CFFO that are available to meet total financial obligations. For example, the value of 1.6 times shown in Table 3.5 under CFFO of $12,000 and the 25% debt choice means that estimated operations produce $1.60 of cash flow for each $1.00 of total financial burden. The larger the amount of cash flow relative to financial burden, the larger the margin of safety, and the lower the firm's financial risk.

The burden coverage ratio values shown in Table 3.5 also reveal the degree of financial risk to which Perplexed would be exposed at higher levels of debt financing. Under normal business conditions, Perplexed would generate barely enough cash flow to cover its financial obligations if 75% debt financing is used. With a coverage ratio of 1.1 times, there is only a $0.10 (10 cents) buffer between positive cash flow and inability to meet debt obligations. If CFFO were to drop during a business slump to the expected level of $12,000, Perplexed would be in a financial bind with either the 50% or 75% capital structure. With the 50% debt choice, only $0.80 (80 cents) of CFFO is expected for each $1.00 of burden, and only $0.50 (50 cents) per $1.00 is expected with 75% debt financing.

Given this information, Perplexed's management would certainly eliminate the 75% capital structure from consideration and argue strongly against the 50% debt alternative. In the former case, the risk is too great. Perplexed would be able to cover its financial expense only if the best possible conditions were to continue indefinitely. A prospect even an eternal optimist would find unlikely. With the 50% capital structure, the risk of insolvency is reduced, but the risk is still significant.

Be aware that the worst-case scenario could occur at any time. Many small businesses do not have the financial resources to withstand either a severe business slump or a prolonged financial crisis. This weakness renders the business vulnerable to total loss; a risk which you will want to avoid.

Cash-Flow Analysis

Back in Chapter 2, the discussion of leverage ratios emphasized two important points:

- The ability to service debt is measured by cash flow.
- Financial risk is created by fixed or mandatory cash outflows that must be met from unpredictable cash inflows.

What's more, as you add to the element of fixed cash outflows — this includes fixed asset costs and fixed operating expenses as well as mandatory financial charges — the threat from prolonged declines in inflows is increased. As a result, any serious consideration of financial risk and the quest for an appropriate debt level must include an analysis of the behavior of future cash flows.

Knowing this, however, raises another question: Which future time periods should be analyzed? Certainly periods of prosperity pose little or no serious threat of insolvency to a well-managed small business. When things are going well, a business is able to generate sufficient cash flow to meet all its needs, including debt service. The opposite is true when adversity strikes. When business activity slumps, CFFO falls to dangerously low levels, and the risk of insolvency becomes a critical issue. Thus, as the small business manager, it is the behavior of cash flows during business slumps that should be the focal point of your concern. In short, the proportion of debt in your firm's capital structure should be determined by planning for the worst-case scenario. To do this type of planning, read the following discussions on cash-flow analysis.

The method used to estimate the upper limit on debt financing involves nothing more than preparing a series of cash-flow estimates under:

Setting Debt Limits

- Different assumed economic conditions; and
- Alternative amounts of debt financing.

These forecasts are evaluated by comparing the minimum expected net cash-flow figure to the total financial burden associated with each capital structure alternative. The appropriate debt ceiling is the approximate point at which the worst-case net cash flow is just sufficient to cover the financial charges related to a given capital structure. While the financial planning tool known as the cash budget — this tool is discussed in Chapter 4 — is the preferential technique for this type of analysis, any format for organizing estimated cash flows can be used. The important point is to use reliable data based on an analysis of your firm's historical financial performance during different periods of business activity and your informed judgment on the impact a business recession would have on sales, operating costs, and cash flows. To illustrate this approach, continue to use the Perplexed Company example.

You may recall that Perplexed's management is in the process of establishing an acceptable financing mix to fund the firm's $100,000 asset base. Debt financing is assumed to have an interest rate of 10% with the principal repaid in five equal annual installments. Based on an analysis of a series of historical cash budgets and financial statements, Perplexed's management estimates that during a typical 12- to 18-month business recession, the firm would experience a cash-flow pattern that is outlined below on Table 3.6.

Table 3.6

PERPLEXED COMPANY
Expected Recessionary Cash Flows

	1st Qtr.	2nd Qtr.	3rd Qtr.	4th Qtr.
Cash Inflows:				
Sales & Accts Rec.	$55,000	$44,000	$36,000	$40,000
Cash Outflows:				
Operating Costs	22,000	20,000	18,000	19,000
Working Capital Expenditures	10,000	8,000	6,000	7,000
Fixed Assets Expenditures	5,000	0	0	0
Total Outflows	$37,000	$28,000	$24,000	$26,000
Cash Flow Before Financial Charges	$18,000	$16,000	$12,000	$14,000

The sales and accounts receivable figures reflect forecast cash sales, and the anticipated pattern of credit sales collections. These gross inflows are expected to decline through the first three quarters of the recession and reach a low during the third quarter. The increase in inflows during the fourth quarter reflects the forecast of an upturn in business activity during that period.

Cash operating costs include normal operating expenses such as payroll, utilities, and insurance. The decline in operating costs through the first three quarters reflects the cost cutting effort that would be implemented as the slowdown in business activity is recognized by management. Working capital and fixed asset expenditures represent outlays for inventory purchases and equipment replacement that are absolutely essential to maintain operations. The difference between planned inflows and total outflows is the net cash flow that should be available to meet financial charges. As indicated on Table 3.6, this figure is expected to reach its minimum during the third quarter. This cash flow minimum is the worst-case focal point of the debt-level analysis.

The minimum $12,000 expected net cash flow figure, along with the mandatory financial charges for several possible capital structure choices, are shown on Table 3.7. The interest and principal payments are calculated in the same manner as shown in previous examples: interest cost equals the amount of debt multiplied by 10%, and the principal payments are determined by dividing the amount of principal by five years.

Table 3.7

PERPLEXED COMPANY
Worst-Case Cash-Flow Comparisons

	25%	40%	50%	75%
Minimum Cash Flow	$12,000	$12,000	$12,000	$ 12,000
Financial Burden:				
Interest Expense	$ 2,500	$ 4,000	$ 5,000	$ 7,500
Annual Principal	5,000	8,000	10,000	15,000
Total Burden	$ 7,500	$12,000	$ 15,000	$ 22,500
Free Cash Flow	$ 4,500	$ 0	$ (3,000)	$ (10,500)

By comparing the worst-case cash flow figure to the financial burden for each capital structure possibility, Perplexed's management can determine at what point the firm's maximum debt capacity lies. For example, the data on Table 3.7 indicates that if a financing mix consisting of 25% debt is used, Perplexed would have excess debt capacity. With this financing mix, cash flow before financing charges is greater than the amount of financial burden. The result is a positive free cash flow of $4,500. If the proportion of debt financing exceeds 40%, Perplexed would be unable to service its debt during a business slowdown. Both the 50% and 75% debt alternatives create negative free cash flow.

To this point then, an answer to the question of an upper limit on debt financing is clearly no more than 40%. At this level of debt, Perplexed is expected to meet all essential operating and financial needs in spite of a business slowdown.

While Perplexed may be able to borrow up to the limits allowed by its expected free cash flow, prudence requires a more cautious approach to debt financing. Rather than borrow to its limit, some of the firm's valuable debt capacity should be held as a reserve to minimize risk and maintain financial flexibility. Financial flexibility refers to a financial cushion which allows management to adjust to unexpected changes in circumstances. If the firm borrows to the limit of its debt capacity, there is no reserve borrowing power to neutralize the problems created by forecasting errors or an unexpected adversity or which allows management to take advantage of an unforeseen favorable opportunity.

Maintaining a Financial Cushion

There are strong arguments for maintaining some degree of financial flexibility. The most obvious is the need to allow for errors in judgment. At best, all decision making including financial planning is an imperfect art. Experience teaches that even management's best informed judgment is sometimes wrong. When this happens, a firm needs the financial cushion to survive the consequences.

Beyond this is the more important concern that all too often those opportunities which prove to be critical in the development and growth of a firm are often beyond a manager's ability to predict. The critical need or opportunity may be just around the corner and that may be the very time when other means of financing, such as raising new equity, may be either unavailable or unattractive. You, therefore, should maintain a certain amount of financial slack so your business is in position to react.

Possibly the strongest of all arguments for financial flexibility should be your concern over the dangers of too much risk. Small firms have a high degree of business risk, and you should be reluctant to compound this problem with unnecessary financial risk. Living on the edge may be exciting and may offer the potential for large profits, but the reality is a devastating down side. At stake is the value of the business as well as your time, effort, and personal wealth.

A Final Word on Risk

In the final analysis, the decision on debt financing is a decision on risk. Unfortunately, this is not an area where hard-and-fast rules are available that will automatically establish your firm's financial policy. It is an area requiring both the art and science of management. You must rely on a combination of sound judgment, an understanding of the nature and consequences of the risk involved, a clear idea of how much risk you are willing to tolerate, and a logical approach to the decision process.

The decision process should begin with the analysis suggested in this chapter. This approach allows you to eliminate the extreme alternatives from consideration and focus attention on the critical elements of the decision. For example, if cash flow prospects are sufficient to safely allow some debt financing, you would logically reject an all equity capital structure. Using debt when there is a comfortable margin of safety allows you to enjoy the gains from favorable leverage and to finance opportunities that may not otherwise be possible. Likewise, when a given level of debt financing would virtually eliminate all margin of safety — recall the 50% and 75% debt alternative in the Perplexed example — you eliminate that choice from consideration.

Decisions within the extremes are not as straightforward. Choosing between alternatives belonging to the gray areas is a matter of informed judgment and your subjective attitude toward risk. Regardless of the nature of a business decision, there simply is no substitute for the expertise that a well-informed manager brings to the decision process. This is not to suggest that experienced managers should ignore sound techniques and make seat-of-the pants decisions. Rather, it means that good managers use sound tools to provide insights that complement their knowledge and experience.

Additionally, each decision on risk has, by necessity, a critical subjective dimension: the level of exposure that you can live with. The tools described above assist you in identifying risk, but there are no generalized rules for defining what is a personally acceptable level. Attitude and tolerance toward risk are matters of personal preference, and such matters are decided individually. For example, this chapter's analysis indicated Perplexed could carry 40% debt in its capital structure. To accomplish this would mean absolutely no financial slack if an unexpected adversity occurred.

Only you can decide whether you are able to sleep soundly with the risk that such a capital structure represents.

Chapter 4

Planning Your Firm's Financing Needs

One of the important lessons from chapters 2 and 3 is the Jekyll and Hyde personality of debt financing. While it produces benefits for a borrowing firm, it also creates risk for both the user and the supplier of funds. If creditors are to provide debt financing on a consistent basis, there must be evidence of sound, responsible management of your business' finances. Justifiably, creditors expect you to be capable of identifying and substantiating the amount of funds needed, the purpose for which the funds are needed, and how and when the financing will be repaid.

Accomplishing these tasks requires careful financial planning. Forecasting and planning your firm's financial requirements are at the heart of the financial management process of any business, small or large. This chapter investigates the tools used to plan a firm's short- and long-term financing needs.

Planning Short-Term Financing Needs

The basic planning tool for any business is a budget. While any number of definitions for a budget are possible, it is nothing more than management's written recipe for what a firm is expected to accomplish over a specific time period and how this should be done. A budget is often expressed in numbers, which identify goals for the period and the resources that will be required to achieve them. These values also serve

Planning Through Budgeting

as standards by which a business' actual performance in a particular budgeted area can be measured and evaluated.

For example, a production budget may specify a goal of producing X number of units over the next year at a cost of Y dollars per unit. The budget would also indicate the labor, materials, production methods, and scheduling that would be required to accomplish this goal. As actual production during the budget period takes place, output and unit cost can be compared to budgeted standards to determine if operations are on or deviating from the plan. If deviations are detected, remedial action can be taken before problems get out of hand.

Budgets can be prepared for any of a firm's activities (financial, marketing, production, etc.) and usually cover a one-year planning horizon. This time frame can be divided into convenient budget intervals such as quarters, months, or weeks. Dividing the planning horizon into short intervals eases the forecasting burden and allows you the opportunity for timely comparisons of budgeted and actual results. You need to note that a budget is not just another accounting record. Accountants record historical transactions; budgeting deals with estimates of the future.

In short, budgeting is planning, and planning is a management function. Budgeting is the essence of sound business management and should be the foundation for your entire financial decision-making process.

The Cash Budget

Forecasting and planning your firm's short-term financing needs is an integral part of the planning/budgeting process, and to do this, you will need a cash budget. A cash budget is simply a projection of the amount and timing of anticipated cash inflows and outflows over a short-term planning horizon. Projected cash flows include both operating and nonoperating cash inflows (cash receipts) and operating and nonoperating cash outflows (cash disbursements).

Cash inflows result from any transaction that causes cash to flow into the business. These include:

- The cash receipts produced by normal operations, such as cash sales and the collection of accounts receivable; and
- Any cash receipts arising from nonoperating sources, such as a tax refund or the sale of a fixed asset.

Cash outflows include:

- The cash disbursements associated with normal operations, such as payments on accounts payable, payroll, or tax obligations; and
- Any nonoperating cash disbursements associated with a firm's investment, financing, and dividend activities, such as interest and principal payments on debt financing, the purchase of fixed assets, or dividend payments (owner's withdrawals).

The projections that make up the cash budget will reflect the impact of your operating plans on cash flows. For example, projected cash outflows for payroll and the payment of accounts payable are determined by the planned level of activity for the budget period and expected inventory purchases. The planned level of activity is based on expected sales which, when combined with the expected collection pattern on accounts receivable, determines the cash flow from operations a firm is able to generate.

Preparing your operating plan and cash budget is one of the more important activities you can perform. By having plans, you create a detailed blueprint of your firm's future direction and what resources it will take to get you there. The largest benefit gained from preparing plans and budgets, however, is being forced to re-examine your business. All too often, as a small business manager, you become so absorbed in day-to-day activities that you lose sight of the factors critical to your business' success. By thinking through the planning process, you have to identify, monitor, and evaluate what is important.

The cash budget plays a vital role in the planning process, because it is the only tool that focuses on the financial variable most critical to your firm's overall performance — the behavior of cash flow. A well-prepared cash budget provides information on when cash deficits and cash surpluses are likely to occur. This information is essential in planning your firm's financing needs and for estimating when and how this financing can be repaid. For these reasons, the cash budget is the single most powerful financial planning tool available to you.

Selecting Budget Intervals

Your cash budget's forecast period should coincide with what is used to measure your short-term operating plans. For most businesses, this is usually one year or less. The length of the budget intervals (weeks, months, etc.) depends on the circumstances peculiar to a business. In general, the interval used depends on the volume of cash flows experienced by a business, the degree of fluctuation in these cash flows, and the amount of risk or uncertainty to which a business is exposed. The greater the volume, fluctuation, or uncertainty of cash flows, the more critical the cash flow forecast, and the shorter the budget interval should be. For many small businesses, monthly intervals are a reasonable compromise.

Getting Started on the Cash Budget

Technically, the cash budgeting process begins with a sales forecast and an estimate of the collection pattern on accounts receivable. If you are a first-time planner, however, it is probably wise to begin by examining the past. This means organizing historical cash flows into the format used for an actual cash budget. To accomplish this task, examine your cash records — cash receipts and disbursements journal, check register, etc. covering past fiscal periods. From these periods you would then identify and organize the various inflows and outflows into their appropriate cash budget categories.

Plugging historical cash flows into their proper budget classifications lets you experience and learn:

- How to work with cash flow data and the budget format;
- How specific cash flow items behave and what factors are influencing this behavior; this understanding improves the quality of cash forecasts and eases the task of projecting cash flows;
- How to interpret the cash budget; and
- How to maintain cash control; this means comparing actual cash flows for a completed budget interval to forecast cash flows, and then identifying the reasons why forecasts were right or wrong.

Before examining a cash budget in further detail, you need to understand more about estimating future cash flows.

Estimating Sales

As with all planning activities, the process of projecting cash flows begins with an estimate of sales for each budget interval in the planning horizon; for example, 12 monthly projections for a one-year horizon. This estimate, and the estimate for the collection pattern on accounts receivable, are the two most critical processes in cash budget preparation. All other budget estimates, by comparison, are relatively easy to make.

To make the sales estimates for each budget interval, begin with the actual sales figures for the corresponding intervals from the previous year. That is, use the sales figure for the previous January as the first projection for January of the budget period; the historical February value for the second, and so on. These historical amounts, however, are only starting points for your forecast. A cash budget should reflect anticipated future conditions, and what has happened in the past may or may not be appropriate to the future. In order to convert historical sales to usable projections, make these adjustments for these potential activities:

- **Trends.** Adjust historical sales figures for any past trend that is expected to continue in the future. For example, if past sales have enjoyed a 5% annual growth rate and this trend is expected to continue, adjust the historical sales figures by this amount.
- **Planned operations.** Adjust trend-modified sales figures to reflect the impact of planned operations. For example, Ideal is planning an addition to its retail store and an expansion of its service facility. As a result, sales are expected to increase by approximately 18% for 19X3 and 19X4; this percentage should be reflected in the projections for those years.
- **Changing conditions.** Adjust corrected historical figures for any anticipated changes in general economic conditions over the planning horizon. For example, if a slowdown in product demand or a general business recession is expected to occur during the planning horizon, the impact of these phenomena must be reflected in sales estimates.

Using this approach, Ideal's management has made the hypothetical sales projections shown on Table 4.1. In practice, an annual forecast is more

Table 4.1

THE IDEAL LEVERAGE COMPANY
Breakdown of 19X3 Forecast Sales

Period	Sales
January	$ 36,000
February	34,000
March	40,000
2nd Quarter	150,000
3rd Quarter	159,000
4th Quarter	171,000
Total 19X3 Forecast Sales	$590,000

detailed in the early months and less detailed in the latter periods. Thus, the first quarter is broken down by month: January, February, and March. The second, third, and fourth quarters are aggregated. The $590,000 is the total for all four quarters of 19X3. These estimates reflect management's expectation of approximately 18% growth over 19X2. This high rate of growth is expected to persist for the next two years and then level off.

The receivables collection pattern is nothing more than the estimated set of percentages that indicate the expected rate of collection on receivables. A given collection percentage represents the proportion of sales from a given period that should be collected in each subsequent period. For example, a monthly collection pattern of 30%, 50%, and 20% means that 30% of sales from a given month should be collected in that same month; 50% in the month following the month of sale; and 20% in two months following the month of sale. So, if forecast credit sales for January are $100,000, $30,000 of this amount is expected to be collected in January, $50,000 in February, and $20,000 in March.

Estimating the Receivables Collection Pattern

The collection pattern percentages can be established using information from your firm's historical sales and receivables records and a technique known as the payments pattern approach. The payments pattern approach uses customer receipts data to determine the percentage of customers that pay at various times after the date of sale. For example, if your cash budget is divided into monthly intervals, you would first compile historical credit sales by month. Then, using customer payment records you would identify what percentage of a given month's credit sales had been collected in that particular month as well as the subsequent months.

Use the steps listed below to establish your collection pattern percentages.

- Select a representative sample of historical credit sales figures from past periods that correspond to the budget intervals you have selected. For example, if your budget spans an entire year in monthly intervals, compile historical sales figures by month for a year. When doing so, keep this important point in mind: If your business is seasonal or sales fluctuate significantly during the year, the pattern of credit sales and collections will not be the same for each month. It is necessary, therefore, to calculate the collection pattern percentages for similar periods. For example, the percentages used to estimate collections for June, the first quarter, or the fall holiday season should be derived from the historical values for June, the first quarter, or the fall holiday season.

- Separate historical credit sales for each period by individual customer. This is done to identify what percentage of specific sales is paid out at various times after the date of sale. This task can be simplified by identifying the purchases of your firm's larger customers, those who account for a significant percentage of sales. These customers' sales figures should be tracked separately, and sales for your remaining customers can be lumped together.

- Trace individual customer payments made on credit sales for a given month. These payments are converted to percentages of sales for the month of sale. The percentages for each month in the analysis are your estimated receivables collection pattern.

To illustrate the above steps, examine a representative sample of Ideal's credit sales for the month of October. Management selected October because it was considered typical of the firm's sales and collection experience. During this month, sales and service revenues totaled $60,000. The analysis revealed that cash sales were $12,000 or 20% of the total, and credit sales made up the remaining $48,000 or 80%. The breakdown of credit sales per major customer is shown on Table 4.2.

Table 4.2

THE IDEAL LEVERAGE COMPANY
October Credit Sales by Customer

Customer	Sales
Debi D's	$18,000
State College	12,000
Avanti	11,000
All Other Credit Sales	7,000
Total Credit Sales for October	$48,000

Further analysis of this information produced the customer payment pattern for October credit sales shown on Table 4.3. Note that these dollar amounts represent collections on sales originating in October.

Table 4.3

THE IDEAL LEVERAGE COMPANY
Collection Pattern for October Credit Sales

Customer	November		December
Debi D's	$18,000		$ 0
State College	0		12,000
Avanti	5,000		6,000
All Other Credit Sales	1,000		6,000
Total Payments	$24,000		$24,000
		$ 24,000	
		+ 24,000	
October Credit Sales		$ 48,000	
Percentage of October Sales Collected In:	50%		50%

Remember, the goal is to associate payments received in a given month with the month in which the associated sale was made.

The collection pattern for October credit sales is indicated by the percentages in the last line of the table. The 50% figure under the November column represents the proportion of October credit sales collected one month after the month of sale. To arrive at this percentage, you divide the total payments for November ($24,000) by the total credit sales for October ($48,000) and then multiply by 100. Likewise, the 50% figure for December represents the percentage of credit sales collected two months after the month of sale ($24,000 divided by $48,000).

To make certain that October was a representative month, Ideal's management performed the same analysis for several other sample periods. The collection pattern for these samples was about the same as for October, as a result, the 50%-50% estimates were used in the actual cash budget projections for 19X3.

Estimating Cash Inflows

Given the necessary estimates, projected cash inflows are determined by applying the percentages for cash sales and receivables collection to projected sales. For Ideal, the percentage of cash sales for October 19X2 was 20% or $12,000 of the total sales services revenues, $60,000. As just determined in Table 4.3, the receivables collection percentage is 50%-50%. The 19X3 cash inflow estimates for Ideal appear on Table 4.4.

This worksheet is simply a tool for making the more detailed calculations required for the cash budget. Appropriate totals from the worksheet, such as total cash receipts, are subsequently brought forward to the cash budget.

The historical sales figures for the last two months of 19X2, and the projected sales figures for 19X3 are shown at the top of the worksheet. The two months of historical credit sales figures must be included in this case because of Ideal's collection lag. While the historical sales figures have no part in the actual cash budget, they do affect the calculation of Ideal's cash inflows for the first two months of the budget period.

Note that for each budget period, the cash sales figure is 20% of sales for that month. For example, estimated sales for March are $40,000 and cash sales are expected to be $8,000 (20% multiplied by $40,000). Credit sales, however, involve a one- and two-month lag. This means that the cash inflows from collections for a given month are a function of sales from the previous two months. Or, stated alternatively, the credit sales for a given month will not be completely converted to cash for two months.

For example, cash inflows from collections in January are the result of sales in the previous December ($40,000) and November ($38,000). The $20,000 shown on the one-month lag row is 50% times the $40,000 of credit sales for December; and the $19,000 for the two-month lag row is 50% times the $38,000 of credit sales for November. Likewise, the two $18,000 collections for the two lag periods in March are the result of expected credit sales of $36,000 in both January and February.

The quarterly collection figures shown on the worksheet reflect the assumption that total sales figure for a quarter are divided equally among the three months of that quarter. For instance, the second quarter sales figure of $150,000 is assumed to occur at the rate of $50,000 for each month of the quarter. Expected collections are determined by applying the assumed collection pattern to the prorated sales figures.

If cash inflows from sources other than operations are anticipated, these inflows should be included in the budget. Note that in Ideal's case, management anticipates an additional $10,000 inflow in the third quarter under other cash receipts. This cash flow represents the expected sale of used service equipment that will be replaced in that quarter.

On Table 4.4, total receipts for a given month are the sum of cash sales, the receivables collected in that month, and any other cash receipts. Remember, the sales and purchase figures for a given month are listed simply as a reference and are not used in actual cash budget worksheet calculations.

Estimating Purchases and Payments

The remaining calculations shown on Table 4.4 reflect expected payments the accounts payable created by inventory purchases. Ideal's inventory purchases policy reflects the nature of its retail business. Purchases are made approximately one-and-one-half months in advance of the following quarter and are based on the projected sales figure for that quarter. For example, the purchases figure in February ($90,000) is based on projected sales for the second quarter ($150,000), and purchases for the second quarter ($95,000) on the sales projection for the third quarter ($159,000).

Table 4.4

THE IDEAL LEVERAGE COMPANY

Cash Budget Worksheet

(Figures Rounded to the Nearest $1)

	19X2 Sales		Projected Sales For 19X3					
	Nov	Dec	Jan	Feb	Mar	2nd Qtr	3rd Qtr	4th Qtr
Sales	$38,000	$40,000	$36,000	$36,000	$40,000	$150,000	$159,000	$171,000
Cash Receipts:								
Cash Sales			$ 7,000	$ 7,000	$ 8,000	$ 30,000	$ 33,000	$ 34,000
Collections:								
1 Month Lag			20,000	18,000	18,000	60,000	62,000	79,000
2 Month Lag			19,000	20,000	18,000	55,000	61,000	75,000
Other Cash Receipts			0	0	0	0	10,000	0
Total Receipts			$46,000	$45,000	$44,000	$145,000	$166,000	$188,000

	Nov 19X2	Jan	Feb	Mar	2nd Qtr	3rd Qtr	4th Qtr
Purchases	$67,200	0	$90,000	0	$ 95,000	$103,000	N/A
Payments for Purchases		$67,200	0	0	$ 90,000	$ 95,000	$103,000

The dollar amount of the advance purchases is calculated by applying the average cost-of-sales percentage (60%) — as shown on Ideal's income statement in Chapter 1 — to projected sales. This percentage is used because management feels it is a reasonable approximation of the cost at which inventory will be purchased.

Calculation of purchases and associated payments involves nothing more than accounting for advanced purchasing and the lag between purchases and payments. For example, during November of 19X2, actual purchases were $67,200. This amount is 60% of the projected sales figure for the first quarter of the 19X3 budget period, $112,000. Likewise, the purchases figure in February, $90,000, is based on anticipated sales for the second quarter of $150,000 and the 60% cost figure. It is important to note that in Ideal's case, the purchase amounts are not cash flows and will not appear on the cash budget. They are accounts payable that are carried on the books until paid. The purchase figures shown on the worksheet serve only as reference numbers that facilitate the calculation of the payment amounts. These figures are the cash flows that will be transferred to the cash budget.

The delay between purchases and payments reflected on Table 4.4 stems from the 45-day credit terms now offered by Ideal's trade supplier. Note, for example, that the $67,200 of purchases made in November 19X2 will be paid 45 days later in January 19X3. Each of the other payment figures shown on Table 4.4 reflect the same 45-day lag.

Estimating Other Cash Outflows — Fixed Costs

The remaining cash outflows which appear on the cash budget can be grouped into two categories: fixed cash costs and variable cash costs.

Fixed cash costs are those expense items that will not change in amount during the budget period. For example, the lease, insurance, and accounting and legal expenses shown on Ideal's income statement are fixed amounts for the year. These items are projected by adjusting the historical amount for any anticipated price change. The appropriate value is then transferred to the cash budget. Ideal's lease and insurance payments are made quarterly, and accounting and legal expenses are paid monthly.

Estimating Other Cash Outflows — Variable Costs

Variable cash costs are those expense items that tend to change in amount with changes in sales. As sales increase or decrease, the cost of variable items increases or decreases as well. To project these amounts, you can use a simple procedure known as the percent-of-sales method.

The reasoning behind using this approach is this: The activity responsible for all other activities in a firm is sales or the anticipation of sales, and variable expense items change as sales change. So, if sales increase next year, then the cash outflows for these items will increase. If there are no major changes in the way you will do business from this year to the next, then it is reasonable to assume that operating expenses will bear the same percentage relationship to sales next year as they did last year. That is, if an expense item such as selling expense was 10% of sales this year, then barring a major change in operations, it is expected to be 10% of sales next year.

To obtain the variable expense percentages that are applied to projected sales, Ideal's management used the percent-of-sales figures shown on the firm's 19X2 income statement. These percentages are applied to projected sales for each budget period to obtain the estimated cash outflow.

For example, the percent of sales column on Ideal's 19X2 income statement in Chapter 1 shows that the selling and administrative expenses item was 1% of sales for that year. To obtain the projected cash outflow for selling and administrative expense for January of the 19X3 budget year, estimated sales of $36,000 is multiplied by 1%.

Cash Outflow = Projected Sales x Percent of Sales

$$= \$36,000 \times 1\%$$
$$= \$360$$

Other variable cash costs are calculated in the same manner. If Ideal's management anticipates changes in any of the historical relationships, the appropriate adjustments would be made to the percent-of-sales values. This was true of the anticipated cash costs for maintenance and repairs and for supplies. In Ideal's judgment, the higher level of activity created by the planned expansion would increase these costs to the level indicated on the 19X3 cast budget on Table 4.5 on page 70.

Financing and Investment Expenditures

Remaining cash outflows yet to be considered are existing loan payments, capital expenditures resulting from the purchase of additional fixed assets, and expected dividend payments (owner's withdrawals). Ideal's existing loan payments are $2,000 per year or $500 per quarter. The anticipated expansion of the retail facility and the purchase of service equipment will require cash outlays of $30,000 per quarter. Because of the anticipated drain on funds caused by the expansion, Ideal does not intend to make dividend distributions during 19X3.

Ideal's estimated cash inflows and outflows appear on the 19X3 cash budget on the following page.

How to Interpret the Cash Budget

It is useful to think of a cash budget as consisting of two parts: the data shown above net cash flow and that shown below that figure. Net cash flow, which is a period-by-period indicator of the cash required to support operating activity, is one of the three major focal points of the budget. It is calculated as the difference between projected cash inflows and outflows. For instance, the negative $40,100 net cash flow figure for January is calculated as the difference between total cash receipts of $46,000 and total cash disbursements of $86,100. Note that Ideal's budget also indicates a negative net cash flow figure for the second quarter ($19,000) and the third quarter ($5,000).

The area below net cash flow is usually referred to as the financing section of the budget. This section indicates when operations are expected to produce excess cash, or when financing will be required to support

Table 4.5

THE IDEAL LEVERAGE COMPANY
19X3 Cash Budget

	Jan	Feb	Mar	2nd Qtr	3rd Qtr	4th Qtr
Cash Inflows	$ 46,000	$45,000	$44,000	$ 145,000	$166,000	$188,000
Cash Outflows:						
Purchases Payments	$ 67,200	$ 0	$ 0	$ 90,000	$ 95,000	$103,000
Wages & Taxes	5,180	5,200	6,340	21,600	22,900	24,620
Lease Payments	2,000	0	0	2,000	2,000	2,000
Utilities	360	360	440	1,500	1,590	1,710
Insurance	2,250	0	0	2,250	2,250	2,250
Selling & Adm.	400	390	470	1,480	1,620	1,760
Mtce. & Repairs	1,000	1,000	1,000	3,000	3,000	3,000
Supplies	1,000	1,000	1,000	3,000	3,000	3,000
Acct. & Legal	250	250	250	750	750	750
Loan Payments	670	0	0	670	670	670
Income Taxes	5,790	0	0	7,750	8,220	8,840
Capital Expend.	0	30,000	0	30,000	30,000	30,000
Total Outflows	$ 86,100	$38,200	$ 9,500	$ 164,000	$171,000	$181,600
Net Cash Flow	(40,100)	6,800	34,500	(19,000)	(5,000)	6,400
+ Beginning Cash	900	2,000	2,000	2,000	2,000	2,000
Total Cash	$(39,200)	$ 8,800	$36,500	$(17,000)	$ (3,000)	$ 8,400
- Min. Cash Balance	2,000	2,000	2,000	2,000	2,000	2,000
Required Financing	(41,200)	0	0	(19,000)	(5,000)	0
Excess Cash	$ 0	$ 6,800	$34,500	$ 0	$ 0	$ 6,400

operating activity. This section of the budget also provides information on two other key variables contained on the cash budget: required financing and excess cash.

The beginning cash figure shown below net cash flow is the amount of cash expected to be on hand at the start of each budget interval. Adding beginning cash to net cash flow produces total cash for the period. Notice that the January beginning cash figure of $900 is the amount of cash on hand at the end of 19X2. Each subsequent beginning cash figure is the minimum balance amount, $2,000, set by management. This minimum balance is the liquid balance that must be maintained to protect against unforeseen, adverse developments, and forecasting errors, Holding liquid balances to protect against contingencies is the price the business must pay for living in an uncertain world.

The required financing figure for each period indicates the external financing that must be raised to support planned operations, planned capital expenditures on buildings and equipment, debt service obligations, and the minimum cash balance requirement. Notice that required financing is signaled for January ($41,200), the second quarter ($19,000), and the third quarter ($5,000). As will be discussed below, the largest required-financing value appearing on the budget is an important figure. It represents the amount of short-term financing Ideal must raise to meet expected working capital needs.

The excess cash figure indicates the amount available for use over and above the minimum cash balance requirement. It is calculated as $0 for periods when financing is required and as total cash minus the minimum balance requirement for periods not requiring financing. For example, excess cash is $0 in January because financing is required. The amount of total cash, ($39,200), is less than the required minimum cash balance, $2,000, and the sum of these two amounts ($41,200) must be borrowed. In February, excess cash is $6,800 because total cash of $8,800 is $6,800 greater than the required minimum balance of $2,000.

The excess cash figure is also important to Ideal's management. By knowing when cash will be available, Ideal can make advance plans to ensure that it will be used effectively. If cash balances are allowed to remain idle, the business suffers an opportunity cost in the form of lost earnings.

Interpreting the Financing Section

The financing section of the cash budget produces the information necessary to identify and make advance preparation for the short-term financing needed to support planned operations. This information is contained in the largest required financing figure for the period.

In Ideal's case, this figure is the ($41,200) shown for January. It implies that if planned operations materialize as suggested, the $41,200 borrowed in January will meet Ideal's financing needs for the entire budget horizon. This figure also implies that assuming any excess cash available during the budget period is used to repay outstanding debt, a positive

Using the Cash Budget to Estimate Short-Term Financing Needs

excess cash figure at the end of the budget period means all required financing will be repaid. This was true for Ideal. Its cash budget showed an excess cash figure of $6,400 for the 4th quarter.

In short, the required financing figure provides an answer to two of the most important questions the banker will ask when confronted with a loan request: How much money is needed, and when and how will it be repaid? In this case, $41,200 is needed, and it will be repaid from normal operations before the year end.

Planning Long-Term Financing Needs

Planning for near-term horizons, such as the monthly intervals used by Ideal, offers one important advantage over long-term planning. Forecasting is easier and less risky. In the short run, the possibility of encountering an unforeseen event that could not have been forecast is considerably lower. On the other hand, the likelihood of such an event increases your attempt to project further into the future. As seen from Ideal's cash budget, this short-run advantage offers any firm the opportunity to estimate, plan for, and control cash flows on an item-by-item basis.

Such detail is not possible, and fortunately not necessary, for extended-term planning horizons. Because uncertainty increases as the length of the forecasting period increases, long-term plans are by necessity broad in scope and deal with general financial relationships rather than detailed values. Briefly, a long-term financial plan provides you with a financial profile of your business based on broad assumptions about future sales growth and the level of planned operations.

Pro Forma Statements

The financial profile that emerges from long-term financial planning is often expressed in the form of projected financial statements: the income statement and balance sheet. These projected statements are referred to as pro forma statements, and they are constructed by substituting projected or estimated values for the actual historical values used by the accountant. This approach to long-term financial planning is based on basic financial logic that is important for you to understand and interpret pro forma statements.

The reasoning goes like this: For your firm to produce sales and maintain a given level of operations, it must have the necessary amount of current assets (cash, receivables, and inventory) and fixed assets (plant and equipment). There is an important relationship between sales, the level of operations, and assets. But, in order to make the investment in assets, you must have financing. Usually, the necessary financing is obtained from a combination of external and internal sources. Some comes from recurring short-term liabilities such as accounts payable (trade credit) and accrued liabilities. Finance people refer to this form of financing as spontaneous, since it does not have to be negotiated, and the amount used tends to increase and decrease with changes in the level of operations. Creditors' funds are also obtained through negotiated short-term liabilities, such as bank loans (notes payable), and long-term liabilities, such as a long-term equipment or a mortgage loan. Owners' funds are provided by paid-in capital and through internally generated cash flows that are retained in the business.

Thus, there is another important relationship between sales, the level of operations, assets, and financing. If any changes in the volume of operations, the level of sales, or the asset base take place, your firm's financial resources are effected. For example, even if the volume of sales and level of operations remain constant from period to period, assets wear out or become obsolete and must be replaced. Financing is required to purchase these replacement assets. Or, if you anticipate long-term growth in the level of operations and volume of sales, additional assets must be added to accommodate the increase in activity. Again, this investment must be financed.

Pro forma statements are developed using the logical relationship between volume of operations, level of sales, size of the asset base, and amount of financing. To accomplish this, you need a sales estimate for each period in the planning horizon and an estimate of the relationship between sales and the various income statement and balance sheet accounts. While a number of techniques may be used to express the necessary sales relationships, the most commonly used approach is the percent-of-sales method.

Pro forma statements not only provide a financial profile of long-term operating plans, they also furnish information on long-term financing needs. The pro forma balance sheet serves as a broad source and use-of-funds statement indicating the investment in assets and how much is required to make this investment.

The first step in preparing pro forma statements is the calculation of historical percentage relationships between sales and appropriate balance sheet and income statement items. The historical statements used to calculate the percent-of-sales values may be those from the previous year, percentages from the previous year adjusted for estimated changes in conditions, or an average of several previous years. Use the source that best reflects estimated future conditions for your small business.

How to Construct Pro Forma Statements

After the percent-of-sales values have been calculated, apply these percentages to projected sales. To illustrate the process as well as learn how the balance sheet can be used to project long-term financial requirements, examine the condensed pro forma statements prepared by The Ideal Leverage Company's management for the two-year planning period, 19X3 and 19X4. These statements are shown as tables 4.6 and 4.7 on the following page.

Table 4.6

THE IDEAL LEVERAGE COMPANY
Condensed 19X3 and 19X4 Pro Forma Income Statements (Rounded)

	% of Sales	19X3	19X4
Sales	Projected Amt.	$590,000	$696,000
Cost of Sales	60.0%	354,000	418,000
Gross Profit	40.0%	$236,000	$278,000
Total Operating Expenses	24.4%	144,000	170,000
Net Operating Income	15.6%	$92,000	$108,000
Net Income	10.0%	$59,000	$70,000

Schedules of the Change in Retained Earnings

	19X3	19X4
Retained Earnings - Previous Year	$120,000	$149,000
Plus: Current Net Income	59,000	70,000
Less: Estimated Dividends	30,000	40,000
Year-End Retained Earnings	$149,000	$179,000

Table 4.7

THE IDEAL LEVERAGE COMPANY
Condensed 19X3 and 19X4 Pro Forma Balance Sheets (Rounded)

	% of Sales	19X3	19X4
Current Assets	50%	$295,000	$348,000
Net Fixed Assets	Projected Amt.	270,000	390,000
Total Assets		$565,000	$738,000
Current Liabilities:			
Notes Payable 19X2	Projected Amt.	$ 40,000	$ 40,000
Spontaneous Liabilities	24%	142,000	167,000
Total Current Liabilities		$182,000	$207,000
Long-Term Liabilities	Projected Amt.	65,000	60,000
Total Liabilities		$247,000	$267,000
Owner's Equity:			
Capital Stock	Projected Amt.	50,000	50,000
Retained Earnings	From Schedule	149,000	179,000
Total Owner's Equity		$199,000	$229,000
Total Liabilities & Equity		$446,000	$496,000
Additional External Financing Required		$119,000	$242,000

The percentages used to calculate Ideal's pro forma income statement values were taken from the percent of sales column of the actual 19X2 income statement in Chapter 1, and the balance sheet percentages were calculated by dividing the appropriate 19X2 balance sheet item by the 19X2 sales figure of $500,000. For example, the net income, percent of sales value of 10% shown on Table 4.6 is calculated as follows:

Percent of Sales = 19X2 Net Income ÷ 19X2 Sales
$$= \$50,000 \div \$500,000 \times 100$$
$$= 10\%$$

Likewise, the current asset, percent of sales value of 50% shown on Table 4.7 was arrived at by:

Percent of Sales = 19X2 Current Assets ÷ 19X2 Sales
$$= \$250,000 \div \$500,000 \times 100$$
$$= 50\%$$

The projected sales and capital expenditure figures were produced by management estimate. Recall from the cash budget information that management anticipates an 18% sales growth rate for 19X3 and 19X4, and capital expenditures of $120,000 in each of those years. Based on these estimates, projected sales for 19X3 is $590,000 (1.18 multiplied by 19X2 sales of $500,000), and $696,000 for 19X4 (1.18 multiplied by $590,000). The 1.18 figure is calculated by adding 1 plus the percentage (.18); for example, to increase 100 by 18%, multiply 100 by 1.18 which equals 118.

The statement values shown on tables 4.6 and 4.7 were obtained by applying the percent of sales values to forecast sales or by entering the indicated management-determined dollar amounts. For example, the gross profit figures on Table 4.6 were calculated as:

19X3 Projected Gross Profit = Projected Sales x Gross Profit Percent of Sales
$$= \$590,000 \times 40\%$$
$$= \$236,000$$

Likewise, the current asset figures on the balance sheets on Table 4.7 were calculated as:

19X3 Projected Current Assets = Projected Sales x Current Asset Percent of Sales
$$= \$590,000 \times 50\%$$
$$= \$295,000$$

19X4 Projected Current Assets = Projected Sales x Current Asset Percent of Sales
$$= \$696,000 \times 50\%$$
$$= \$348,000$$

Once the pro forma account values have been determined, the statements are prepared using the following instructions. These instructions can help you better understand how the pro forma income statement and the balance sheet are used to make long-term financing estimates.

The Pro Forma Income Statement

The income statements and balance sheets on tables 4.6 and 4.7 have been abbreviated to show only key statement accounts. While each detailed expense, asset, and liability item could have been calculated, it is not always necessary to do so. If, as in this case, the statements are used only to obtain a rough estimate of long-term financing requirements, only the net income figure and aggregated balance sheet values are needed. On the other hand, if the statement were used as part of a loan proposal, the complete statement would be prepared.

As explained earlier, the projected dollar amounts on the pro forma income statements are obtained by multiplying the sales estimates by the appropriate percent of sales values. For example, the 19X4 net income value is calculated as:

19X4 Net Income = 19X4 Projected Sales x Net Income Percent of Sales
= $696,000 x 10%
= $70,000 (rounded)

The retained earnings schedules shown below the income statements on Table 4.6 reveal how the retained earnings values which appear on the pro forma balance sheets are calculated. In accordance with accounting convention, the year-end retained earnings figure (projected in this case) is determined as the retained earnings figure from the previous year-end balance sheet, plus net income for the period, and minus dividends (owner's withdrawals). On the pro forma balance sheets, these figures serve as substitutes for cash flow from operations (CFFO) or internally generated financing.

The Pro Forma Balance Sheet

The pro forma balance sheets shown on Table 4.7 were prepared by applying the appropriate percent of sales values to projected sales and by entering the estimated dollar amounts. The net fixed asset figure for 19X3 was calculated as the 19X2 net fixed asset value of $150,000, plus the annual $120,000 capital expenditure estimated by management. The 19X4 net fixed asset value reflects the 19X3 value plus the estimated $120,000 expenditure for that year.

The projected values for notes payable, $40,000, are the same as those for 19X2. There are two reasons for extending these historical amounts. First, management has assumed that Ideal is able to continue borrowing at least this amount of short-term financing in the future. Second, as discussed below, any borrowing above this amount will be included in the estimate of the additional external financing required.

Spontaneous liabilities, which consists of accounts payable and accrued expenses, is that form of short-term, non-negotiated financing that tends to expand and contract automatically with changes in the level of sales activity. It is financing in the form of delayed payments, and for Ideal, these two accounts were a combined 24% of sales in 19X2. The long-term liability values on the pro forma balance sheets reflect an assumption of a $5,000 per year reduction of principal on the existing mortgage loan. Ideal's stockholders plan no additional investment (purchase of additional shares) over the planning horizon so the value of the capital stock accounts remain unchanged from 19X2. The retained earnings values reflect the changes detailed on the schedules shown on Table 4.6.

The balance sheet should balance: the value of total assets (uses of funds) should equal the value of total liabilities and owner's equity (sources of funds). Note, however, that the pro forma balance sheets on Table 4.7 do not balance. In 19X3 for example, the projected total asset value is $565,000, while total liabilities and equity is $446,000. How can this be? The answer is also the reason that the pro forma balance sheet is used to provide an estimate of the financing needed to support long-term plans.

Estimating Additional Financing Needs

The imbalance between total assets and total liabilities and equity means that Ideal will require additional financing to pay for the increase in assets that result from planned sales growth. Some financing is available from the current level of notes payable borrowing ($40,000), spontaneous financing ($142,000 and $167,000), and from internally generated funds (the increase in retained earnings of $149,000 and $179,000), but it is not enough. If management is to carry out its plans, additional external financing in the form of either notes payable, long-term debt, additional owner's investment, or some combination of the three must be raised.

The amount of this required financing is shown as the additional external financing required (AFR) figure on the pro forma balance sheets. This balancing "plug figure" is calculated as:

AFR = Total Assets – Total Liabilities & Equity

If the AFR figure is positive, as is the case for Ideal, additional financing is indicated. At the time these plans are finalized, Ideal's management should begin making advance preparation for raising $361,000, $119,000 ($565,000 minus $446,000) in 19X3, and $242,000 ($738,000 minus $496,000) in 19X4. If the AFR value were zero, no additional external financing is indicated. That is, spontaneous financing, notes payable, and CFFO are sufficient to meet planned needs, and sources and uses of funds are equal. If the AFR value were negative, excess funds are expected. In this case, the combination of existing notes payable, spontaneous financing, and internally generated funds is more than sufficient to meet expected needs.

A Bonus from the Financial Planning Process

In addition to the valuable financing information provided to you through the cash budget and pro forma statements, the mere act of preparing these planning documents produces other equally valuable benefits. Through financial planning, you:

- Are provided a clear understanding of the key factors affecting the success and financial position of your business;
- Have the data necessary to evaluate the success of your financial plan, or to determine what, if anything, went wrong;
- Increase your expertise and thereby your effectiveness in future planning efforts; and
- Are able to formulate a more convincing business plan and loan proposal because of the insights gained from direct involvement in the planning exercise.

In short, planning forces you to identify, gather information on, and evaluate what is important. As a result, the real benefit from financial planning may not be the financial plans produced, but rather what you learn about your business and its operations in the process.

Acquiring Debt Financing

Chapter 5:
Financing for Short-Term Needs

Chapter 6:
Extended-Term Financing for Your Small Firm

Chapter 7:
Understanding Your Banker

Chapter 8:
Preparing and Presenting a Business Plan
and Financing Proposal

Chapter 5

Financing for Short-Term Needs

Short-term credit is of particular importance to any small firm, because unlike a larger firm, a small firm has at best only restricted access to long-term external financing. This limitation forces greater reliance on short-term credit. In many small firms, short-term financing and cash flow from operations are virtually the only available sources of funds.

In the acquisition and management of short-term financing, you need to know:

- How much should be used; and
- The specific sources that should be used.

As indicated in Chapter 1, the amount of short-term financing used depends on the amount of temporary working capital that must be financed. That is, short-term temporary needs should be matched with short-term financing. For example, the temporary need for working capital during seasonal peaks in operations would be financed with short-term sources. This chapter examines the important factors that must be considered when using a specific form of short-term financing.

What Is Short-Term Debt?

Short-term debt is commonly characterized as obligations that mature within one year. That is, the principal amount and associated interest will be outstanding or repaid in one year or less. This is in contrast to extended-term financing which has a maturity of longer than one year. While it is convenient to identify financing sources by maturity, it is more useful for you to view the difference between short- and extended-term financing in terms of how the funds are used and the means of repayment.

Ideally, short-term financing is used to satisfy seasonal or temporary working capital needs, such as a retailer's build-up of inventory and accounts receivable during the winter holiday season. Repayment of this short-term credit should come from the cash flow generated by the sale of inventory and collection of receivables. On the other hand, extended-term financing can be used to finance permanent additions to your firm's asset base, such as fixed assets or a permanent increase in the level of working capital. Funds to repay such loans usually come from cash flows generated over a period of several years and not from liquidation of the assets being financed.

Short-term obligations appear on your firm's balance sheet as current liabilities. While the term "current liability" may have a negative connotation for some, there is nothing unfavorable about these obligations. Liabilities, if properly managed, are a normal part of the operations of virtually all businesses, and they meet two important needs in your firm's financing scheme.

- Short-term financing provides the temporary funds required to support current assets, conduct day-to-day operations, and keep the business productive. Since short-term cash inflows are rarely synchronized with the temporary need for working capital, your firm will turn to short-term financing sources to meet its needs.

- Short-term financing can be used to bridge the gap between current needs and the time when the required long-term financing can be secured. For example, a short-term bank loan may be used by a construction firm as stop-gap funding of the early stages of an apartment complex or real estate development. When construction has progressed to the point that the project qualifies for extended-term financing, a long-term loan would be negotiated.

Types of Short-Term Debt Financing

Short-term credit sources are usually grouped into two basic categories: unsecured and secured. Unsecured credit has traditionally been defined as financing obtained without the borrower's pledge of specific assets to serve as collateral. In the event of borrower default, the lender has the legal right to sue for breach of contract, but has no claim on any particular asset of the business. Rather, the unsecured creditor shares proportionately with all other general creditors in the available pool of unsecured assets.

Unsecured bank financing, which is often referred to as cash-flow lending, is actually based on the assumed ability of the borrower to make the mandatory interest and principal payments.

To qualify for this type of financing, a borrowing firm must have unquestioned credit capability. This means a business is viewed by the banker as having a strong financial position, a history of demonstrated earning power, an impeccable record of debt repayment, and a highly certain future for continued financial performance. The qualifying standards for trade credit, which is the other major source of unsecured financing for any small firm, are often less stringent than those imposed by commercial banks.

Unsecured Credit

Although the ultimate security behind every business loan is the earning power of a firm, the future of any small business is highly uncertain. Lenders, therefore, require many small businesses to secure financing with various types of collateral. This type of financing, which is often called asset lending by bankers, involves providing the lender with a prior, legal claim on a specific asset or group of assets in the event of default. The primary source of collateral for secured short-term financing is a firm's working capital (cash, accounts receivable, or inventory) and, if necessary, the personal endorsement or guarantee of the loan by the owner(s).

Secured Credit

Under a typical asset financing agreement, the lender takes a security interest in all or a part of an asset or group of assets and provides funds equal to a percentage of the asset's value. For example, if accounts receivable are used to secure a bank loan, the bank will advance funds in the range of 65% to 85% of the face value of acceptable receivables. The actual percentage advanced in this case depends on the quality of the accounts receivable as measured by past collection and bad-debt experience and the riskiness of the business. Where inventory is used as loan collateral, the security interest arrangements suggested by the lender may be even more elaborate.

Factors Influencing Short-Term Credit Selection

While short-term financing is most often used by businesses to support seasonal working capital needs, the various methods for raising these funds do not have uniform characteristics. The many differences between sources of short-term financing require you to carefully evaluate the features of a particular opportunity to ensure that it is compatible with the needs and capabilities of your firm. In choosing a source of short-term financing, you need to consider availability, reliability, restrictions, cost, and flexibility.

Availability

Because a typical small firm has only limited financing opportunities, accessibility often becomes the primary consideration when evaluating a supplier of credit. When limited financing opportunity is a problem, you must be certain that the particular financing arrangement is cost-justified, and the associated contractual obligations do not unreasonably restrict management or jeopardize your firm's existence.

Reliability

Not only must funds be available, but they must be available when and as often as needed. To ensure reliability, you need to make every effort to nurture the relationship with your financing source and to cultivate a public image as a credit-worthy borrower. The essential foundation for both of these actions is sound financial management and a responsible attitude toward debt obligations.

Restrictions

Loan restrictions take the form of contractual covenants that limit your freedom of action or that specify explicit financial standards your firm must maintain, or both. Examples of limiting or restrictive covenants are restrictions on salaries or on freedom to sell fixed assets without prior approval of the lender. Imposed financial standards can include such measures as maintenance of a specified working capital position or limitations on dividend payments.

A lender's incentive to impose restrictive covenants will vary with the financial position of your firm, the quality of your management, and the degree of risk perceived in extending credit. In general, the stronger the financial position of a firm, the more negotiating leverage available to management, and the more favorable the terms obtained.

Cost

If all other considerations are equal, lowest cost is the factor to use when choosing among financing alternatives. After satisfactorily resolving the other important factors influencing the short-term financing decision, seek the financing arrangement offering the lowest effective annual rate of interest. It is important when considering effective cost to include not only interest charges but any fees or other dollar costs incurred — for example, a service charge, commitment fee, or the mandatory purchase of insurance — as well as any specific arrangements that affect the amount of money actually available for use by your firm, such as a discounted loan or compensating balance requirement.

Flexibility

Flexibility in this context refers to the degree to which the amount of financing used is readily increased or decreased with changes in the volume of operations. As a general rule, short-term financing is inherently more flexible than extended-term financing. Flexibility becomes increasingly more important as the degree of business risk to which your firm is exposed increases. Flexibility, however, is not present to the same degree in all sources of short-term financing.

Unsecured Sources of Short-Term Financing

There are two sources of unsecured financing available to you: 1) your small business; and 2) commercial banks. The first, your small business, not only creates the need for funds, but it can also produce two significant types of sources of unsecured financing: trade credit and accruals. The second, commercial banks, can offer you loans. Trade credit and accruals are discussed below, and the discussion on commercial banks is on page 90.

Trade Credit and Accruals

Among short-term financing sources, trade credit and accruals are unique. Neither involves the direct loan of funds to a firm. Rather, they take the form of delayed payment for goods or services received. The purchase of inventory on credit (trade credit) gives rise to accounts payable, and the use of services, such as labor (accruals), creates the balance sheet liability of accrued wage expense.

Trade credit and accruals are spontaneous or self-generating. For instance, once a firm establishes the relationship with a supplier of goods or services, the amount of credit used rises and falls in response to changes in the volume of operations without negotiation or conscious decisions on the part of management — such as when accounts payable swell automatically as the purchase of inventory increases in response to growing sales. Taken together, trade credit and accruals constitute a substantial offset to a firm's short-term financing needs. Trade credit, however, is the most important of these two sources.

Trade Credit

Trade credit is credit extended by one firm to another in conjunction with the sale of goods or services that are used in the normal course of business. For the purchasing firm, using trade credit is the equivalent of a consumer charge account at a department store; goods are purchased but payment can be delayed to the extent of the specified credit terms. For the length of the credit period, the purchaser has a debt outstanding to the supplier. This debt is recorded on the books (balance sheet) of the purchasing firm as the current liability or accounts payable. The corresponding entry for the trade supplier is accounts receivable.

If a purchasing firm has an established relationship with its trade supplier, goods are ordered as the level of activity dictates. These orders are placed without the continual renegotiation that would be required with a bank loan. The payment delay provided by the seller's credit terms is an important source of working capital financing. Although technically this financing does not involve a direct loan of funds, the option to delay payment is the equivalent of having an interest free loan for the period of the credit terms.

Advantages of Trade Credit

As a financing source, trade credit has a number of advantages, such as:

- **Availability and Consistency.** Trade credit is often the most available and consistent source of financing. For instance, when you are a trade supplier (or vendor), you have a distinct advantage over the typical financial institution making a loan when extending credit. When a financial institution makes a loan, it receives in return only the fixed interest yield on the loan and the repaid principal. Conversely, the profit margin on the goods sold by the vendor provides a much higher rate of return on the transaction. This profit margin is normally sufficient to cover both the cost of credit extended and the normal profit margin on the goods. Because of the higher return, the vendor can assume more risk and sell to customers with credit standings that would be less than acceptable to a financial institution making a loan of funds. For small firms having only a marginal credit rating, this point is crucial. This means trade credit may be the only form of available financing on a consistent basis.

- **Flexibility.** The amount of trade credit used is automatically increased and reduced as a normal part of a firm's operations, without the burden of continual renegotiation. Trade credit is also granted on an informal basis making any contract or other formal agreement representing the debt unnecessary.

- **Cost.** Trade credit provides a distinct cost advantage over conventional forms of financing. If the credit terms do not include the opportunity for a cash discount, or if a cash discount is available and taken, there is no explicit cost associated with this method of financing. However, if a cash discount is offered as part of the credit terms, and the buyer does not pay within the discount period, there can be a substantial effective cost to missing the discount.

Understanding Credit Terms

The terms of sale offered by a supplier are stated on the invoice that accompanies the shipment of goods. The more common forms of credit terms include a net period and, if offered, a discount for early payment. The net period is the maximum length of time for which credit is extended. It is shown as the letter "n" followed by the number of days. For example, credit terms with a net period of 30 days are shown as n30.

If a cash discount is offered, the amount of the discount and the number of days the discount is in effect are expressed as the discount percentage/discount period. For example, if a 1% discount from the invoice price is offered for payment within 15 days, or the full amount of the invoice must be paid in 30 days, the credit terms would appear as 1/15, n30.

In practice, a small firm most often encounters the above credit-term format. There are, however, a myriad of variations depending on the industry of the selling firm, common practice, the buyer's credit standing, and the seller's financial strength and cash-flow cycle. Table 5.1 contains examples and explanations of different terms under which goods are sold.

The Cost of Using Trade Credit

Your first reaction to the idea that there is a cost associated with trade credit might be: "Wrong, there is no interest payment associated with using trade credit, so there is no cost. Trade credit is free financing." This

Table 5.1 – Example Credit Terms

Terms	Definition	Type of User
Cash on Delivery (C.O.D.)	Goods are shipped and customer makes payment before taking possession.	High risk, or one for which credit information is lacking.
Cash Before Delivery (C.B.D.)	Goods are not shipped until payment is received.	High risk, usually poor payment record.
Net Cash (e.g., net 30 days)	Invoice must be paid in full by the period indicated.	Normal credit risk. Commonly used in many lines of retailing.
Bill to Bill	Requires payment on previous invoice when new delivery is made.	Normal credit risk. Also used in many lines of retailing.
Ordinary Terms (e.g., 2/10, n30, or 1/15, n60)	Provide the indicated percent discount if payment is made within the discount date; otherwise, payment in full is required by the indicated net date.	Many different lines of business. Most commonly used credit terms.
Monthly Billing (e.g., 8/10, E.O.M. or 2/10, prox. n30)	A single payment for all purchases made before the 25th of one month is made in the next month. Terms may include the indicated cash discount. E.O.M. means end of month. "Prox." is an abbreviation for the Latin word *proximo* meaning, next.	Widely used in industries where it is common to place several orders during a given month, such as apparel, lumber, or books.
Seasonal Dating (e.g., n30, May 1; or 2/10, n30, May 1)	Payment for all goods shipped prior to the indicated date is due according to the indicated terms.	Highly seasonal industries, such as toys and Christmas cards.
Consignment	The seller acts as agent and receives a commission for that sale. Title to goods remains with the manufacturer. The seller remits payment less commission after the goods are sold.	May be used in any appropriate business. The most common application is in rack sales of books and magazines in supermarkets.

statement is true as long as no cash discount is offered; or, if one is offered, payment is made within the discount period. If, however, a cash discount is offered as part of the credit terms, and the discount is not taken, a firm incurs a cost for missing the discount. Depending on the credit terms being offered, this cost can be substantial.

The cost associated with missing a cash discount is not an explicit, measurable interest charge as in the case of bank financing. Rather, it is a hidden cost that preys on the unsuspecting. Finance people refer to this cost as an opportunity cost; the cost of a foregone opportunity. While the opportunity cost of missing a cash discount is not obvious because no check is written for payment, the impact on a firm's cash account is real.

The Opportunity Cost of Trade Credit

By foregoing a cash discount, you elect to delay payment until the more distant net date rather than the earlier discount date. To gain these additional days of financing — the difference between the discount date and the net date — you lose the discount amount. This loss represents a real cost. It is the cost of paying the full invoice price rather than the lower discount price.

For example, assume your firm's supplier offers terms of 2/10, n30. With these terms, you can gain a 2% discount by making payment on or before the 10th day. If you choose to take the longer credit period and pay at the end of 30 days, you pay the full amount of the invoice. Delaying payment until the 30th day provides an extra 20 days of financing (day 10 to day 30), but this additional time is not free. In this case, the cost of the additional 20 days of financing is the missed 2% discount.

You might feel that 2% is not much of an opportunity cost to suffer for missing the discount. This would be true if 2% were the opportunity cost for the entire year, but it is not. In this case, the cost is 2% for 20 days. If you purchase from this supplier on a regular basis, 2% for every 20 day period in a year amounts to an annual effective cost of 37.23% for foregoing discounts. This is a sizable cost to suffer for the extra 20 days of financing gained.

Calculating the Cost of Missing a Cash Discount

To calculate the annual effective cost of missing a cash discount, you simply need two fractions. The first fraction consists of the percentage discount divided by one minus the percentage discount, and the second involves dividing 365 by the difference in days between the net period and the discount period. These two fractions are then multiplied to obtain the annual effective cost or rate (AER) of missing a cash discount.

$$\text{Annual Effective Cost} = \frac{\text{Percentage Discount}}{1 - \text{Percentage Discount}} \times \frac{365}{\text{Net Period} - \text{Discount Period}}$$

In the above example, the annual effective cost of missing the cash discount when credit terms are 2/10 n30 was 37.23%. This was the calculation:

$$AER = (.02 \div 1 - .02) \times (365 \div 30 - 10)$$
$$= (.02 \div .98) \times (365 \div 20)$$
$$= .0204 \times 18.25 \times 100$$
$$= 37.23\%$$

Table 5.2 contains selected examples of the cost of missing a cash discount under various credit terms. Each listed cost was calculated using the AER formula illustrated above. As a learning exercise, verify the cost figures by making the necessary AER calculations.

Table 5.2

Annual Effective Cost of Missing Cash Discount with Various Credit Terms

Credit Terms	Annual Cost
1/10, n30	18.4%
2/10, n30	37.2%
3/10, n30	56.4%
1/15, n60	8.2%
3/15, n60	24.6%
5/15, n60	41.0%
8/10, E.O.M.	157.7%

The examples in Table 5.2 help clarify three important considerations associated with cash discounts. First, the cost of missing a cash discount depends on the specific credit terms offered. In general, the longer the net period or the lower the discount percentage, the lower the annual effective cost of missing the discount. For example, the AER for missing a cash discount when terms are 2/10, n30 is 37.23%. If the terms were 2/10, n60, the AER drops to 12.41%.

Second, as a general rule, missing cash discounts is a costly method of financing. If the cash is available, take the discount unless your firm can earn considerably more than the AER by using the cash in an alternative investment. For example, if your firm's return on its asset base (ROI) is greater than the AER, and there is an investment alternative available, there is a sound reason for missing the discount. Otherwise, the discount should be taken.

Third, if the cash necessary to take the discount is not available, consider borrowing the funds to make the early payment. If the firm has the necessary credit capability, and the interest cost of borrowing is less than the AER, there is a definite financial advantage to borrowing the funds and taking the discount. It is important to note, however, that any advantage to borrowing to take the discount assumes the loan will be repaid on the net date. This is the date the supplier would have to be paid if the discount is not taken.

Accruals

Virtually every business firm is provided services on a continuing basis that are not paid for at the time the service is rendered. For example, employees provide services to the firm each day they work; yet, they are usually not paid until some specified future payroll date. When preparing your firm's financial statements, such services are treated as expenses at the time they are rendered. Since payment is delayed, however, your firm receives a form of credit similar to that provided by trade suppliers. The unpaid portion of this credit appears on the balance sheet as a current liability under titles such as accrued wages payable or accrued taxes payable.

The time period over which your firm postpones payments for accrued items is predetermined and fixed — for example, the pay period or tax date — and the degree to which such services are employed is determined by the volume of operations; for example, increased production means increased labor hours. Thus, the amount of accrued liabilities shown on the balance sheet tends to rise and fall with the level of activity. This provides your firm with the equivalent of temporary financing.

Unsecured Commercial Bank Financing

Commercial banks are the second major source of unsecured, short-term financing for qualified small firms. Although banks today make a variety of loans and are more aggressive lenders than in the past, they remain the primary suppliers of short term, self-liquidating loans to businesses. Self-liquidating loans are used to finance temporary increases in working capital: inventory, accounts receivable, and liquid cash balances. As these assets are liquidated, they provide the cash flow to repay the loan. Traditional bankers have viewed this type of loan as having low default risk and ideally suited to the nature of a banking operation.

Unlike accounts payable created by trade credit, the amount of notes payable resulting from a bank loan does not rise spontaneously with increases in the volume of operations. A bank loan is a negotiated transactions evidenced by a legally binding promissory note. This instrument is a signed agreement covering the terms of repayment and may take the form of a demand note, which is payable on demand by the bank, or one payable in a specified number of days as, for example, a 90-day note.

A transaction loan or a line of credit are two types of unsecured, short-term bank loans. Since both represent short-term financing, they have maturities of one year or less. The interest rates on these loans vary with the credit worthiness of the borrower and the general level of interest rates in the economy. Before discussing the particulars of these financing arrangements, take a closer look at the cost of bank loans.

Within limits, the interest rates on business loans are set by negotiation between the borrower and the bank. In general, the greater the perceived risk of the borrower, the higher the rate of interest the bank will require as compensation. However, because banks are basically conservative lending institutions, and because they receive only the limited return provided by the interest on the loan, they have characteristically denied credit to high-risk borrowers. Bankers are fond of saying, "We are not in the venture capital business." While some of the banking recklessness of the 1980s seems to contradict this statement, it is still basically true, especially for the small firm borrower.

In general, a bank's lending rates are scaled upward from its prime interest rate. The prime is the interest rate the bank charges its most credit worthy customers on short-term loans. It is established by the bank itself and adjusted periodically to reflect changing market rates of interest for short-term money. As such, it serves as the floor for bank loans, and the base rate to which premiums are added as perceived customer risk increases.

The manner in which the interest on a loan is actually paid is also the subject of negotiation between the borrowing firm and the bank. One of three methods can be used: ordinary or simple interest, discounted interest, and a floating rate of interest.

- **Ordinary-Interest Method.** With this method, interest is paid on the full amount of the principal on the note's maturity date. For example, assume Ideal borrows $50,000 for 90 days at 12% to cover seasonal working capital needs. If the ordinary-interest method is used, Ideal would repay the $50,000 loan principal plus $1,500 in interest cost ($50,000 multiplied by .12 multiplied by 90 divided by 360) at the end of 90 days. In this case, the annual effective rate of interest on the loan (true cost) is the same as the stated rate of 12%. Ideal had use of the full amount of the principal for the entire period of the loan and paid interest only on what was used for the time period it was used.

- **Discounted-Interest Method.** If the loan agreement in the above situation had specified the interest to be discounted, the bank would have first deducted the amount of interest on the loan before Ideal received the loan proceeds. In this case, Ideal would have had only $48,500 ($50,000 minus $1,500) available for use. As will be discussed in the next section, discounting the loan in this manner increases the annual effective cost (AER) of borrowing.

- **Floating-Rate Method.** Under a floating- or variable-rate agreement, which in recent years has been the most common type of business loan, the interest rate is not fixed. Rather, it varies with the bank's prime rate according to the relationship specified in the loan agreement. For example, if Ideal's short-term borrowing rate were specified as prime plus 4%, interest would be calculated each day by adding 4% to the existing prime rate, adjusting this percentage to a daily basis, and multiplying it by the principal, as illustrated on the following page.

Interest Rates on Bank Loans

Interest Cost = [(Prime Rate + 4%) ÷ 365] x Principal

Each month Ideal would have to pay the interest owed from the previous month. At maturity, the principal plus the remaining interest would be paid. With a floating-rate agreement, the amount of interest paid and the effective cost of the loan cannot be determined until the loan has been paid at maturity.

Calculating the Effective Cost of Unsecured Bank Loans

The annual effective cost of a particular loan arrangement is calculated using the appropriate variation of the general annual effective cost or rate (AER) formula. The basic form of this relationship is:

$$AER = \frac{\text{Total Dollar Cost}}{\text{Amount Available}}$$

In this formula, total dollar cost includes interest charges, plus any other costs the firm incurs to obtain the loan. These may include such charges as service fees, loan origination fees, or the mandatory purchase of life insurance on the firm's principal officer(s). The amount available is the funds from the loan that the firm can actually use to meet its needs. Under some loan arrangements, this will be the loan principal. In other cases, such as when the loan is discounted or a compensating balance is required, the amount available for use will be less than the principal of the loan. The following examples demonstrate how the AER formula can work in different situations.

Assume initially that Ideal is able to borrow $50,000 from Friendly Bank for one year at 12% ordinary interest. Under this arrangement the total dollar cost is the interest charge on the loan of $6,000 ($50,000 multiplied by .12 multiplied by 365 divided by 365). Since the loan arrangement specifies the ordinary-interest method for paying interest, the interest and principal are due on the maturity date. Thus, Ideal has the full amount of the principal ($50,000) available for use for the entire year. The AER in this case is simply the 12% stated rate on the loan. It is calculated as:

AER = Total Dollar Cost ÷ Amount Available
    = $6,000 ÷ $50,000 x 100
    = 12%

Now assume that Ideal borrows the $50,000 at 12% ordinary interest for 90 days rather than one year. The AER in this case is calculated in two steps. First, the interest for the 90-day loan period is calculated. Second, the AER formula is adjusted for the portion of a year represented by the loan. The interest on the loan of $1,479 is calculated as:

Interest Charge = Principal x Rate x Portion of Year
$$= \$50,000 \times .12 \times \frac{90}{365}$$
$$= \$50,000 \times .12 \times .2465$$
$$= \$1,479$$

To adjust the AER formula for the portion of a year the loan is outstanding requires nothing more than adding an annualizing fraction to the AER formula. An annualizing fraction is the number of days in a year (365) divided by the number of days in the loan period (90 days in this case). The relationship now appears as:

AER = (Interest for the Period ÷ Principal) x Annualizing Fraction

The annual effective rate of interest on Ideal's 90-day loan is calculated as:

AER = (Interest for the Period ÷ Principal) x Annualizing Fraction

$$= \text{(90-Day Interest} \div \text{Principal)} \times \tfrac{365}{90}$$
$$= (\$1,479 \div \$50,000) \times (365 \div 90)$$
$$= .02958 \times 4.05 \times 100$$
$$= 12\%$$

Notice the effective rate is the same as the stated rate, 12%. The reason is also the same as that in the case of the one-year loan. Ideal had the full amount of the principal for the entire 90 days, and interest was paid only on the principal actually available for use.

To understand how things can change under other bank loan arrangements, assume now that Ideal borrows the $50,000 for 90-days but at 12% interest discounted. Recall that discounting the loan means the interest is deducted from the loan proceeds in advance. Under this arrangement, the AER increases to 12.4% which is calculated as follows.

AER = (90-Day Interest ÷ Amount Available) x Annualizing Fraction

$$= \$1,479 \div (\$50,000 - \$1,479) \times \tfrac{365}{90}$$
$$= (\$1,479 \div \$48,521) \times (365 \div 90)$$
$$= .03048 \times 4.05 \times 100$$
$$= 12.4\%$$

Note that the difference between the 12% AER under nondiscounted and the 12.4% under the discounted loan is the amount of principal actually available for use. Ideal has borrowed, pays interest on, and repays $50,000 of principal, but has only $48,521 ($50,000 principal minus $1,479 discounted interest) to use during the time period of the loan.

A loan agreement with a similar effect on the AER is a compensating balance requirement. Under this arrangement, which is commonly used with a line of credit granted by a bank, the borrowing firm is required to maintain a stipulated percentage of the loan as a minimum average deposit in its checking accounting with that bank. For example, a 20% compensating balance requires the borrower to maintain a minimum checking account balance of 20% of the line of credit. As is true of a discounted loan, the effect of the compensating balance requirement is to reduce the amount of the loan actually available for use. In this case, only 80% of the credit line is available to meet the firm's needs.

For example, assume that Ideal has been granted a $100,000 line of credit at 12% ordinary interest, with a 20% compensating balance requirement (CBR). If Ideal uses the the full amount of the credit line for 180 days, the AER is 15.2%.

AER = (180-Day Interest ÷ Amount Available) x Annualizing Fraction

$$= [\text{180-Day Interest} \div \text{Principal} \times (1 - \text{CBR})]) \times \frac{365}{180}$$

$$= (\$6,000 \div \$100,000 \times .8) \times (365 \div 180)$$

$$= 15.2\%$$

Again, the AER increases when reducing the amount of the loan actually available for use. Since the 20% compensating balance requirement leaves only $80,000 available to meet Ideal's needs, the AER jumps from 12% to 15.2%.

Being more familiar with the concept of interest cost on bank loans, you can now look at two types of unsecured bank financing — the transaction loan and the line of credit — in greater detail.

Transaction Loan

A short-term, unsecured transaction loan is a direct, single payment financing arrangement which is evidenced by a promissory note. The maturity on this type of loan is usually between one and six months, but can range up to slightly less than one year. While it is often possible for you to pay the existing interest cost and renegotiate or roll over a transaction loan at maturity, commercial banks generally require that you "clean up" loans for a 30- to 60-day period each year. This means you must be free from short-term bank debt for that period. The purpose of this requirement is to ensure that you are not attempting to meet long-term needs by substituting lower cost, short-term bank credit for higher-rate, long-term funds.

Borrowing arrangements for transaction loans often include discounting the loan or a compensating balance requirement, or both. As indicated above, both procedures have a significant impact on the effective cost of borrowing.

Line of Credit

A line of credit is a commitment from a bank to its regular, credit worthy business customers to provide a stated maximum amount of short-term financing for a specified time period. This time period, which is intended to coincide with a firm's working capital cycle, may extend to as long as 11 months. As is true of the transaction loan, the bank expects the credit line to be "cleaned up" once per year. The credit line is often granted with a compensating balance requirement, and the floating or variable-rate method of interest payment is used. For small borrowers this usually means an interest cost of two to four percentage points above the bank's prime rate.

If the bank's credit line commitment is informal, there is no legal obligation to guarantee the availability of funds during the loan period. Banks, however, tend to treat even informal commitments as morally binding unless a firm's circumstances change materially during the credit period. If the commitment involves a formal arrangement the bank's obligation is legally enforceable. In this case, a firm will usually be charged a commitment fee whether or not it borrows against or draws on the credit line. This fee, which is paid in addition to interest on the loan, can range from one-fourth of one percent to as much as one percent of the unused portion of the credit line.

Assume Ideal, after identifying its working capital needs through the cash budget process, approaches its bank with a credit line request in the amount of $50,000. The loan request is accompanied by the cash budget, a financing plan, and the firm's most recent financial statements. These documents serve to support Ideal's estimate of the amount, purpose, and timing of the firm's need for funds, and to clearly identify when and how the proposed loans will be repaid.

The bank's loan officer will evaluate Ideal's financial position, the supporting documents, and the credit line request. If the request is approved, Ideal will receive a formal letter acknowledging the bank's commitment. The letter will identify the terms of the credit line including the size of the commitment, the interest rate, the commitment fee if any, the clean-up period, and the required compensating balance. Upon receipt of the letter, Ideal is able to draw on the line by notifying the bank of its intentions and signing a promissory note for the amount of the draw.

To illustrate how the true cost of the credit line is determined, assume the following terms for Ideal's $50,000, six-month (182 days) credit line:

- An interest rate of prime plus 4%;
- An annual fee of one-half of one percent (.005) on the unused portion of the credit line; and
- A compensating balance requirement of 10%.

Assume further the following pattern for Ideal's borrowings against the credit line and for the changes in the prime rate of interest during these periods:

- Twenty thousand dollars is borrowed for a period of 60 days, with the full amount repaid at that time. The prime rate during this period was 8%, and Ideal's borrowing rate was, therefore, 12% (8% plus 4%).
- Fifty thousand dollars is borrowed for 120 days, with the full amount repaid at that time. The prime rate during this period was $8^1/4$%, and Ideal's borrowing rate was $12^1/4$%.

Since the bank's prime rate may fluctuate during the loan period and Ideal does not know in advance precisely when and how much of the credit line will be used, the effective cost of this financing source cannot be calculated until after the fact. The steps in this somewhat more complicated calculation are shown on the following page.

Calculating the Effective Cost of a Credit Line

Step 1: Determine the total dollar cost of the credit line.

This includes the cost of both the commitment fee and the interest.

Commitment Fee = Unused Balance x Annual Fee x Portion of Year

First 60 Days = ($50,000 − $20,000) x (.005) x (60 ÷ 365)

= $41.10

Next 120 Days = ($50,000 − $50,000) x (.005) x (120 ÷ 365)

= $0

Interest Cost = Financing x Interest Rate x Portion of Year

First 60 Days = $20,000 x .12 x (60 ÷ 365)

= $394.52

Next 120 Days = $50,000 x .1225 x (120 ÷ 365)

= $2013.70

Total Dollar Cost = Commitment Fee for First 60 Days and Next 120 Days

+ Interest Cost for First 60 Days and Next 120 Days

= $41.10 + $0.00 + $394.52 + $2013.70

= $2,449.32

Step 2: Determine the average amount of financing used.

Average Financing = First Amount Borrowed x Portion of Credit Period

+ Second Amount Borrowed x Portion of Credit Period

= $20,000 x (60 ÷ 182) + $50,000 x (120 ÷ 182)

= $39,560.44

Step 3: Determine the annual effective cost or rate.

AER = (Total Dollar Cost ÷ Average Financing) x Portion of Year

= ($2,449.32 ÷ $39,560.44) x (365 ÷ 180)

= 12.6%

Advantages of Unsecured Bank Financing

If you qualify for unsecured bank financing, you gain several important advantages. These include:

- **Availability.** The ability to borrow from a bank means you have solved your most pressing short-term financing problem: where to find a reliable, consistent source of outside financing. For many small firms, this problem is insurmountable, and financing for these entities is limited to owner's capital and funds from operations. Once you attain a financial position which qualifies you for bank financing, your hard work is essential in maintaining this critical relationship between you and the bank. The topic of establishing and maintaining a banking relationship is discussed further in Chapter 7.

- **Prestige.** The mere fact that your business has the financial position to qualify for unsecured bank credit has prestige and public relations value. This enviable status draws notice from your suppliers, competitors, customers, and other financiers. The ability to borrow from a bank on an unsecured basis is literally a stamp of approval by a qualified financial institution on your firm's financial position, its payment practices, and business prospects.

- **Cost.** Next to trade credit, unsecured bank credit is usually the cheapest source of financing available to any firm. Secured financing with a bank or with another financial institution will entail higher interest rates because it represents more risk for the lender.

- **Reliability.** Contrary to common misconceptions, banking is a competitive industry, and most banks work hard at maintaining their relationship with good customers. One example is found in the typical banker's feeling of responsibility toward meeting the financing needs of its valued customers. To a small business, such an attitude may be the most essential aspect of its banking relationship. Once a small business reaches the status of a valued customer, the bank becomes a reliable source of ongoing short-term financing.

- **Flexibility.** Once a credit line has been negotiated, your firm has a loan commitment in the form of a drawing account which serves as low-cost insurance against a temporary shortage of funds. The funds are used only as needed, and if the credit line is represented by an informal commitment, there is no cost for the unused portion of the line. What's more, barring a change in your firm's financial position or business prospects, this financing source can be renewed with little difficulty.

- **Advice and Information.** In addition to extending credit, banks can provide you with a number of valuable services. These services may include such things as credit information on potential customers, advice on business or financial decisions, and information on business conditions or prospects.

While there may be disadvantages associated with bank financing, when viewed in perspective, they tend to be minor inconveniences at most. Possible disadvantages may include:

Disadvantages of Unsecured Bank Financing

- **Qualifying.** Because of a bank's narrow margin-of-return between the rate it must pay to raise funds and the interest rate it earns on short-term loans, the credit criteria used to determine who shall receive short-term unsecured financing may be quite stringent. This means that you may find it difficult to qualify for unsecured bank financing.

- **Impermanence.** Banks usually regard credit line borrowing as financing for a firm's temporary working capital needs and not as a source of permanent short-term debt. Since a clean-up provision accompanies the credit line commitment, a firm will have to make alternative arrangements to meet its needs during the clean-up period.

- **Inconvenience.** Unlike trade credit, bank financing is not spontaneous. Each time financing is required, the arrangement must be renegotiated. The bank will also require a firm to provide regular financial reports and other necessary business information.

Secured Short-Term Financing

For new firms, firms with a marginal credit rating, or for those that have exhausted unsecured short-term debt capacity, providing the lender with acceptable collateral may offer a financing opportunity that would otherwise not exist. The entire process surrounding pledging and securing collateral is, however, more involved and more costly than unsecured financing for both borrower and lender. For a borrower or lender to voluntarily elect to secure a loan, if the circumstances did not dictate the need to do so, is a rare situation.

While virtually any legal asset acceptable to both borrower and lender can be used as collateral for short-term financing, creditors typically prefer a security interest in a highly liquid asset. Since current assets are the most liquid assets of any firm, short-term financing is frequently secured with these assets.

Characteristics of Secured Short-Term Financing

There are some common characteristics regarding secured short-term financing you should know. They include collateral, security interests, the percentage advance, and cost.

Collateral

Pledging collateral as security for a loan is widely believed to reduce the risk exposure for the lender. Lenders usually do not view loans in this way. A time-honored banking adage reflects the typical view on collateral: "Good collateral does not make a bad loan good." Although a security interest in assets pledged as collateral may reduce the lender's losses if the borrower defaults, the existence of collateral does not improve the risk of borrower default. Default risk is a function of a business' ability to generate the cash flows necessary to repay the loan and the borrower's integrity and attitude toward meeting debt obligations.

Since traditional financial institutions, such as banks, can earn only limited returns on loans, the probability of borrower default is the major consideration in the loan evaluation process. In general, lenders prefer to make a low risk, unsecured loan at a lower interest rates than a loan with a high probability of borrower default. If default occurs, the lender suffers the physical and legal problems associated with seizing and liquidating the pledged asset(s).

Where collateral is deemed necessary, lenders prefer to secure assets that have whose economic life is closely matched to the term of the loan. Viewed from the lender's perspective, highly desirable collateral would include that:

- The asset is easily liquidated in the event of default.
- The resale value of the asset is relatively stable.
- The legal claim to the asset is easily verified in the event of default.
- The lender would have little difficulty maintaining control over the physical whereabouts of the asset.

In many cases, current assets — such as highly liquid, short-term investments in savings certificates or marketable securities, accounts receivable, and to varying degrees inventory — serve as acceptable collateral for short-term financing. If your small firm is incorporated, the lender may require your personal endorsement of the promissory note. This simple act places your personal assets as well as those of the business at risk in the event of default.

A security interest is a legal claim to the ownership of a pledged asset in the event of borrower default. The lender obtains this claim by first entering into a contract with the borrower and meeting the laws of the governing state. This contract, which in legalese is known as the security agreement, specifies the detail surrounding the financing arrangement. Included are a description of the collateral held and the detailed terms of the loan. As the small firm borrower, your greatest concerns regarding the loan terms are the interest rate to be paid, the loan repayment schedule, loan restrictions, and the conditions required for the security interest to be removed.

Security Interest

In order for the lender to legally establish the security interest in the pledged asset, a copy of the security agreement is filed in a designated public office within the resident state. This is usually a county or state court. In addition to establishing the lender's legal claim, the filing also enables other prospective lenders to know which assets of a borrowing firm are unavailable as collateral.

To serve as acceptable collateral, the lender must be able to liquidate the secured asset if the borrower defaults. Since the future value of any asset is not known with certainty, a lender rarely allows 100% of the decided current worth of an asset as collateral value. The percentage advance allowed on a pledged asset depends on its type, the ease with which it can be liquidated, and the lender's assessment of the riskiness of the future assets value. The percentage advance can range from as much as 100% on a bank saving certificate owned by the borrower, to as little as 20% of the value of work-in-process inventory. In general, to qualify as acceptable collateral an asset should:

The Percentage Advance

- Have a current market value that is at least equal to or, in most cases, greater than the amount of the loan;
- Be in a form that is easy to identify; for example, large appliances as opposed to unprocessed coffee beans;
- Be in a form that makes it easy for the lender to maintain legal and physical control; for example, goods in a bonded warehouse as opposed to work-in-process inventory; and
- Have a readily accessible, active secondary market making it easy for the lender to liquidate in the event of borrower default.

The interest rate charged on secured short-term loans varies depending on the nature of the loan and the quality of the collateral, but secured short-

Cost

term financing is usually more costly than unsecured borrowing because the lender perceives a higher risk of default. If the lending institution envisions sufficient default risk to require collateral, a higher interest rate will be charged. Also, because a secured loan is more troublesome to negotiate and administer than an unsecured loan, the lender will usually require added compensation in some other form, such as a service fee.

Sources of Secured Short-Term Financing

As a small business borrower, you need to know that there are four primary sources of secured short-term financing: commercial banks, commercial finance companies, the U.S. Small Business Administration (SBA), and factors.

Commercial Banks

A commercial bank is a financial institution that obtains most of its working capital by accepting deposits from its customers. Depositors' funds are then used to conduct the bank's primary business of making loans and investments. Refer to Chapter 7 for more details on commercial banks and the other types of financing they offer.

Commercial Finance Companies

Commercial finance companies are lending institutions that make only secured short- and long-term loans to businesses. They are the business-world counterpart to consumer finance companies. Unlike banks, finance companies are not permitted to hold checking and savings account deposits. The business of these institutions is solely that of lending money. To do so, they raise funds by borrowing in the open market. Because they must cover the cost of these borrowed funds and because they lend to higher-risk borrowers, the interest rates charged borrowers by commercial finance companies is generally higher than that of banks. Commercial finance companies also offer extended-term financing to small businesses. See Chapter 6.

U.S. Small Business Administration

The U.S. Small Business Administration (SBA) is a federal government agency which assists small businesses by providing financing, counseling, and workshops. For further SBA financing information, see Chapter 6.

Factors

Factors are financial institutions which specialize in providing short-term financing to small business through an accounts receivable financing process known as factoring. Factoring is when a financial institution actually purchases the accounts receivables of a business, assumes the title and risk of those receivable, and in return provides that business with its needed funds. Factoring and another method of accounts receivable financing called pledging are discussed on the following pages.

The two most common methods of accounts receivable financing are pledging and factoring. Both commercial banks and commercial finance companies make secured loans against pledged receivables. Factoring, on the other hand, is done in large part by approximately 20 factors located throughout the United States, and only to a minor degree, by commercial banks and finance companies.

Accounts Receivable Financing

Accounts receivable represent the money owed to a business from credit sales to its customers. Next to cash, receivables are the most liquid of any firm's assets and, if management has carefully administered and controlled the credit granting process, they are converted to cash within a short period of time. These qualities make receivables a desirable asset for any firm to hold, and for the same reason, often make desirable collateral for a loan.

Pledging Accounts Receivables

Any financing agreement using receivables as collateral has three important components:

- The specific receivables that will be accepted as collateral;
- The percentage of the face value of the receivables that will be advanced; and
- The notification system that will be used.

The collateral value of a particular receivable or group of accounts depends on the credit standing of your firm's customer(s), your returns and allowances record, and your honesty and integrity. In general, the higher the overall quality of the receivables pledged, the lower your firm's sales-returns-and-allowances experience; and the higher your firm's standing as a customer of the lending institution, the larger the percentage of the face value of the receivables that will be advanced.

If your firm is perceived as an acceptable credit risk, the loan against pledged receivables will normally be made on a non-notification basis. This means the borrowing firm's customers are not notified of the financing arrangement, and payment of the outstanding receivable is made to the seller in the normal manner. Under the non-notification arrangement, the lender must either trust that you will remit customer payments as they are received or conduct periodic audits of your books to ensure that they are being made. Under a notification arrangement, the customers whose accounts have been used as collateral are instructed to make payments directly to the lender.

A pledging arrangement will take one of two basic forms: a general lien or selective receivables financing.

A General Lien Arrangement

A general lien agreement is the simplest and least expensive of the two alternatives but entails the most risk for the lending institution. Under a general lien arrangement, the lender accepts all of a borrower's accounts receivable as collateral for the loan or credit line. In doing so, the lender also accepts the default risk associated with those receivables. The higher or lower the overall default risk of the receivables, the smaller or larger the percentage advance. This figure will usually range from a low of about 35% to 40% when the overall quality of the receivables is questionable, to a high of about 75% to 80% when the receivables are of good quality.

Selective Receivables Financing

Under selective receivables financing, the lender evaluates the quality of your firm's receivables and chooses the accounts on which to base the loan or credit line. Since the lender has control over which receivables are pledged, there is less risk exposure and the advance can range up to 100% of the face value of the receivables selected. The advantage of the larger percent advance, is somewhat offset by the cost of an administrative fee the lender imposes for evaluating your receivables. This fee, which can range from 1% to 3% of the amount loaned, is paid in addition to the normal interest charges on the loan. The following example illustrates the selective financing process.

Assume Ideal approaches The Friendly Bank with a line-of-credit request secured by the list of customer accounts shown on Table 5.3. To establish the amount of the credit line, The Friendly Bank will evaluate the receivables to identify which qualify as acceptable collateral. The bank's first task is to weed out any past due accounts. Since Ideal's credit terms are 2/10, net 30, Customer C who is 11 days past due (41 minus 30) is immediately eliminated from consideration.

Table 5.3

THE IDEAL LEVERAGE COMPANY
Accounts Receivable Data

Customer	Outstanding Amount	Days Outstanding	Average Payment Period
A	$10,000	18	29
B	4,000	4	36
C	3,000	41	45
D	21,000	7	20
E	15,000	10	30
F	17,000	10	28
G	8,000	20	30
H	12,000	19	25
I	6,000	7	40

The Friendly Bank will next study the payment history of Ideal's customers to determine the average number of days taken before payment is received and then will exclude from consideration those accounts with a history of late payments. The information from the bank's study is shown in the last column of Table 5.3. Based on this data, the accounts of customers B and I are also eliminated. Note that although neither B nor I is currently past due, the analysis of their payment history identifies them as chronic late payers.

Having eliminated the accounts of C, B, and I, Friendly is left with $83,000 of acceptable collateral from customers A, D, E, F, G, and H. This dollar amount will be adjusted for both Ideal's average sales-returns-and-allowances history and for the overall quality of the receivables. If Ideal has an average of one-half of one percent (1.00 minus .005 or .995) of its sales returned by dissatisfied customers, and Friendly determines a percent advance of 90%, the credit line commitment would be $74,326 ($83,000 x .995 x .90). If Ideal agrees to these terms, Friendly would file a lien to establish its security interest on the pledged receivables.

Interest rates on commercial bank loans secured by accounts receivable range from 2% to 6% above the prime rate. The rates charged by commercial finance companies on these loans will usually be slightly higher than this range. In addition to the stated interest rate, the lending institution adds an administrative fee of 1% to 3% of the amount loaned. This fee compensates the lender for the cost of evaluating the borrower's receivables and administering the loan.

Pledging Cost

The primary advantages of securing a loan or credit line by pledging accounts receivable are availability and flexibility. By having acceptable collateral, you have a financing opportunity that may not otherwise exist. In addition, when receivables financing is used on a continuous basis, your firm gains some of the flexibility associated with spontaneous funds. As the volume of operations and the level of sales increase, new receivables are created. These additional accounts become the collateral for additional financing.

Advantages of Pledging Receivables

A major disadvantage associated with pledging receivables is cost. This cost includes the interest cost, which can be substantially above the prime rate, and the additional administrative fee, which increases the annual effective rate of this method of borrowing. The cost consideration must, however, be balanced against the advantage of availability. In short, if your firm can earn rates of return on the loan proceeds that is greater than the cost of financing, the cost disadvantage becomes secondary.

Disadvantages of Pledging Receivables

Factoring accounts receivable differs considerably from that of pledging accounts receivable. Factoring involves the actual sale of the asset and, in contrast to pledging, title and risk pass to the factor. Also, a factor plays a major role in administering a firm's credit function and in determining its credit policy. While factoring receivables is not a very common practice

Factoring Accounts Receivables

in all industries, it is normal business practice for many firms in textile products, furniture manufacturing, and apparel goods.

A factor performs three important functions: financing, credit analysis and collection, and risk bearing.

- **Financing.** A factor provides funds for a firm through either of two methods: maturity factoring or advance factoring. Under maturity factoring, a firm receives payment for receivables sold to the factor on either the date the customer's payment is received, or on the last day of the credit period, whichever comes first. When advance or discount factoring is used, a factor advances funds to a firm when the customer is invoiced for the purchase.

- **Credit analysis and collection.** As a normal part of the factoring arrangement, the factor evaluates the credit worthiness of each of a firm's customers. The customers' receivables not meeting a factor's credit standards will not be accepted for purchase. If a firm chooses to extend credit to these customers, it must carry the receivables and bear the risk of bad debt loss. On the other hand, a factor takes full responsibility for collecting all amounts due and any bad debt loss on all accepted receivables. By performing the credit and collection functions, a factor relieves a firm of the cost and responsibility of each.

- **Risk bearing.** Most factoring arrangements call for the purchase of receivables on a nonrecourse basis. This means that the factor must absorb the loss of a customer default. The nonrecourse arrangement passes title as well as default risk to the factor, and also relieves a firm of bad-debt expense.

The Factoring Process

The procedures, conditions, and charges associated with factoring are detailed in a contract known as the factoring agreement. The maturity factoring and advance factoring arrangements used in the factoring agreement are best illustrated with an example.

Assume that Ideal has entered into a factoring arrangement with the TLC Factoring Company. After performing the credit analysis on each of Ideal's customers, TLC sets up an account for each customer that has been identified as an acceptable risk. As payment on account is received from one of these customers, or funds are advanced against an acceptable but uncollected receivable, TLC makes a deposit in the appropriate account. Ideal is then free to draw against these funds as needed. If Ideal leaves funds in any account, a surplus will exist on which TLC will pay interest.

Assume further that on May 1 Ideal had the list of acceptable receivables and outstanding balances shown in the first two columns of Table 5.4. The third column of this table indicates the type of agreement used, maturity or advance factoring, and the last column reveals the customers' status on May 30, the last day of the credit period.

Since Ideal used advance factoring to borrow against accounts D and E, TLC immediately deposits the value of these accounts, $36,000, minus the normal factoring commissions and the percentage reserve held against

Table 5.4

THE IDEAL LEVERAGE COMPANY
Accounts Receivable Data

Customer	Outstanding Amount	Arrangement	Status May 30th
A	$10,000	Maturity	Collected 5/22
D	21,000	Advance	Collected 5/30
E	15,000	Advance	Collected 5/30
F	17,000	Maturity	Uncollected
G	8,000	Maturity	Uncollected
H	12,000	Maturity	Collected 5/25

advanced funds. On May 22 and May 25, TLC deposits the amounts collected for customers A and H less the factoring commission on these receivables. On May 30, the value of the receivables of F and G, less the factoring commission, is made available to Ideal even though these receivables are not collected as of that date. Recall that the maturity factoring arrangement provides for either payment at the time the account is collected or on the last day of the credit period, whichever comes first.

The Cost of Factoring Receivables

Factoring costs include a commission on either maturity- or advance-factored receivables and interest on advances. The commission, which compensates the factor for credit evaluation, administration, and collection expense, can range from 1% to 3% of the face amount of the receivables. The interest cost on advance factoring generally ranges from two to four percentage points above the prime rate. In addition, the factor will usually hold some percentage of the face value of the receivables as a reserve for potential sales returns and allowances. The size of the percentage reserve depends on the firm's past sales-returns-and-allowances experience. Any amounts held in reserve are remitted to the firm when the receivable is collected by the factor.

To illustrate the calculation of the effective cost of factoring, assume that TLC charges a 2% commission on all receivables factored and 4% interest on advances above prime. Since the prime rate is currently 8%, Ideal will pay an interest rate of 12% on any advanced funds. Because Ideal's experience on returns and allowances is excellent, a minimal 1% reserve is held against advances.

The annual effective cost on the maturity-factored account of Customer A is calculated on the next page. Since Customer A pays in 30 days or about 12 times per year, the number 12 instead of (365 divided by 30) is used as the portion of the year value in the AER equation.

AER = (Amount of Commission ÷ Available Amount) x Portion of Year

$$= (\$10,000 \times .02) \div (\$10,000 \times .98) \times 12$$

$$= (\$200 \div \$9,800) \times 12 \times 100$$

$$= 24.5\%$$

Table 5.5

THE IDEAL LEVERAGE COMPANY
Dollar Cost and Net Proceeds Calculations

Value of Customer D's Account	$21,000.00
Less: Reserve at 1%	(210.00)
Less: Factoring Commission at 2%	(420.00)
Funds Available for Advance	$20,370.00
Less: Interest on Advance ($20,370 x .12 x 1/12)	204.00
Net Proceeds from Advance	$20,166.00
Total Dollar Cost of Factoring:	
Commission	$420.00
Interest	204.00
Opportunity Cost on Reserve Funds	3.50
Total	$627.50

The AER on advance-factored receivables has three cost components: the factoring commission, the interest charge on the advanced funds, and the opportunity cost of the reserve held by the factor. This latter item is not an explicit, out-of-pocket cost as is the factor's commission or the interest charge. Rather, it is a hidden cost that stems from Ideal's inability to use the funds that are held in reserve. If Ideal had these funds, they could be invested in working assets. Because these funds are not available, Ideal loses the return on investment (ROI) that could be earned if they were available for use. While this loss does not show up in the firm's financial records, it is real.

The AER calculation on advanced-factored receivables is illustrated on Table 5.5 using the information for Customer D and an assumed ROI for Ideal of 20%. The first step in the process is to determine the dollar cost of the advance and the net proceeds Ideal will have available for use.

The opportunity cost on the amount held as reserve is calculated as:

Opportunity Cost = Reserve Amount x ROI x Portion of Year

$$= \$210 \times .20 \times \frac{1}{12}$$

$$= \$3.50$$

And finally, the AER is calculated as:

AER = (Total Dollar Cost ÷ Available Amount) x Portion of Year
    = [($420 + $204 + $3.50) ÷ $20,166] x 12
    = 37.3%

If factoring is used only as an intermittent form of financing, the obvious disadvantage, as shown in the above examples, is cost. Given the administrative complexity of the factoring arrangement, firms that use this method of short-term financing typically employ it on a continuous basis. When used in this manner, factoring provides services for a firm that extend beyond the opportunity to raise financing. The factor assumes responsibility for evaluating the credit worthiness of a firm's customers and for the administration and collection of factored accounts. In essence, the factor administers a firm's credit and collection functions, thereby relieving the firm of the cost and effort of doing so. For small firms unable to effectively administer credit and collection policy, this advantage may offset the high annual effective cost of factoring.

Advantages of Factoring

Possibly of equal importance, maturity factoring removes a major cause of uncertainty in a firm's cash-flow pattern. Because a firm knows it will receive its funds no later than the last day of the credit period when maturity factoring is used, the arrangement ensures a known pattern of cash inflows from operations.

There is one potential down side associated with factoring on a continuous basis, and that is, you should carefully consider that the advantage of having the factor administer the credit function may be offset by the danger of your business inadvertently adopting a credit policy that has been established by the factor. Since the factor determines the criteria for judging whether a customer's account is acceptable, there is a natural tendency to limit sales to those customers; therefore, consider whether the factor's credit standards are appropriate for all your customers.

Disadvantages of Factoring

The opportunity to pledge acceptable inventory to secure a loan may also provide financing for your small firm that would otherwise be denied. The process surrounding inventory financing is, in principle, the same as that of pledging receivables. The lender can use a general lien that secures all of your inventory holdings or one that pinpoints specific items as collateral. Also, the amount loaned against inventory and the interest rate charged depends upon the quality of the inventory offered as collateral.

Short-Term Inventory Financing

For inventory to qualify as collateral, it must be easy for the lender to maintain legal and physical control over the inventory and to repossess and liquidate the inventory in the event of borrower default. The more liquid the goods and the easier it is for the lender to maintain control over the pledged items, the higher the collateral value of the inventory.

For example, widely used, nonperishable raw materials, such as grain, crude oil, or integrated electronic circuits sold in active markets at reasonably stable prices, are desirable collateral. Finished goods, such as automobiles or major appliances, that are easily identified, readily sold if the borrower defaults, and easily monitored or controlled by the lender, are also considered suitable collateral. On the other hand, work-in-process inventory which is in various stages of completion is not desirable collateral.

The various security devices the lender may use to establish legal control over secured inventory also depends on the nature of the inventory, your credit standing, and the degree of trust that exists between you and the lender. The three legal or physical control devices available to the lender are a floating lien, a trust receipt, and a bonded warehouse receipt.

Floating Lien Inventory Loans

A floating or blanket lien is used to secure goods that are not easily identified, such as unprocessed food stuffs or work-in-process inventory, or that consist of a large number of inexpensive items, such as hardware inventory or tires. Through a floating lien, the lender establishes legal claim to your entire inventory for as long as the loan is outstanding. While the floating lien is the simplest legal claim to administer, it is the most risky form of inventory financing for the lender.

The risk stems from the difficulty of maintaining close physical control over the inventory and from the absence of a stable inventory value. Because of the type of inventory pledged under a floating lien — mostly raw materials or work-in-process — it must remain in the borrower's (your) hands. During this time period, the amount held, its character, and its value are continuously changing. With the security behind the loan out of the lender's control, it is difficult if not impossible to verify its presence at any given moment, to exercise the legal claim, and to liquidate the inventory if as the borrower, you default. Given these disadvantages, banks and commercial finance companies will generally advance less than 50% of the cost of the inventory, and the interest rate will range from approximately 4% to 6% above prime.

To illustrate the floating lien arrangement, assume that Ideal's management has estimated the firm will need $50,000 to finance its working capital requirements for the upcoming season. Management is willing to make the firm's entire inventory available as collateral for the 60-day loan period. The Friendly Bank has agreed to a loan secured by a floating lien. Friendly will advance 40% of the average cost of the inventory at the prime interest rate, plus 4%. With a 40% advance, Ideal must pledge inventory in the amount of $125,000 to meet its $50,000 working capital requirement. This is calculated as:

Amount Pledged = Amount of Financing Required ÷ Percent Advance

$$= \$50,000 \div .4$$
$$= \$125,000$$

A trust receipt is a lien used to secure specific items of inventory. It is widely used in the financing of relatively expensive items that are easily identified by serial number or description. These so called floor planning loans are made by banks, commercial finance companies, and by the financing subsidiaries of many large manufacturers. For example, General Motors (GM) finances the inventory of GM dealers through its financing wing, General Motors Acceptance Corporation (GMAC).

Trust Receipt Inventory Loans

Similar to a floating lien arrangement, trust receipt financing allows the secured inventory to remain in your control. You are free to sell the goods but are trusted to remit the principal and outstanding interest on the item sold at the time of sale. Unlike the floating lien, however, each piece of secured inventory can be easily identified. This allows the lender to keep detailed records on each item, and these records are kept current through frequent audits of your premises. If an inventory item is not found during the audit, it is assumed sold and the loan amount, plus interest, is due.

Because of the type of inventory secured through trust receipt financing, the lender has more control and can repossess and liquidate the asset more easily than under a floating lien arrangement. These factors combine to reduce the lender's risk exposure and to make a larger percentage advance against the goods pledged possible. Advances that are from 80% to 100% of inventory value are not uncommon with trust receipt financing, and interest rates on this type financing are in line with other forms of secured loans. If you are a qualified small firm borrower, you can expect to incur interest rates which are 2% to 6% above the current prime rate.

Warehouse receipt financing is used by banks and commercial finance companies to secure loans against readily salable finished goods inventory. The secured goods can be stored by the lender in either of two bonded warehousing facilities: a terminal warehouse or a field warehouse. The terminal warehouse is a public facility located on the premises of the warehouseman. A field warehouse is a bonded facility established and controlled by the warehouseman but located on your premises. This arrangement is used to secure inventory that is not easily transported. The secured inventory is physically separated from other inventory, and the warehouseman maintains a guard at that location.

Warehouse Receipt Loans

Regardless of which form of warehousing is used, the lender is able to maintain rigid control over the secured goods. Since the lender holds the warehouse receipt for the stored inventory, the warehouseman will not release the goods to you without written approval from the lender. The increased control and liquidity provided by warehouse financing over a floating lien arrangement reduces risk and allows for a more generous percentage advance. Advances of 90% or better of the cost basis of the inventory are common with this arrangement.

The annual effective cost of warehouse financing is higher than other forms of secured lending because of the combination of interest charges and storage fees. Interest rates are in line with other secured lending, 2%

to 6% above prime, but you also pay the warehousing fee. This latter cost can range from 1% to 3% of the amount of the loan. The following example illustrates the AER calculation of a warehouse receipt loan.

Assume the Friendly Bank has agreed to an inventory loan of $50,000 for two months using Ideal's finished goods inventory as collateral. Friendly will advance 95% of the cost basis of the inventory at prime plus 4%, but the terms of the loan require the goods to be stored in a public warehouse until the time of sale. The warehouse fee is one and one-half percent (.015) of the value of the loan. In order to obtain the needed $50,000 with an 95% advance, Ideal must pledge inventory with a cost value of $52,632 ($50,000 divided by .95). If the current prime rate is 8%, the AER of 21.6% is calculated as follows:

Step 1: Determine the total dollar cost of the loan.

$$\text{Warehouse Fee} = \$50,000 \times .015$$
$$= \$750$$

$$\text{Interest Charges} = \$52,632 \times .12 \times \frac{2}{12}$$
$$= \$1,053$$

$$\text{Total Dollar Cost} = \$750 + \$1,053$$
$$= \$1,803$$

Step 2: Calculate the AER.

$$\text{AER} = (\$1,803 \div \$50,000) \times \frac{12}{2}$$
$$= 21.6\%$$

Advantages of Inventory Financing

As is true with receivables financing, the major advantages of inventory financing are availability and flexibility. By having acceptable inventory to secure a loan, you have the opportunity to obtain financing that may otherwise be unavailable on an unsecured basis. Inventory also provides some degree of financing flexibility. As your firm's volume of operations increases, so does the amount of inventory that can be used as collateral to secure the needed financing.

Disadvantages of Inventory Financing

The major disadvantage of secured inventory financing may be cost. In addition to interest charges, lender's often tack on loan-origination or service fees for the additional paperwork and administrative effort required to secure and monitor an inventory loan. These fees, along with the warehouse fee that must be paid if the goods are stored, raise the annual effective cost of this form of financing. As is the case with any financing alternative, however, whether the total effective cost of inventory financing is prohibitive depends on the rate of return your firm can earn on the borrowed funds.

Table 5.6 – Short-Term Financing Summary

Type	Source	Qualification	Cost
Trade Credit (Accts. Payable)	Normal trade supplier.	Good customer standing and good payment record.	No explicit charges but usually a sizable opportunity cost for missing offered cash discounts.
Accruals	Normal delayed payments for labor, taxes, etc.	Normal business relations.	None, as long as there is no penalty for delay.
Unsecured Transaction Loan	Commercial banks.	Established firms with strong financial position.	Interest cost is negotiable but will range from prime to prime plus several percentage points. A commitment fee and compensating balance may also be required.
Pledged Accounts Receivable	Commercial banks and commercial finance companies.	Firms with acceptable credit standing and sufficient, liquid accounts receivable.	Interest cost will range from 2% to 6% above prime. The receivables will be discounted heavily under general lien financing and much less under selective financing. The lender also adds an administrative fee of 1% to 3% of the loan's face value.
Factored Accounts Receivable	Commercial banks, commercial finance companies, and factors.	Firms with acceptable credit standing and sufficient, liquid accounts receivable.	Commissions on maturity factoring range from 1% to 3% of the receivables' face value. Interest on advance factoring ranges from 2% to 4% above prime. Factor retains a reserve against the advance which creates an opportunity cost for the firm.
Pledged Inventory	Commercial banks, commercial finance companies, and some manufacturers.	Firms with acceptable credit standing and sufficient, liquid inventory.	Interest cost on any security arrangement ranges from 2% to 6% above prime. The percentage advance is less than 50% of the inventory value with floating lien, and ranges between 80% and 100% for trust or warehouse receipt arrangements. The latter arrangement also requires the borrower to pay storage fees of 1% to 3% of the loan amount.

A Summary of Short-Term Financing Sources

In the final analysis, the types and costs of the various sources of financing available to you are determined by your business' specific characteristics. Such factors as the nature of the firm's product or service, the types of assets it holds, and its financial position are important determinates of its financing possibilities. The most critical of all factors, however, is your firm's credit standing. In the world of borrowing money there is no substitute for the well-managed, financially sound business with a proven track record for generating compensatory cash flow and profit. In short, the more effective your firm's financial management, the greater its financing opportunities, and the lower the cost of this financing.

Table 5.6 provides a capsule view of the major characteristics of the various types and sources of short-term financing.

Chapter 6

Extended-Term Financing for Your Small Firm

Chapter 5 examined alternative means for meeting your small business' short-term credit needs. This chapter investigates the subject of extended-term financing alternatives. These include both intermediate-term obligations with maturities between 1 and 10 years and long-term financing with maturities greater than 10 years.

The Nature and Characteristics of Extended-Term Financing

Extended-term financing refers to multi-year debt obligations which are repaid in periodic installments beginning within one year of the loan agreement date. As opposed to short-term credit, this financing represents an important component of the typical small firm's permanent capital and is used to finance the expansion of permanent levels of current assets, to acquire vehicles and equipment, or to purchase or construct real property.

Small businesses are often viewed by most creditors as having a highly uncertain future, and making an extended-term loan to such a business means being locked into a high-risk agreement for a prolonged period. To make this type of loan, therefore, a lender must feel comfortable with your business and the quality of its management, be compensated for the additional risk exposure, and take precautions to minimize risk and potential loss. Compensation comes in the form of interest rates higher

Interest Cost and Collateral Requirements

than those charged for short-term financing, and loss and risk minimizing methods include collateral requirements and the imposition of restrictive or protective covenants in the loan agreement.

Stated interest rates on extended-term financing vary with your risk characteristics and with changes in market rates of interest. During the past 10 years, interest rates have ranged from a low of approximately 14% to a high of more than 20% per annum. Interest charges can be specified in the loan agreement as a fixed rate over the life of the financing or as a variable (floating) rate which is tied to the prime interest rate. The annual effective cost of the extended-term financing is calculated for you and appears in the loan agreement as the annual percentage rate (APR).

The required collateral for extended-term financing usually consists of the asset(s) purchased with the proceeds of the financing, other available business assets, and possibly your own personal assets. To pledge personal assets as collateral, you personally endorse the promissory note.

A loan agreement's restrictive covenants are designed to protect a creditor's claim on your firm's assets and liquidity position. Examples of the more common provisions found in small business, extended-term financing agreements include requirements that the firm:

- Limit the use of the loan proceeds to the purpose(s) specified in the agreement;
- Purchase life insurance on its principal(s) naming the lender as beneficiary;
- Maintain a minimum working capital position;
- Maintain adequate accounting records and furnish financial statements and specified reports on a regular basis;
- Is prohibited from selling any of its fixed assets without the lender's authorization;
- Is prohibited from creating additional liens on existing assets or taking any other actions that would weaken the lender's claim on the firm's asset base;
- Is prohibited from additional extended-term borrowing without authorization from the lender;
- Is prohibited from purchasing additional fixed assets without the lender's authorization;
- Limit dividend payments (owner's withdrawals) to amounts specified in the agreement;
- Is prohibited from repurchasing the business' stock or buying another owner's interest without the lender's authorization;
- Limit salaries, bonuses, and other compensation for the firm's officers and directors to the amounts specified in the agreement; and
- Limit the uses of surplus cash to those specified in the agreement.

While the existence of restrictive provisions is virtually a foregone conclusion in a small business, extended-term loan agreement, many of the restrictions can often be negotiated. Your goal is to successfully negotiate an agreement that minimizes this burden.

One distinguishing characteristic of extended-term financing is what finance people call amortization of the loan by regular and equal installments over its life. This means that each monthly, quarterly, or semiannual payment provides the lender with both the stated interest return on the amount of the principal outstanding since the last payment and the

Repayment Schedules on Extended-Term Financing

Table 6.1

THE IDEAL LEVERAGE COMPANY
Quarterly Amortization Schedule for a $100,000 Loan

Quarter	Beginning Balance	Quarterly Payment	Interest @ 16%	Toward Principal	Ending Balance
1	$100,000	$6,001	$4,000	$2,001	$97,999
2	97,999	6,001	3,920	2,081	95,917
3	95,917	6,001	3,837	2,165	93,753
4	93,753	6,001	3,750	2,251	91,502
5	91,502	6,001	3,660	2,341	89,160
6	89,160	6,001	3,566	2,435	86,725
7	86,725	6,001	3,469	2,532	84,193
8	84,193	6,001	3,368	2,634	81,560
9	81,560	6,001	3,262	2,739	78,821
10	78,821	6,001	3,153	2,848	75,972
11	75,972	6,001	3,039	2,962	73,010
12	73,010	6,001	2,920	3,081	69,929
13	69,929	6,001	2,797	3,204	66,725
14	66,725	6,001	2,669	3,332	63,392
15	63,392	6,001	2,536	3,466	59,927
16	59,927	6,001	2,397	3,604	56,323
17	56,323	6,001	2,253	3,748	52,574
18	52,574	6,001	2,103	3,898	48,676
19	48,676	6,001	1,947	4,054	44,622
20	44,622	6,001	1,785	4,216	40,405
21	40,405	6,001	1,616	4,385	36,020
22	36,020	6,001	1,441	4,560	31,460
23	31,460	6,001	1,258	4,743	26,717
24	26,717	6,001	1,069	4,933	21,784
25	21,784	6,001	871	5,130	16,654
26	16,654	6,001	666	5,335	11,319
27	11,319	6,001	453	5,549	5,770
28	5,770	6,001	231	5,770	0

return of a portion of the outstanding principal. In short, amortization of a debt obligation provides for both interest and the gradual retirement of the principal over the life of the agreement. On the previous page, Table 6.1 displays the amortization schedule for a 16%, $100,000, seven-year, equipment loan that Ideal negotiated with Friendly Bank. The loan was amortized with quarterly payments of $6,001.

Each of Table 6.1's quarterly payments accomplishes two important goals for the lender. First, the payment provides for the interest earned on the outstanding portion of the principal (remaining balance) during each quarterly period. For example, the interest payment of $4,000 on the $100,000 outstanding principal during the first quarterly period is calculated as:

Interest = Principal x Interest x Portion of Year

$$= \$100,000 \times .16 \times \frac{3}{12}$$

$$= \$4,000$$

Second, each quarterly installment also provides the lender with the return of a portion of the outstanding principal. The amount of the payment that is applied to the principal is calculated by subtracting the payment's interest portion from its full amount. For example, the $2,001 of the first quarterly payment applied to the beginning principal is calculated as:

Amount Applied to Principal = Payment – Interest for the Period

$$= \$6,001 - \$4,000$$

$$= \$2,001$$

The remaining balance on the loan after each installment payment is calculated as the beginning balance minus the amount applied to principal. For example, the ending balance for the first quarter is determined as:

Ending Balance = Beginning Balance – Amount Applied to Principal

$$= \$100,000 - \$2,001$$

$$= \$97,999$$

Note that the ending balance for one period becomes the beginning balance for the next. The procedure is then repeated for each subsequent payment.

Loan Repayments and Taxes

Of particular interest to Ideal's management is the tax effects of the scheduled loan payments shown on Table 6.1. Since interest paid is a tax-deductible business expense, the after-tax cash outflows required to service the loan are less than the actual loan payments. The reason for this seeming contradiction is the tax savings provided by the interest-expense tax shield. Even though the interest must be paid to the lender, each dollar of interest reduces the firm's taxable income by one dollar. Lower taxable income means a lower tax payment. If the business is in the 34% tax bracket as is The Ideal Leverage Company, a dollar of interest expense saves $0.34 (34 cents) in income tax.

Interest Expense Tax Savings = Amount of Interest x Tax Rate

$$= \$1.00 \times .34$$
$$= \$0.34$$

Applying this principle to Ideal's loan payments produces the after-tax cash flow data shown on Table 6.2. The interest expense tax savings shown in Table 6.2's second column are calculated as the interest portion of the loan payment each period times Ideal's 34% tax rate.

Table 6.2

THE IDEAL LEVERAGE COMPANY
Quarterly After-Tax Cash Outflow on $100,000 Loan

Quarter	Quarterly Payment	Interest Shield Tax Savings	After-Tax Cash Outflow
1	$6,001	$1,360	$4,641
2	6,001	1,333	4,668
3	6,001	1,305	4,696
4	6,001	1,275	4,726
5	6,001	1,244	4,757
6	6,001	1,212	4,789
7	6,001	1,179	4,822
8	6,001	1,145	4,856
9	6,001	1,109	4,892
10	6,001	1,072	4,929
11	6,001	1,033	4,968
12	6,001	993	5,008
13	6,001	951	5,050
14	6,001	907	5,094
15	6,001	862	5,139
16	6,001	815	5,186
17	6,001	766	5,235
18	6,001	715	5,286
19	6,001	662	5,339
20	6,001	607	5,394
21	6,001	549	5,452
22	6,001	490	5,511
23	6,001	428	5,573
24	6,001	363	5,638
25	6,001	296	5,705
26	6,001	226	5,775
27	6,001	154	5,847
28	6,001	79	5,922

For example, the tax savings of $1,360 for the first quarterly period is determined as:

Interest Tax Savings (1st Period) = Amount of Interest x Tax Rate
$$= \$4,000 \times .34$$
$$= \$1,360$$

The after-tax cash flow values shown in the last column of Table 6.2 are found by subtracting the interest-expense tax savings for a period from the loan payment for that same period. For example, the after-tax cash outflow for the first quarterly period of $4,641 is calculated as:

After-Tax Cash Outflow = Loan Payment – Interest Tax Savings
$$= \$6,001 - \$1,360$$
$$= \$4,641$$

Keep in mind the after-tax cash flow benefit of the interest-expense tax shield. While Ideal must make a loan payment of $6,001 each period, the tax savings provided by the interest portion of the payment reduces the after-tax burden of this cash outflow.

Factors Influencing the Use of Extended-Term Financing

An extended-term financing agreement involves mandatory payments and binding contract provisions that must be honored regardless of your firm's financial performance; accepting this risk is a major consideration. Before doing so, give careful consideration to its ramifications and to the many factors that influence the decision. Primary among these factors are maturity, availability, risk/return tradeoff, cost, hidden factors, flexibility, and owner control.

Appropriate Maturity

The first step in the financing decision is to decide the correct maturity or length of borrowing period for the proposed financing arrangement. To determine whether or not you should choose short- or long-term financing, you first need to take a look at the nature of the asset you wish to finance.

As the expected life of the asset to be financed increases, the maturity of the financing should increase. For example, ideally, short-term or temporary assets, such as seasonal increases in inventory and receivables, should be financed with short-term credit. Long-term assets, which include both the permanent component of working capital and fixed assets, should be financed with extended-term financing. The permanent component of working capital equals the dollars that are permanently invested in inventory, receivables, and cash.

For large businesses, the task of raising permanent capital is usually a matter of management preference for debt or equity; however, equity financing for a small firm, other than additional investment by the existing owner, is rarely a realistic alternative. Most small businesses lack the growth potential found appealing by equity investors. This lack of equity financing opportunities, and the often prohibitive costs for doing so even when the necessary appeal exists, leaves you with two realistic capital structure choices: extended-term debt financing or internally generated cash flow. The result has been the heavy reliance of small firms on debt capital.

Availability

As discussed in Chapter 2, there is a significant difference in the degree of risk between debt and equity financing. While debt financing produces the potential for increasing the return to you, the owner, through favorable leverage, it also creates the risk associated with meeting fixed financial obligations. On the other hand, while equity financing offers no leveraging opportunity, it does avoid the risk of mandatory financial burden. These differences are important to both you and potential financiers. Before providing extended-term financing, lenders will satisfy themselves that your firm's existing and proposed debt ratios are acceptable, and there is a high probability of sufficient cash flow to meet financial charges. If the loan pushes your firm beyond what is perceived as acceptable limits for these measures, you are faced with two formidable tasks: justifying the risk to yourself and to the lender.

Acceptable Risk/Return Tradeoff

If your small firm is capable of attracting external equity capital, you will find that the annual effective cost (or AER) is high. (External equity is addressed at length in chapters 9 and 10, and effective cost is addressed in Chapter 5.) On the other hand, the effective cost of judicious amounts of debt financing is considerably cheaper than external equity capital. Adding to the advantage of lower effective cost is the tax shield provided by interest expense. Because the government subsidizes a portion of the cost of debt financing for your firm, the after-tax cost of debt is lower than the before-tax borrowing cost. In Ideal's case, the after-tax cost of the 16% loan described earlier is 10.56% (16% multiplied by 1 minus .34).

Effective Cost

While the natural tendency is to seek the cheapest form of financing possible, potential problems are created if cost is the only factor considered in the decision. Often, nonquantitative issues are as critical to a successful financing as the effective interest rate. The noncost factors most important to the financing decision are availability, restrictive covenants, and personal guarantees.

Hidden Factors

- **Availability.** Given the small business' continuing struggle to find adequate financing, availability is often a critical consideration. If your firm has a strong relationship with a lender which provides continued access to financing, borrowing from this source even at slightly higher rates may be more important than shopping for bargain prices.

- **Restrictive covenants.** The protective covenants imposed by a lender may also represent an important implicit cost. While a major objective of these covenants is to impose prudent financial management principles on your business, they may become a burden if your business' circumstances change. You need to evaluate proposed loan covenants to determine if your firm can reasonably live with the restrictions for an extended period. It is important to note that contract provisions are negotiable and the severity of protective covenants demanded by the lender depends on your credit strength. The stronger your credit position, the more leverage you have in the negotiation and the less stringent the restrictions.

- **Personal loan guarantees.** You also need to consider the opportunity cost of a personal loan guarantee. In most cases, the loan will depend on your personal endorsement; however, such an endorsement restricts your discretions over the collateral and places the collateral at risk for the entire period of the loan.

Flexibility

Financial flexibility refers to your firm's ability to adjust financing amounts as needs change. The more flexible your firm's financing sources, the lower its financial risk. Flexibility is difficult if not impossible to achieve with equity capital because ownership interest in a business, once created, is not easily retired. Debt, however, provides some measure of flexibility. If operations produce excess cash flow, debt obligations can be reduced through repayment and, where credit capability allows, it can be raised quickly at an acquisition cost substantially lower than equity.

Owner's Control

For small businesses in which the ownership interest is highly concentrated, maintaining majority control is an important consideration in the financing decision. The freedom to make unchallenged decisions depends on your relative interest in the business. Acquiring funds through the sale of new equity can jeopardize this interest since new owners will have a voice in the business. On the other hand, debt financing offers the advantage of leaving your proportionate interest and control of the business undisturbed. If you are able to raise external equity capital, you need to weigh the prospects of equity dilution against the restrictions created by protective loan covenants.

Forms of Extended-Term Financing

While longer-term debt financing opportunities for small firms are limited when compared to those of large businesses, there are bona fide alternatives — which are discussed in this section — available to the credit worthy borrower.

Term Loans

A term loan is the title given by lenders to traditional business installment debt. It is defined as amortized, intermediate-term financing covering a period from 1 to 10 years. As the title implies, the typical term loan is repayable in equal installments over the life of the contract. Occasionally, either of three alternative repayment arrangements may be negotiated: a balloon payment, an equity sweetener, or a recapture clause.

- **Balloon payment.** A balloon payment is a large, lump-sum payment made at the end of the loan period. The payment compensates the lender for payments that are either smaller than normal or limited in number during the loan period.
- **Equity sweetener.** An equity sweetener is a stock option which, in addition to the fixed interest charges on the loan, grants the lender the right to purchase a specified number of shares of common stock in a borrower's firm at an attractive price. The sweetener is designed to compensate the lender for higher risk exposure by raising the potential return above that which is provided by fixed interest charges.
- **Recapture clause.** A recapture clause is an agreement that requires the borrower to repay the loan more quickly if the firm's sales and cash flows, or some other performance measure, exceed expectations.

Term loans made to small businesses are virtually always secured with a lien on the asset(s) purchased from the loan proceeds; with other fixed assets of the firm; or with personal assets of the owner. The maturity of the term loan is usually tied to the expected service life of the purchased asset. The assets most commonly financed through term loans are equipment, real property, and the permanent component of working capital (cash, receivables, inventory).

An offshoot of the standard term loan is a revolving credit loan. This arrangement combines the features of a term loan with those of a line of credit. Under a revolving credit agreement, the lender makes a legally binding commitment to:

- Loan a specified amount of funds over an extended time period, usually up to five years; and
- Continue lending up to the stated amount until the end of the agreement period.

As is the case with a line of credit, a revolving credit loan provides the flexibility to use financing only at the time it is needed. In addition, as the original principal is reduced through repayment, a firm can reborrow up to the stated maximum. For this privilege, a business pays a commitment fee on the unused portion of the loan in addition to the established interest rate on the financing.

Cost of Term-Loan Financing

Because of the lender's increased risk exposure, the stated interest rate on a term loan will almost always be higher than the stated rate on short-term borrowing. The loan agreement may specify a fixed interest rate over the life of the loan or a floating rate that moves directly with the prime rate of interest. In either case, the lender may use one of two methods for calculating interest:

- **The unpaid balance method.** This method calculates the interest applied to the portion of the outstanding principal from each period.
- **The full-amount method.** This method calculates the interest applied to the full amount of the principal for the entire life of the loan.

If interest is calculated on the unpaid balance, the annual percentage rate of the loan, or APR as the banker calls it, is the same as the stated rate. In this case, the borrower pays interest only on the amount actually available for use over the time period it is used. On the other hand, if interest is charged on the full amount of the principal, the APR will be approximately double the stated rate. With this so called add-on method, total interest is added to the principal to determine the amount of the periodic installment payments. For example, if $10,000 is loaned at 12% add-on for three years, the monthly installments would be $377.78. This is calculated as follows:

Step 1: Determine the interest for one year.

> Interest for One Year = Principal x Stated Interest Rate
> = $10,000 x .12
> = $1,200

Step 2: Calculate the total interest for the loan period.

> Total Interest = Interest for One Year x Number of Years of Loan
> = $1,200 x 3
> = $3,600

Step 3: Determine the total amount to be repaid.

> Total Amount Repaid = Total Interest + Principal
> = $3,600 + $10,000
> = $13,600

Step 4: Calculate installment amount to be paid on a monthly basis.

> Monthly Installment Amount = Total Amount Repaid ÷ Number of Installments
> = $13,000 ÷ 36
> = $377.78

While a borrower pays interest on the full amount of the principal for three years, the full amount of the principal is not available for use during the entire three-year period. Each monthly installment reduces the amount of principal outstanding, and a borrower has that much less principal to use after each period.

In addition to the interest cost, the borrower may also be required to maintain a compensating balance, and to pay service charges to cover the costs of credit analysis, loan origination fees, or legal fees. Any of these requirements raises the annual effective cost of the loan.

When evaluating the cost of term-loan financing, focus on the annual percentage rate (APR) of the loan and not the stated rate.

If your business has the necessary credit capability, term-loan financing offers two important advantages.

Advantages of Term-Loan Financing

- Since most small businesses do not have the financial capability to raise funds through the sale of long-term debt securities in the open market, term loans serve as a good substitute form of financing. In addition, term loans can be obtained more quickly and at a substantially lower cost than financing through a public issue.
- Since the loan provisions are established through negotiation, it is possible to have the agreement and the repayment schedule tailored to fit your needs and cash-flow pattern. Equally as important, once the loan is obtained the lender is prevented from cancelling or refusing to renew credit.

Equipment that is owned free of any liens and in good operating order may serve as collateral for extended-term financing. The financing arrangement used is almost always in the form of a term loan with a maturity tied to the remaining service life of the asset. As is true of all secured financing, the lender takes a security interest in the pledged asset and limits the amount of the loan to some percentage of its estimated liquidation value. The liquidation value is often established by a qualified appraiser who must be hired and paid by the borrowing business.

Asset-Based Loans

In some cases, receivables or inventory may be accepted as collateral for asset-based loans. The pledging, security interest, and percent advance arrangements are the same as those used for short-term financing, but the loan maturity will be for an extended period. Similar to short-term receivables or inventory financing, borrowing may be done on a continuous basis as additional assets are created and pledged.

Loan policies on asset-based loans vary among lenders. While some commercial finance companies rely solely on the value of the asset used as security to judge the merits of the loan, commercial banks also require your business to have acceptable credit standing and the ability to generate adequate cash flow.

Asset-based financing provides the same advantages as term loans, but it generally has a slightly higher rate of interest, and the lender often levies a service charge or loan origination fee in addition to the interest charge.

Mortgage lending is simply financing provided by a security interest in real property: land and buildings. Mortgage loans are virtually identical in character to term loans. They are amortized over the life of the agreement, but because of the nature of the asset involved, usually have longer

Mortgage Loans

maturities than term loans. Mortgage loans to businesses are similar in character to those made for residential financing except for slightly shorter maturities and quarterly rather than monthly installments.

The rate of interest charged on commercial mortgage financing depends on the characteristics of the secured property. If the asset has multiple uses, is high in resale value, and is easily liquidated, interest rates will be competitive with the general level of mortgage rates. Conversely, the more specialized the asset, the greater the risk to the lender, and the higher the interest rate demanded.

Sale-and-Leaseback Financing

Sale-and-leaseback (SAL) financing is an alternative form of asset-based lending. For your qualified small firm, this arrangement also provides the opportunity for securing long-term financing at a reasonable cost. The procedure involves the sale of a lien-free, business asset to a lender (lessor) while simultaneously creating a long-term lease agreement through which the selling business (lessee) leases the property back from the lender. The assets used in SAL financing are usually limited to real property, but virtually any type — factory buildings, land, office buildings, warehouses, etc. — is acceptable. This financing strategy allows you to unlock the equity that is tied-up in the property which is particularly effective, if the asset has increased in value.

Sale-and-leaseback financing represents a major decision for you, and before you make that decision, you should feel that:

- There is a definite and clear-cut investment opportunity for the funds provided by the agreement.
- The expected rate of return earned on the use of the proceeds from the sale exceeds the cost of leasing the property.
- Either the lease period offered by the lessor is sufficiently long to meet your needs, or the agreement provides your business with an option for renewal at the end of each lease period.

Advantages of a Sale-and-Leaseback

Because of the SAL decision's importance, you need to carefully weigh the particular advantages and disadvantages associated with SAL financing. The advantages are listed below.

- **Easier to obtain.** The SAL opportunity is not limited to credit worthy firms. It can be used by businesses with marginal credit standing as well as those having financial difficulty. For these firms, the cost of SAL financing may be cheaper than conventional financing.
- **More financing.** SAL financing will typically provide the selling business a greater amount of funds than conventional financing since no down payment is required.
- **Less restrictive.** The resulting lease agreement will have fewer if any restrictions than that of a conventional asset-based loan.
- **Possible tax benefits.** The entire amount of the payments made by you, the borrowing firm, under the lease agreement qualify as tax-deductible rental expenses.

- **Improve liquidity.** Your business is able to reflect an immediate improvement in the net working capital position shown on the balance sheet. At the time of sale, your firm's equity interest in the fixed asset is converted into cash.

Possible disadvantages associated with sale-and-leaseback financing are:

- **Risk.** The lease payments are a fixed financial and legal obligation that must be met to maintain continued use of the property.
- **Loss of ownership rights.** Title to the property passes to the lessor, and your business loses the flexibility associated with ownership of the property.
- **IRS restrictions.** The SAL agreement must be drafted to meet IRS requirements or the tax benefits are lost.

Disadvantages of a Sale-and-Leaseback

If your small firm has adequate credit capability, leasing may be an attractive alternative to borrowing funds in order to finance a fixed-asset investment. Leasing business assets is simply a specialized form of debt financing in which your business (lessee) enters into a binding contract to rent the services of the asset in question. The usual procedure is for the lessor, often a financial institution specializing in industrial leasing, to buy the asset required by your firm and lease its services according to the terms of a binding agreement. This arrangement allows virtually any business asset to be leased, including specialized plant or equipment items.

Lease Financing

The lessor remains the legal owner of the asset and is entitled to the depreciation tax benefits that ownership provides. On the other hand, if the lease agreement meets IRS guidelines, the lessee is able to deduct the entire lease payment from taxable income. IRS guidelines were established to ensure that a lease is not used as a disguised form of an installment sale to gain unwarranted tax deductions. The guidelines include:

- The term of the lease be less than the service life of the asset;
- The lessor have a reasonable rate of return on the lease arrangement; and
- The lessee pay fair market value for the asset if purchased upon expiration of the lease.

The lease agreement may take one of two basic forms: a financial lease or an operating lease. A financial lease, which is referred to by accountants as a capital lease, is used to finance land, buildings, and equipment of any variety. The agreement is a binding, noncancellable contract that obligates the lessor to a specified number of periodic payments. It is written for a time period that is approximately equivalent to the life of the asset, and any residual value of the asset at that time reverts to you, the lessor. The lease payments are sufficient to recapture the cost of the asset for the lessor and to produce a yield or rate of return at least equivalent to the interest yield that could be earned on a comparable loan. As is true with any debt contract, failure by you to make the required payments provides the lessor with the right to sue for breach of contract.

Types of Lease Financing

The financial lease may be a net lease or a service lease. Under a net lease, you are responsible for all service, maintenance, taxes, and insurance on the asset. The lessor provides only the financing for the arrangement. A net lease is commonly used for leasing arrangements made with financial institutions. Under a service lease, the lessor provides financing as well as the required service and maintenance on the asset. The service lease is often used when an asset is leased directly from the manufacturer.

Net financial lease and the service financial lease are debt contracts. The form, content, and specified obligations of the agreement are the same as those of a debt contract, and the lessor has virtually the same legal recourse in the event of default as any other creditor. Given the nature of the transaction, the lessor's primary concern is your ability to meet the obligated lease payments. To make this determination, the lessor will apply the same credit standards when evaluating a potential lessee as would be applied for a comparable term loan.

By contrast, an operating lease is a short-term lease that can be canceled, possibly with a penalty payment, at any time during the term of the agreement. Usually, all that is required for cancellation is reasonable notice from either party to the lease. Short-term in the context of an operating lease agreement means a time period that is considerably shorter than the expected service life of the asset. The lease payments on an operating lease are usually not sufficient to recapture the full cost of the asset, but the the expected residual value compensates the lessor for the difference. This form of leasing is commonly used for equipment with relatively short service or technological lives, such as computers or automobiles, and it is often more costly than borrowing to buy the asset.

Advantages of Lease Financing

For many small businesses, lease financing may be more advantageous than borrowing to buy the asset. The potential advantages are:

- **Increased financing.** With leasing there is no down payment requirement as is often the case with a comparable extended-term loan. Through a financial lease, a firm is able to obtain 100% financing. For example, assume Ideal uses a particular piece of equipment in its production process. Since the firm has the necessary credit capability, the asset can be purchased with the proceeds of a term loan from Friendly Bank, or the services of the asset can be acquired through a financial lease. If the loan alternative is decided, Friendly Bank will likely require an initial down payment that can range from between 5% to 20% of the cost the asset. If the asset is leased, no down payment is required. The only initial cash outflow Ideal would suffer is the first lease payment.
- **Increased financing potential.** Leasing may also make it possible for businesses with marginal credit ratings to obtain the services of an asset that cannot be acquired by borrowing. For these firms, securing a term loan may not be possible or, if it is, only at the cost of undesirable restrictions or a prohibitive interest rate.
- **Avoid restrictive covenants.** Any loan agreement under which you

borrow is certain to contain provisions that to varying degrees restrict your freedom. Lease agreements, however, rarely contain restrictive covenants.

- **Potential tax advantage.** Land, as opposed to other fixed assets, cannot be depreciated for tax purposes. This means that land ownership provides no depreciation tax shield for you. If land is leased, however, the entire lease payment is tax deductible.

- **Shared risk of obsolescence.** If equipment subject to rapid technological change is leased under an operating lease agreement, the lessor shares some of the risk of obsolescence. You can update equipment through the periodic lease renewal. Also, many operating lease agreements provide for the automatic replacement of equipment as technological advances are made.

- **Longer maturity structure.** Since lease agreements are structured for much of the asset's service life, the term of the lease often extends beyond the maturity period available on a comparable loan.

- **Lower liability risk.** Although state laws vary, a firm's liability on a lease default is less than that on a loan. Under a collateralized loan agreement, the lender has both a lien on the specific asset(s) pledged, and a general creditor's claim on all other nonpledged assets. A lessor's claim, however, is usually limited to repossession of the leased asset and a specific number of lease payments.

- **Convenience.** A lease agreement is often less difficult to administer, involves less paperwork and documentation, and can be structured more quickly than a loan contract. In addition, leasing may be attractive because you will have to deal only with one party, the lessor, who provides both the asset and the financing.

Several potential disadvantages — which are listed below — may be associated with lease financing. Whether these considerations are actually negatives, depends on your circumstances and the financing alternatives that are available.

Disadvantages of Lease Financing

- **Cost.** In general, the annual effective cost of leasing is higher than that of a term loan of comparable maturity. Any unfavorable cost differential may, however, be outweighed by the advantages you may gain through leasing. What's more, the cost of leasing can be minimized by careful shopping. As is true of other financial institutions, leasing businesses operate in a competitive environment and have different policies, attitudes toward risk, and required rates of return. Where possible, it is advisable to obtain competitive bids by providing a number of prospective lessors with a description of the required asset.

- **Risk.** The terms of a financial lease are as binding on your firm as those of a comparable debt contract. This may be a problem if the lease does not provide for the automatic upgrade of an asset that has become technologically obsolete. Your business is obligated for the lease payments through the full term of a financial lease, even if the asset becomes unusable.

■ **Loss of ownership interest.** Since the lessor owns the leased asset, you do not build equity in the asset. Moreover, the asset reverts to the lessor at the end of the lease period. This means you lose any residual value the asset may have at that time. This disadvantage may be offset by the typical lease provision allowing you to purchase the asset at the end of the lease period at a price equal to its fair market value.

Industrial Development Financing

Virtually all state or local governments have established economic development agencies acting to promote business and economic growth in their jurisdictions. The incentives offered by these agencies to qualifying businesses take a variety of forms, including financing assistance at often attractive rates. The purpose of these incentives is to create jobs by inducing businesses to locate in their area and to encourage local businesses to make job-creating investments in new plant and equipment. Some agencies also offer leases on land, buildings, or other plant assets on attractive terms. The bulk of the financing plans offered, however, take one of two basic forms: industrial revenue bonds (IRB) or packaged loans.

An IRB, which is commonly referred to in financial circles as a muni or tax-exempt municipal bond, is a long-term bond issue sold to the public under the auspices of a state or municipal economic development agency. The purpose of the bond issue is to raise funds on behalf of, and which will be spent by, the target business. Although the recipient business assumes liability for the interest and principal payments on the bond, it gains a significant financing cost advantage. What distinguishes the IRB from bonds of the federal government or private businesses is the tax-exempt feature. The interest payments received by the bondholder are free from federal income tax, and this allows the bond to be sold at a relatively low interest rate. The cost advantage gained by the target business can serve as a powerful inducement.

An alternative form of economic development financing is a packaged loan. This unique arrangement takes the form of a direct loan made by the development authority to the target firm, but at an interest cost lower than the going market rate. The loan funds are obtained by the agency from combination of governmental and private sources. Often the combination consists of some specified percentage of state government, federal government, and local bank funds. Again, the relatively lower interest cost serves as a strong incentive for the target firm.

Sources of Extended-Term Financing

The opportunities available for the credit worthy small business have grown over the past two decades. Available sources include: commercial banks, savings and loan institutions, commercial finance companies, equipment manufacturers, independent leasing companies, life insurance companies, U.S. government, and venture capitalists.

Commercial Banks

Commercial banks have become increasingly more receptive over the past two decades to the financing needs of small firms. As a result, they rank as the largest single source of extended-term financing for small businesses and provide extended financing primarily through term loans, mortgage loans, and to a lesser extent through industrial leasing. Commercial bank term loans will have either a fixed or floating interest rate, and a loan agreement that follows the pattern previously described in the beginning of this chapter. Mortgage loans are similar to those used for standard residential financing with the exception of a shorter maturity, usually 10 years, and quarterly rather than monthly installment payments.

Benefits from Commercial Bank Financing

Bank financing offers significant advantages to your small firm, including lower interest cost. A commercial bank is only one of two private financing sources for business firms that obtain a large proportion of its loan funds from depositor accounts rather than through the sale of securities in public markets. This means that bank lending costs are lower than those of competitors, and this cost differential can be passed on to you in the form of lower interest rates.

Another significant, but often overlooked benefit of bank borrowing is management assistance. Many large banks have a department that specializes in small business lending, and its loan officers readily provide financial management assistance as well as information on related topics, such as business trends, economic conditions, or investment opportunities. While smaller banks may not have a specialized small business department, its loan officers often have expertise on local conditions and small business operations.

Savings and Loan Institutions

The federal government's deregulation of banks and savings and loan (S&L) institutions in the 1980s dramatically altered the borrowing and lending practices of these two institutions. One of the results of deregulation has been increased competition for funds. Both have responded by finding new and innovative techniques for attracting both depositor funds and loan customers. While the recent S&L and bank debacle questions the wisdom of deregulation, it has opened avenues for small firm financing.

Prior to deregulation, S&L lending was limited primarily to residential mortgages and to temporary financing for the initial stages of residential and commercial construction. Since that time, many S&Ls have attempted to earn higher loan yields by branching into non-traditional lending areas. While current lending practices of S&Ls are not uniform, extended-term mortgage financing should be investigated by contacting a representative sample of these financial institutions.

Commercial Finance Companies

Commercial finance companies are actively involved in equipment financing through installment loans, which are secured by a lien on a business' asset and possibly by your personal assets. Interest rates on installment loans are generally higher than those charged by commercial banks and can range up to 3% to 4% above bank rates.

This relative cost disadvantage may be offset by the tendency of commercial finance companies to accept greater risk exposure in their loan portfolios than commercial banks. Small businesses unable to qualify for a bank loan may be able to obtain extended-term financing from this source. The tendency to accept greater risk also translates into a willingness to be more flexible than a bank when negotiating provisions of the loan agreement. Commercial finance companies often:

- Accept business assets as collateral that are deemed unacceptable by a bank;
- Usually insist on fewer or less restrictive loan provisions; and
- Tend to be more lax about overseeing its customer's activities.

Equipment Manufacturers

Often manufacturers of business equipment make financing available to customers either directly or through a captive financing subsidiary. A captive financing subsidiary is a division or wholly owned subsidiary whose business is providing financing to customers. An example of a captive financing subsidiary is GMAC, which is the financing wing of General Motors. The financing may take the form of a standard term loan — referred to in this case as a conditional sales contract — or an operating or financial lease.

Providing financing for its customers has important advantages for a manufacturer. First, by offering financing, it enhances product sales. Since financing a sale produces both profit margin and interest return, the manufacturer can justify higher risk and extend credit to marginally qualified customers. Also, dealing directly with a manufacturer makes it convenient for you, the customer, to combine the purchasing and financing functions in one transaction. Second, the profit earned on financing activities is an important source of cash flow for many manufacturing firms. Finally, the danger of injuring customer goodwill through reliance on the collection practices of outside finance companies is avoided.

The interest cost of manufacturer financing is higher than that of commercial banks, but it is comparable to rates charged by commercial finance companies. Any cost disadvantage of manufacturer financing may be offset by any of several possible advantages. The manufacturer's willingness to accept higher credit risk offers an opportunity that may not be available from traditional financial institutions. Also, this type financing usually requires a smaller down payment and less stringent loan covenants than a bank loan.

An important, but often overlooked advantage of manufacturer financing is the additional opportunities it may create. Manufacturer's financing subsidiaries customarily make receivables and inventory loans and can provide small businesses with an alternative financing source for meeting working capital needs.

Independent Leasing Companies

The largest volume of business lease financing is provided by distinctive financial institutions known as independent or industrial leasing companies.

These companies tend to specialize in either operating leases or financial leases. An industrial leasing company specializing in operating leases concentrates on the leasing of standardized, short-lived business assets, such as computers and commercial and industrial vehicles. These short-lived, cancellable leases are rarely designed to amortize the cost of the asset and lessor's required rate of return. Rather, the rate of return for the lessor usually depends heavily on the resale value of the asset at the end of the lease period. At that time, the lessor will either release the asset, often to the original lessee, or sell it at fair market value.

An industrial leasing company specializing in financial leases provides financing to purchase the particular asset specified by the lessee. Such leases are fully amortized, alternative form debt contracts that are negotiated solely on the credit strength of the lessee. For these reasons, the lessor is indifferent to the type of asset to be leased.

Life insurance companies, while an important source of long-term debt financing for large businesses, provide only limited assistance to small businesses. The typical life insurance company has large amounts of premium dollars that must be invested on a regular basis in fixed return opportunities. This need often renders smaller loans impractical. Life insurance companies that do make financing available to smaller borrowers engage in industrial leasing, make fixed-rate term and mortgage loans, and buy long-term bonds.

Life Insurance Companies

Insurance company term loans differ from those of commercial banks in several important respects. First, insurance companies are willing to offer longer maturities, often 15 years or more, than the typical commercial bank. Second, in order to meet their portfolio needs, insurance companies want to receive loan repayments for the entire term of the contract. Consequently, the loan agreement often calls for a stiff penalty for prepayments or early retirement of the loan, or prohibit them altogether.

Life insurance companies' business mortgage loans typically have longer maturities than those offered by commercial banks. The typical insurance company loan will have a maturity of up to 30 years as opposed to a 10- to 15-year maturity on a bank loan. Bond financings by insurance companies also have long-term maturities ranging up to as much as 30 years.

A recent trend in insurance company lending has been the addition of an equity sweetener or equity kicker on loans made to more risky businesses. This provision justifies the higher risk by allowing the lender to share in a firm's earnings success as well as enjoy the interest yield on the loan. The sweetener may take the form of a percentage claim on the earnings from the commercial real estate that has been financed; warrants which allow the lender to buy stock in the borrowing business at a stated price; or, in the case of bond financing, a conversion privilege that allows the lender to exchange the bond for a specified number of shares of common stock in the borrowing firm.

U.S. Small Business Administration

In addition to the opportunities provided by state or municipal economic development agencies, agencies of the federal government also make funds available to qualified small businesses. The most prominent of these agencies is the U.S. Small Business Administration (SBA). The SBA is an independent government agency created by Congress in 1953 to provide assistance to small businesses. This assistance helps you by:

- Providing free business and technical counseling;
- Providing educational services through workshops, seminars, and a variety of topical literature on small firm management;
- Ensuring that small businesses receive an equitable proportion of government purchases, contracts, and subcontracts;
- Licensing, regulating, and lending to small business investment companies (SBIC); and
- Helping qualified small businesses obtain financing.

Before investigating the details of SBA financing opportunities, mention should be made of the SBA's management education and assistance programs. While financing may be your uppermost concern, it is not the primary cause of the downfall of failed businesses. The culprit is usually the absence of sufficient management expertise. While many small business owner/managers tend to be well-versed in the technical aspects of their business, they are often inadequately trained or inexperienced in one or more of the critical administrative areas. In such cases, the regional SBA office, with its educational and management assistance services, can be an effective remedy to this problem.

Eligibility for SBA Financing

To be eligible for SBA financing assistance, your business must first meet the SBA's definition of a small business. These standards, however, are not rigidly applied. Rather, they serve as suggestive guidelines for distinguishing eligible independent small businesses from ineligible larger entities. In general, a business is considered small if:

- It is an independent business not dominant in its field, and sales revenue (number of employees for a manufacturing business) does not exceed the approximate limits shown on Table 6.3. Note that the dollar amounts and employee numbers are subject to change.
- It is ineligible for alternative financing from other government agencies.
- It is unable to obtain financing from private sources on reasonable terms.
- There is sufficient evidence that an owner/manager has the capability to operate the business successfully.
- The business and its ownership represent a reasonable credit risk, and the loan is supported with adequate security.
- It has demonstrated past earnings, or has future prospects that provide reasonable assurances the loan will be repaid.

Table 6.3

SBA Definition of what Qualifies as a Small Business

Industry	Criteria
Wholesale	Annual sales must not exceed $9.5 to $22.0 million, depending on the industry.
Retail	Annual sales must not exceed $2.0 to $7.5 million, depending on the industry.
Service	Annual sales must not exceed $2.0 to $8.0 million, depending on the industry.
Manufacturing	Number of employees must not exceed 250 to 1,500, depending on the industry.
Construction	Annual receipts must not exceed $9.5 million, averaged over a three-year period.
Special Trade Construction	Average annual receipts must not exceed $1.0 to $2.0 million for the three most recently completed fiscal years, depending on the industry.
Agriculture	Annual receipts must not exceed $1.0 million.

Even if your business meets this criteria, the SBA will not consider assistance if the business is:

- A nonprofit or charitable organization;
- Engaged in lending for or investing in real estate;
- Engaged in the mass media business, such as the publication of magazines and newspapers or television or radio broadcasting;
- Selling mainly alcoholic beverages, or derives its revenue from gambling;
- Using the proceeds to finance owner's withdrawals or unwarranted changes in ownership; or
- Using the proceeds to establish a monopoly position.

Types of SBA Financing

SBA loan activity takes a variety of forms, including disaster loans, economic injury loans, surety bond guarantees, loans to economic development agencies, loans to SBICs, and direct and participating small business loans. The latter two loan programs are of special interest to the small business owner.

Since its inception, the SBA has maintained, to varying degrees, a direct loan program. The purpose of the program is to fulfill its intended role of "lender of last resort" for qualified businesses unable to raise funds in the private sector. Financing for this program comes directly from Congress through budget appropriations. The amount of these appropriations has declined steadily since 1980, however, and the SBA has increasingly removed itself from direct lending. At the time of this writing, only Vietnam veterans are eligible for a direct business loan from the SBA.

In recent years, the SBA/bank participation (guarantee) loan program has been the primary focus of the agency's financing activity. Under this program, you apply directly to and negotiate with a local commercial bank interested in making such loans. If you are deemed an acceptable credit risk by both the bank and the SBA, the bank makes the loan and the SBA guarantees up to 90% of the outstanding principle for the lending bank. This guarantee removes most of the default risk on the loan making it possible for the bank to lend to higher-risk, small firm borrowers.

Participating loans made to finance permanent working capital and equipment are in the form of standard term loans with maturities of up to approximately 7 years. Principal and interest on these loans are amortized through monthly or quarterly installments. Loans for the purchase or construction of real property may have maturities of up to 20 years. The maximum interest rate on a guaranteed loan is set by the SBA but pegged to the bank prime rate. This rate is slightly less than the going rate for comparable loans without the guarantee.

For more information on SBA financing and services, contact the SBA office nearest you. The SBA also offers a national toll-free telephone hotline which is designed to provide general SBA information. This SBA Answer Desk Hotline is shown below.

SBA Answer Desk
(800) 827-5722

Negotiating an SBA Participating Loan

Since the participating loan is negotiated directly with a lending bank, you have the responsibility for finding a bank interested in such a loan. The process begins with an indication by the bank loan officer that he or she will consider making an SBA guaranteed loan. With the cooperation of the bank's loan officer, you then prepare the detailed SBA loan application and supporting documents. When the loan officer is satisfied with the application, it, along with the bank's report on your business, is sent to the SBA. If any aspect of the application requires clarification, you may be contacted by the SBA. If not, your business will have no contact with the SBA. The bank negotiates the entire process on your behalf.

Finding a local bank involved in SBA-guaranteed lending is not difficult. The most obvious approach is direct inquiry of various local bank loan officers. Information can also be obtained from local business people or from business groups, such as your chamber of commerce or area planning and development commissions. Also, each regional SBA office publishes monthly statistics on which banks participate in SBA programs and the amounts loaned. This data is useful in identifying active banks as well as the types of businesses and industries in which they take an interest.

Because an SBA participating loan is made directly by a traditional financial institution, some aspects of the agreement can be negotiated. Features, such as the manner in which interest is paid (fixed versus floating rate) and collateral requirements, are flexible. The bank will not negotiate fixed items, such as the interest rate on the loan, your personal endorsement of the note, and mandatory life insurance on your firm's principals.

It is important to note that there is no such thing as a standardized SBA participating loan. Banks, as private financial institutions, are subject to varying conditions and changing policies. It is in your best interest to survey several banks before making application and to try a second bank if rejection occurs.

SBICs and Venture Capitalists

For the small business offering attractive growth potential or the start-up firm with a potentially profitable innovation, debt or equity financing may be available from a venture capitalist. Venture capitalists fall into two broad categories: those licensed and regulated by the federal government through the U.S. Small Business Administration and nonregulated businesses. The former group provides financing through long-term debt, which may be in the form of either straight debt or debt with an equity sweetener, and equity financing through the purchase of common stock. The latter group specializes primarily in equity financing. Venture capital financing is covered further in Chapter 9.

Tips for Negotiating Extended-Term Financing

Entering into any contract is an important decision, but the decision is even more critical in the case of an extended-term debt agreement. You are the one that lives with the payment schedule and covenants of the contract for a protracted time period. Needless to say, the decision should not be taken lightly nor should it be made in haste. You are aware that the conditions and circumstances surrounding the business never stay the same. Nothing, that is, but the burden of taxes and the contracts to which the business is legally bound. You need to carefully evaluate and cost-justify every detail of an extended-term contract. This analysis must be made in the context of the conditions under which your firm currently operates and under reasonable assumptions for alternative futures conditions your business may face.

Be Prepared

To effectively and convincingly discuss your firm's extended-term financing needs with a lender, you must be certain what these needs are. If you cannot justify the risk/return tradeoff associated with the financing, the financing request certainly cannot be articulated and justified in a manner that will satisfy a prospective lender.

Formalize the Loan Request

A detailed loan request should be incorporated into a written, formal business plan covering the same time frame as the expected financing. Properly prepared, a business plan is a blueprint for the direction you expect the business to take; its intended operations and activities; and its financial future. A business plan meets two essential prerequisites for raising extended-term financing:

- The preparation process itself is an educational experience.
- It provides insight into aspects of the business and its operations that are sometimes lost under the burden of day-to-day management.

Preparing a business plan also allows you to identify and evaluate factors that are vital to your firm's success.

Equally as important, the business plan provides the lender with the type of information that will be required to make a decision on the loan request. The fact that this information is presented through a formal business plan before the lender has to request it sends a clear message: This business is in the hands of competent management. Remember, the lender's perception of management is often the deciding factor in granting the loan. Chapter 8 provides a detailed discussion of preparing and presenting the financing proposal and business plan.

Consider All Relevant Factors

While cost is an important consideration in any financing decision, non-financial factors may be of equal weight and should be carefully evaluated. In order to remain viable, your small business must be sufficiently flexible to alter operations or change directions as the need arises. Therefore, be certain that provisions in the extended-term contract do not eliminate this potential. Also, many small firms face limited extended-term financing opportunities, and a strong relationship with a financial institution that serves your firm's financing needs may be more important than minor cost savings.

Shop Carefully

There is wide variation in the operating philosophy and policies of financial institutions. Lending practices will differ between different types of financial institutions and often differ between those in the same institutional category. You should shop carefully for extended-term financing. This is especially true if a loan request is rejected. What one lender finds unsuitable may be acceptable to another.

Learn from Rejection

The denial of a loan request can often be a valuable educational experience. Carefully evaluate and identify the underlying reasons why your loan was rejected, and determine if the problem(s) can be remedied. Often, the loan officer with whom the negotiation has been conducted is willing to discuss the specific reasons for the rejection. This knowledge may not only make the difference between success or failure on the next attempt, but it may also provide valuable insight into weaknesses that require your attention.

Chapter 7

Understanding Your Banker

Choosing a suitable bank or banker and maintaining a viable banking relationship is a very important goal for any small business manager. A strong bank affiliation can be a major contributing factor to your small firm's success and the key to its survival during difficult times. Unfortunately, many managers often select a bank on the basis of convenience, and fail to nurture the banker's loyalty. These are costly errors.

Having a bank that you can rely upon to provide financing and services is extremely important. To make a wise choice and achieve the desired level of rapport requires an understanding of both banking fundamentals and the banker's way of thinking. The more informed you are about a particular bank, its procedures, the logic of its operations, and the philosophy of its officers, the more satisfactory and profitable the association.

This chapter provides you with a basic understanding of the nature, characteristics, and philosophy of commercial banking. This knowledge is valuable when attempting to deal effectively with banks and other types of financiers.

The Importance of Good Banking Relations

Certainly the most important reason for establishing and maintaining a strong bank affiliation is financing. With virtually no access to the money and capital markets for your small business, you must rely on institutional lenders to meet your financial needs. Most prominent among this group is the commercial bank. Creating the opportunity for a continuous supply of financing under reasonable terms from a bank may become your most valuable financial asset.

A strong banking relationship also offers your business an important measure of financial flexibility. For example, assume for a moment that you are the owner of a small manufacturing company. On a routine visit to the offices of your largest customer, you are told by the firm's vice-president that they will be opening an additional plant in another city. You are asked in unequivocal terms if your company is in position to make a firm commitment to supply both the existing and new plants, and to do so with same day delivery. The implication behind the inquiry is clear: If you can't meet our needs, we will find another supplier who will. Naturally, the vice-president wants an answer yesterday.

You immediately decide that to make this commitment requires an additional warehouse facility located near the customer's new plant site. A quick mental calculation suggests it would take about $50,000 to lease the space, stock the warehouse, and buy the necessary equipment. Consider the advantage of having a banker that knows you and your business well enough to make an informal commitment for the required financing over the telephone.

While some managers may never experience a dilemma of this magnitude, the story has relevance for all small businesses. Regardless of the reason, sooner or later the need for financing will arise. Your most logical choice for meeting this need is a bank. Unless the proper groundwork has been laid before the fact, however, bank financing is difficult, if not impossible, to obtain on short notice.

The advantage of financial flexibility through an ongoing bank relationship also manifests itself in other ways. Since small firms are typically undercapitalized, they more often than not operate without sufficient cash reserves. This is not a serious problem if the firm has a bank affiliation strong enough to provide emergency financing. In the absence of an existing bank relationship, however, undercapitalization entails enormous risk. Raising financing quickly is a monumental task in itself without the added burden of trying to get acquainted with a banker in the process.

A strong association with a banker is also important for the many services a bank can provide; for example, providing credit information on a potential customer, advice on a business opportunity, or insight into the outlook for business conditions in a firm's market.

The Nature and Characteristics of Commercial Banks

Essentially, a bank is a privately owned dealer in debt. It is a financial institution that obtains most of its working capital by accepting demand

and savings deposits and, to a much lesser extent, occasional borrowing from other lenders and the investment of its stockholders. Depositor's funds, which are debts or liabilities of the bank, are used to conduct its primary business: making loans and investments.

Commercial banks receive the right to operate as a regulated, depository institution through a charter. Charters for national banks, those created and regulated by the federal government, are granted by the U.S. Comptroller of the Currency. State banks receive their charter in the state of incorporation from the state counterpart to the U.S. Comptroller of the Currency. With the charter goes the responsibility to help service the financial needs of the community in which it operates, as well as to generate a profit for its stockholders. The charter also obligates the bank to submit to supervision and to abide by banking regulations.

The U.S. Comptroller of the Currency, and to a lesser extent, the Federal Deposit Insurance Corporation (FDIC) regulate and supervise the activities of national banks. State banks are regulated by a state agency similar to that at the federal level and by the FDIC, if the bank is a member.

The primary focus of bank regulation and supervision is ensuring the protection and responsible management of depositors' money. Regulatory agencies strive to achieve this objective by requiring banks to maintain adequate reserves against deposits, exercise sound judgment in setting loan policies, and to achieve efficiency in their operations. The burden of operating under vigorously enforced restrictions has shaped the conservative attitude toward loans and investments that is held by traditional bankers. While a banker's cautious risk/return perspective may be irritating to a small business manager whose loan request has been rejected, it is necessary in order for banks to maintain the public trust.

Commercial Banking as a Business

While banks have a responsibility to regulators, depositors, and the community in which they reside, they are first and foremost privately owned businesses operating to make a profit for their stockholders. Fortunately, a well-run bank's ultimate goal is long-run profitability through a strong commitment to the economic health of its community. This is accomplished in large part by making sound business loans. While "making a fast buck" is not part of the philosophy of traditional banks, their fundamental objective is still to earn a profit. What distinguishes banks from other profit-seeking financial institutions, however, is the conservative attitude toward risk that is virtually forced on them by the various restrictions governing banking operations.

The basic mechanics of the banking business are relatively simple. The liabilities created by deposits — and to a minor extent stockholders' invested capital — less the reserves that must be set aside, provide the capital for doing business. These funds are literally the raw material of banking. As with any manufacturing business, a bank converts its raw material into finished goods that are offered to customers. In this case, the raw material is depositors' funds, and the finished goods are the bank's loans and investments. The interest return on these loans and investments represents the bank's sales revenue.

The cost of a bank's raw materials, the interest it must pay on deposits, along with the costs of the services provided its customers represent the bank's cost of sales. To be profitable, the interest revenue must be sufficient to cover cost of sales, overhead costs, an appropriate allowance for losses on loans and investments, and to produce a compensatory return on stockholder's invested capital.

Factors Influencing Loans and Investments

Three primary considerations influence a banker's choice of which loans to make or not to make. They are:

- The type of deposits held by the bank;
- The expectations of bank examiners; and
- The risk/return perspective of its officers.

These factors help explain the typical banker's attitude toward lending to small businesses.

Like other businesses, a bank attempts to synchronize its cash inflows and outflows. It does this by attempting to make loans and investments that have a maturity roughly equivalent to that of the deposits that must be protected. If the bulk of the bank's depositors hold checking accounts, it must guard against the instability and sudden cash drains that are characteristics of these short-term balances. This is accomplished by confining the largest portion of its loans and investments to short maturities. For example, short-term, self-liquidating, working capital loans to businesses have traditionally been the mainstay of the banking business because checking accounts often make up the largest proportion of a bank's deposits.

The types of loans and investments banks make are also influenced by the possible adverse reaction of examiners to its activities. As regulated institutions, a bank's portfolio of loans and investments is subject to periodic scrutiny by examiners from the various banking regulatory agencies. If deviations from regulations or acceptable policy are found, the bank is subject to penalties that can range from reprimands to the loss of its charter.

A banker's attitude toward risk is also tempered by a realistic view of the risk/return tradeoff inherent in the choice between lending as opposed to the alternative of investing in low-risk securities. When a bank officer considers making a business loan, he or she naturally compares this use of funds to the return that could be earned on a low-risk investment, such as a security of the federal government. The comparison is made by estimating the degree of default risk inherent in the loan relative to that of the low-risk alternative. To compensate for the higher degree of risk associated with the loan, a banker charges an interest rate higher than what could be earned on the low-risk investment.

Theoretically, banks could make loans with any degree of risk by simply charging a sufficiently high interest rate. In the real world, this is not possible. First, there are state usury laws that set upper limits on interest rates that can be charged. In the case of high-risk loans, banks simply could not legally charge a compensatory interest rate. Also, as a creditor in the loan transaction, a banker does not share in the earnings success of the borrower. Because of the reality of a limited return, a bank is not in a position to suffer the potential loss on a high-risk loan. These factors, when coupled with the responsibility to meet depositor liabilities and the threat of periodic examination, are sobering influences on a bank's lending and investing policies.

To place the effect these limitations have on shaping bank lending policy into perspective, consider two comparisons: 1) bank credit versus trade credit; and 2) credit owner's investment capital versus that of a creditor on a fixed-interest loan.

Bank Credit Versus Trade Credit

The return earned by a bank to compensate for the risk of a typical business loan is in striking contrast to that of a business firm extending trade credit to a customer. A business firm has the potential for a greater return than what a bank earns on the loan and can, therefore, accept a greater risk.

For example, assume a manufacturing business with 30-day credit terms is considering a $10,000 credit sale to a customer with only a marginal credit standing. The customer is expected to pay in 30 days and to repeat the $10,000 purchase each month. These transactions would generate $120,000 of annual sales for the manufacturer. Since the customer will pay the outstanding balance on the account each month, the manufacturer will have only an average of $10,000 [$120,000 multiplied by (30 divided by 360)] of capital tied up in accounts receivable or at risk at any one time. If the manufacturer's before-tax return on sales is 20%, the $120,000 of annual credit sales to the customer will generate $24,000 of pre-tax profit ($120,000 multiplied by .20).

Now assume that Friendly Bank is considering either making a $10,000, one-year loan to the same customer at the going interest rate of 14%, or investing the $10,000 in a government bond yielding 9%. In making the loan, the bank will incur a $200 cost for credit investigation and other associated loan costs. If the loan is made, Friendly can expect a net return before taxes of $1,200 [($10,000 multiplied by .14) minus $200]. If, on the other hand, Friendly chooses to invest in the government bond it would earn a risk-free $900. The decision for Friendly boils down to whether the expected additional $300 ($1,200 minus $900) earned from a loan to a customer with marginal credit is sufficient to compensate for the additional risk.

If the bank's position is contrasted to that of the manufacturer, the difference is startling. The manufacturer generates an expected annual return of $24,000 for assuming risk. The same risk assumption for the bank nets $3,600 ($300 multiplied by 12 months) if the loan is repeated each month. Obviously, Friendly must take an entirely different view of risk assumption than the manufacturer. A responsibility to protect depositors' funds dictates that potential loss of principal through borrower default is a primary concern.

Owner Return Versus Creditor Return

Further understanding of a bank's perspective on a potential small business loan can be gained by comparing a creditor's position to that of an ownership interest. The point can be best illustrated with an example.

Assume that Friendly Bank has been approached for a loan by an entrepreneur interested in starting a new business. The venture holds the prospects for substantial profits, but it is risky. Valuable personal assets of the entrepreneur would secure the loan, and the proceeds along with the entrepreneur's investment would provide the start-up capital for the business.

If the loan is made and the business succeeds, Friendly earns only the fixed interest rate on the loan. On the other hand, the entrepreneur earns the promised high rate of return on the profits generated by the business. If the business fails, Friendly suffers the cost of repossessing, establishing legal title to, and selling the pledged personal assets, which probably means a considerable loss.

Here again, it is virtually impossible for a bank to justify the type of risk associated with loans to start-up or other high-risk businesses. To rationally assume that degree of risk, an investor would have to expect the potential for high returns. Banks, which receive only the limited interest return, cannot logically do so.

How Banks Differ

So far the discussion has centered on commercial banking as an institution and perhaps has mistakenly implied that the policies and practices of all banks are uniform; however, this is not the case. Banks may differ in such important areas as the types of financing made available, interest rates charged, willingness to accept risk, staff expertise, services offered, and in their attitude toward small business loans. Understanding and identifying these differences will help you select a suitable bank.

The more important factors accounting for the difference between banks include:

- **Type of bank.** The importance of business loans to a particular bank will influence the reaction of a loan officer to a small business loan application. For example, banks specializing in consumer loans and home mortgages may be much less interested in making small business loans than smaller banks that routinely do this type of lending.

- **Specialization.** As bank officers become familiar with a particular industry through repeated lending, they gain confidence in their ability to gauge risk. This often leads to a preference for specializing in particular categories of loans. While this is a plus for the small firm in the bank's speciality area, it also means that there may be much less interest on the part of the bank in making other types of business loans.

- **Risk perception.** Even though bankers tend to be conservative, there can be substantial differences between banks in terms of attitude toward risk and loan policy. Some are simply more conservative than others and tend to be highly selective in the types of loans made. Other banks may be more willing to accept higher degrees of risk and actively solicit small business loans. Estimating risk is more judgment than science, and the simple fact is that personal judgments, including risk perceptions, differ.
- **Current conditions.** Prevailing conditions — such as a bank's current portfolio of loans and investments, the amount of reserves it has available for lending, or the the Federal Reserve System's existing monetary policy — will strongly influence the willingness to undertake new or more questionable loans. When banks are loaned up or credit conditions are tight, there is a natural tendency to choose only the most desirable lending or investing alternatives.

Establish and Maintain a Strong Banking Relationship

Narrowing the Field

The search for a suitable bank should begin with a clear distinction between the types of banks and an understanding of a bank's service area. Banks can be broadly classified as retail banks, wholesale banks, and combination banks.

- Retail banks are geared toward the needs of household accounts. They specialize in personal loans such as those for automobiles or home improvement.
- Wholesale banks specialize in business loans. Their personnel are trained in business matters, and often have expertise in the local business economy or particular industries in which lending activities are concentrated.
- Combination banks do both retailing and wholesaling.

Your task is to find a business-oriented bank that will provide the financial assistance, expertise, and services your business requires now and is likely to require in the future.

The fact that there are a large number of banking offices in the nation is of little benefit because selection of a bank is essentially limited to choices from the local community. Banks outside of your local area are not anxious to make loans to your firm because of the higher costs of checking credit and of collecting the loan in the event of default. Moreover, a bank will typically not make business loans to any size business unless a checking account or money market account is maintained. Out-of-town banks know that nonlocal firms are not likely to keep meaningful deposits at their institution because it is too costly in both time and expense to do so.

Asking the Right Questions

The first step in identifying a bank that will meet your needs is to ask knowledgeable parties about the banks and bankers in the area. Inquiries about bank services, attitudes, and expertise can be directed to other business owners and to bankers themselves. Often, a useful source of information is a bank's business development officer. As the title implies, these individuals have the specific task of seeking new business accounts for the bank. Contact with a business development officer provides useful information for weeding out banks that do not meet your selection criteria.

When the search is narrowed to the most likely candidate(s), you should make personal contact with a ranking bank officer. In this meeting, you should discuss your business, its needs, what you are looking for in a banking relationship, and whether the bank can meet those needs. Be sure to let the banker know that financing will eventually be sought if you choose his or her bank, and you hope that the banker will begin learning about your business before the need arises. If the bank appears to meet your firm's needs, request that a loan officer start a data file on your firm and offer to supply whatever information may be required for this purpose.

Making the Choice

The choice of an appropriate bank boils down to finding the institution that meets your established criteria. While some of this criteria may be strictly subjective considerations, there are several major factors that should govern your choice. These factors are discussed below.

Banker's Attitude

One critical question that must be answered about a bank is its attitude toward lending and assisting small businesses. If a bank tends to shy away from loans to smaller businesses, it will be difficult to obtain funds if your firm's credit standing is or becomes the least bit marginal. During the interview process, see if there is tangible evidence that substantiates the bank's willingness to assist small businesses. For example, question the bank officer about such specifics as what percentage of the bank's business loans are made to small and medium-sized firms or if the bank actively seeks SBA-guaranteed loans.

Lending Policy

Closely related to the bank's overall attitude toward small firms is the issue of the types of loans it will make. To do so, you need to inquire about the bank's willingness to make a verbal or written commitment for a line of credit; about its compensating balance requirements; and about the specific provisions that are normally included in extended-term loan agreements. With this latter point, determine both the extent to which collateral is required and the type of collateral considered acceptable. For example, a bank that does not make inventory loans is of little value to a business whose most valuable asset is inventory.

Services

After discussing the bank's basic lending philosophy, focus on available services. For example, does the bank offer such amenities as payroll check preparation, financial counseling for small business managers, credit reference checks on a firm's prospective customers, international financial services, and possibly personal services for a firm's management. By knowing the range and depth of a bank's services, you also gain insight into how progressive and imaginative its staff is, and if they would be likely to find creative solutions to a particular problem your business may face in the future.

Overdraft Policy

Despite efforts, virtually all smaller businesses face unexpected, temporary cash shortages at one time or another. Often, a convenient alternative for handling the problem is an overdraw on the firm's checking account balance. Some banks allow this to be done by automatically treating an overdraw as a loan to be repaid with interest. Those that do not allow this option consider an overdraw a blemish on a customer's record.

Who Will Be Your Loan Officer?

In the typical bank, the extent of a particular loan officer's authority to make loans, make loans above a given dollar amount, or influence the bank's loan committee usually depends on rank, tenure, and experience. Keep these latter qualities in mind when seeking your firm's loan officer. Typically, banks assign loan officers on the basis of the size and the importance of an account. A small business may automatically be assigned a junior staff member rather than an officer of the bank — officer usually means a rank of at least assistant vice-president. Determine who will be assigned and if you have a say in that assignment. You want to do your banking with an officer of the highest possible rank.

What to Look Out For

In the process of weighing these various factors, you need to guard against a particular bank's overemphasis on low-interest rates or being lured by a bank that seems to be offering nothing but low rates. The seeming advantage of lower interest cost is sometimes fleeting at best. First, conditions for banks change, and when this happens, changes in interest rates are usually quick to follow. Even more important is the fact that the seeming advantage of small rate differentials can easily be outweighed by qualitative considerations, such as bank loyalty or its first-rate service.

Beginning the Relationship

When your business has a financial crisis and you have to literally introduce yourself to a banker, the chances of obtaining financial assistance are minimal at best. Bankers are basically conservative lenders with an overriding concern for minimizing risk. They feel that this is best accomplished by limiting loans to businesses they know and trust.

A common mistake among managers of small firms is to wait until a pressing need arises before approaching a bank. This is usually the worst possible time for doing so. A firm's financial statements will reflect the crisis and give the impression its managers are unable to plan. Failing to plan is, in the mind of most bankers, a sure sign of inept management. It substantiates the small business stereotype of technical incompetence and administrative weakness.

In short, a strong bank affiliation that produces a continuing supply of credit for a small business is based on mutual understanding and trust. Since it takes time for these bonds to develop, building a favorable climate for a loan request should begin long before the funds are actually needed. You should devote time and effort to building a background of information and goodwill with your bank of choice, not to mention getting to know the loan officer you will be dealing with.

Your new banking relationship should most logically start with your firm's deposit. Deposits are the raw material of the banking business, and the size and/or stability of a checking account can be a major influence on a firm's ability to obtain credit.

The next task is to prove to the bank that you are capable of guiding your business through difficult times and have the integrity to live up to the letter and spirit of your repayment responsibilities. This degree of trust is not built overnight. It takes time, effort, and information.

Your bank will want to learn about and evaluate your business; therefore, you should provide the appropriate information regularly and voluntarily. Include a brief narrative on your firm's history and its officers; copies of its traditional financial statements, plus a cash-flow report; and your written review of the results and progress of the firm during that particular period. Give the bank a list of your firm's major suppliers and key customers along with the offer to contact them for references. As a vital part of this orientation process, you can invite your loan officer to visit your business and become familiar with the operation and its key people.

One word of caution about providing information to the bank: Make certain that the information is timely, provided voluntarily, and is complete. Don't conceal facts or omit pertinent financial data. Loan officers are inherently suspicious people, and incomplete information is a signal that the customer is hiding something. This is absolutely the worst possible signal you could send.

Maintaining the Relationship

A good banking relationship, like a good marriage, requires hard work. If well-maintained, a good banking relationship should grow stronger over the years and become your most valuable intangible asset. To reach this plateau, you need to demonstrate two virtues: honesty and responsibility.

The most effective method for demonstrating candor and honesty is to openly discuss, without prodding, your business' plans, results, fortunes, and misfortunes on a regular basis. This means literally briefing the loan officer on what went right, what went wrong, and what steps were taken to prevent future occurrences of what went wrong. However distasteful this may seem, it is often the single most important activity that can be done to develop rapport with a banker.

The result of keeping the banker informed avoids having adverse developments come as a surprise. The bank has an important financial stake in your business and, consequently, the right to the prompt notice of major developments. If storm clouds are developing, do not hide the problem until it becomes unmanageable. Candid admission of problems, and an open discussion of what you and the bank can do to solve them will go a long way toward building the banker's trust and confidence.

An experienced banker knows full well that every firm encounters occasional difficulties. The question in the banker's mind is how will you handle these problems. Evidence of a thorough approach to identifying and planning solutions to problems cannot help but impress a banker.

Another responsible attitude toward debt is accomplished by taking loans, repaying them on schedule, and meeting all facets of the agreement in both letter and spirit. By doing so, you gain the banker's trust and loyalty, and he or she will consider your business a valued customer, favor it with privileges, and make it easier for you to obtain needed future financing.

How a Loan Request Is Analyzed by a Banker

Fortunately, loan negotiations between a small business and its bank are not a confrontation ultimately decided by a winner and a loser. Lending is the essence of the banking business, and making mutually beneficial loans is as important to the success of the bank as it is to the small business. This does not mean, however, that you should avoid negotiating the best possible terms for a loan. Indeed, it is in your firm's best interest to do so. Rather, it means that understanding what information a loan officer seeks, and providing the evidence required to ease normal banking concerns, is the most effective prescription for getting what is needed.

Since the loan evaluation process is part science and part art, it is impossible to determine in advance the exact criteria used by a particular loan officer to evaluate a loan request. A sound proposal should, however, contain information that expands on the following points:

- What is the specific purpose(s) of the loan?
- Exactly how much is required?
- What is the exact source of repayment for the loan?
- What evidence is available to substantiate the assumptions that the expected source of repayment is reliable?
- What alternative source of repayment is available if management's plans fail?
- What business or personal assets, or both, are available to collateralize the loan?
- What evidence is available to substantiate the competence and ability of a business' management?

Even a cursory examination of these points suggests the need for you to do your homework before making a loan request. It is a virtual certainty that an experienced loan officer will ask probing questions about each of them. Failure to anticipate these inquiries or to provide acceptable answers is damaging evidence that you may not completely understand the business or are incapable of planning for your firm's needs.

To present you and your business in the best possible light, the loan request should be based on and accompanied by a complete business plan. This document is the single most important planning activity that you can perform. As will be discussed in the next chapter, a business plan is more than a device for getting financing; it is the vehicle that makes you examine, evaluate, and plan for all aspects of your business. A business plan's existence proves to your banker that you are doing all the right activities.

Chapter 8

Preparing and Presenting a Business Plan and Financing Proposal

With the necessary background on the the fundamentals of debt financing, sources of this financing, and the mind set of a typical banker, you can now investigate the topic of preparing and presenting a business plan and financing proposal. Unfortunately, this is an area plagued with myths, and these misunderstandings are often the root cause of an entrepreneur's inability to secure needed funds.

One of the more common fallacies shared by small business owners is the mistaken notion that their business speaks for itself, and a formal, written presentation is not needed to secure financing. An experienced financier knows better than most that nothing in life is as it appears on the surface, particularly a business firm. Rarely, if ever, will financing be provided before a careful appraisal is made of a firm's financial condition, the quality of its management, and its risk as a financing candidate. This appraisal requires factual data. What's more, a financier expects a small business manager to have the understanding needed to prepare this information, and failure to do so raises questions about management ability.

Another common misconception is that loans are obtained through personal contacts, friendly relations, or an effective sales pitch. Such extras will certainly help if the important criteria has been met, but seldom, is an experienced financier talked out of money. What any supplier of funds really wants to talk about are facts, and it is facts about the business, its future, and the quality of its management that will ultimately determine a firm's ability to obtain financing. These facts should be presented to the financier in a carefully prepared financing proposal. This proposal is an essential component of the firm's overall business plan.

The Foundation of a Good Financing Proposal

All too often small business people are denied financing — even when they deserve it — because of an ineffective or poorly prepared presentation. They simply do not know how to relate their firm's needs to the financier; are unaware of what questions he or she will ask; and are unable to provide satisfactory answers to these queries. In short, they do not realize that obtaining money is like any other business transaction.

As with any business arrangement, both parties must have a reasonable expectation that their objectives will be achieved. To do so, you provide evidence that the need is legitimate, and the repayment schedule and other terms of the arrangement will be honored. The financier, on the other hand, must have confidence in your ability to do what has been promised. In order for both parties to make the necessary judgments to complete the transaction requires facts, figures, and a well-conceived plan for the future. In order to get an idea of the type of information needed to prepare a sound financing proposal, examine the information a typical bank loan officer would require when considering a loan.

What a Typical Loan Officer Wants to Know

Unfortunately, there is no exact formula for deciding which information requirements and criteria will be used by a loan officer to determine an acceptable loan. A part of the lending process involves personal judgment, and acceptance standards will vary slightly from one financial institution to the next. For any small business borrower, however, two virtually universal truths will govern the decision of the lending institution:

- Sound business and financial criteria will be used to judge the merits of the loan request.
- Certain essential questions about a firm and its management must be answered satisfactorily.

How Much Money Is Needed?

Your loan request should be supported by evidence of sound business and financial planning. Plans are the tools through which you identify and justify what is needed and how and when the needed financing will be repaid. Information on these key considerations is what a loan officer uses to evaluate the validity of a request.

Well-thought out plans also enhance the likelihood you are seeking an appropriate amount of financing. Borrowing and lending the right amount of funds benefits both the debtor and creditor. If too little financing is requested and granted, planned operations will suffer from insufficient capital. If too much is loaned, the financial burden may be too great to repay.

A well-conceived, carefully documented plan indicates you:

- Understand the factors that determine your firm's success;
- Have carefully considered where your firm is going and what resources are needed to get it there;

- Take positive actions to meet established goals rather than simply reacting to events as they occur; and
- Anticipate problems and their solutions before a crisis occurs.

In short, evidence of sound planning is the single best indicator of competent management.

How Will the Financing Be Used?

In general, a loan's purpose is for both parties to make money and to help satisfy the lender that you have carefully thought through the need for financing, a detailed explanation of how you will use and apply the loan proceeds is required. For example, if plans call for an increase in fixed assets, each particular asset should be identified and accompanied by such details as cost, manufacturer, intended use, and estimated life. Or, if additional working capital is required to support a seasonal increase in operations, the amounts used to purchase inventory and to support increased credit sales should be fully explained.

How Will the Loan Be Repaid?

In general, the cash flow from operations (CFFO) financed by the loan is the basis for repayment; however, an experienced loan officer looks for a clear, well-supported discussion of how and when this cash flow will be available. The most convincing method for providing this information is a well-prepared cash budget. See Chapter 4.

How Will the Loan Be Protected if Plans Go Awry?

How will you repay the bank if something goes wrong? There are two satisfactory answers to this question: 1) evidence that a contingency plan is in place; and 2) evidence of available collateral to secure the loan.

The Final Analysis

In the final analysis, the decision on whether financing will be made available to your small business rests primarily on the financier's confidence in your management ability. The existence of formal plans bolsters this confidence.

Since the foundation for a good financing proposal is sound planning, it follows that a business plan and financing proposal should precede the financing request.

The Business Plan and Financing Proposal

A business plan is a written, formalized expression of what and who the business is, its objectives, and the strategies and programs needed to achieve them. Simply stated, the business plan is both an actual and planned blueprint for your firm. It identifies where your firm currently is, where you expect to take it, and the physical and financial resources required to do so. As the basis for the financing request, this document serves two important uses:

- **Promotes understanding.** A business plan and financing proposal provide the information necessary for a prospective financier to understand and evaluate the nature and operations of your business as well as identify the key ingredients to its success. These latter items are those few crucial variables upon which your firm's sales, cash flows, and profits depend.

- **Sends the right message.** Careful analysis and planning are the heart of the administrative process; it is what managers are supposed to do. By indicating a complete knowledge of all aspects of the business as well as the ability to direct its future with sound realistic plans, you make a strong statement about your management capability.

Whether the complete business plan and the financing proposal are included as separate documents in the presentation package, or the relevant parts of the business plan are summarized as part of the financing proposal depends on the stage of your firm's life cycle, the type of financing required, and the strength of the relationship with the target financier. In general, the closer your firm is to the embryo or development stage or the less familiar the financier is with your firm, the greater the need for a separate business plan and financing proposal. If the proposal is written for a mature firm and presented to an established financing source, the business plan can often be omitted. In this latter case, the essential components of the plan would then be included in the financing proposal.

Components of a Good Business Plan

The purpose of a formal business plan and financing proposal is to provide the prospective financier with the information needed to make a decision on whether a firm and its management represent a credit worthy financing candidate. To do so effectively, the business plan must contain certain essential facts based on sound research and analysis. Included are facts about the nature of the business; the quality of its management; the nature of its industry, products and markets; its competitive position; and its needs. Each of these basic components of the plan is discussed in turn.

Business Description and History

A description of the business and its history identifies who the business is and how it came into existence. These two elements — description and history — make up the first part of your business plan.

You should write your business description as if the financier knows nothing about your business, its markets, or method of operations. Write in a simple, narrative style and be sure to include your company name and its location(s); the form of organization under which you conduct business (proprietorship, partnership, or corporation); your principal business; the industry and principal markets in which you operate; and your name and position and those of any other key management personnel.

The second part of this section should be a succinct, approximately one-page discussion of your business' history. Your focus in this historical overview should be:

- The date and place of origin of your business and the name(s) of its original founders;
- The original purpose of your business: its industry, products, and principal markets; and
- A concise description of the major milestones in the firm's history. Milestones are events, such as organizational changes, or changes in the nature of the business, its products, key personnel, or markets. Any critical turning points in your firm's history should be described and accompanied by an explanation of how your firm was able to adapt to these changes and grow from the experience. For example, if a major change had occurred in your firm's market as the result of new competition or new products, emphasize the measures taken by your management to counteract this adversity. Or, if the firm's existence was threatened during a recession, explain how certain tactics enabled your firm to weather the storm.

Ideally, this section will serve as a subtle portrayal of your firm as a solid, stable business run by capable, effective management.

If your business is in an embryo stage, there obviously would be no business history. In this case, the writing should be slanted toward your intended future. For example, your narrative would address questions, such as:

- How will your business be organized?
- Where will it be located?
- Who are its principals?
- What type of business will be conducted?
- What are its planned major milestones, and when are they expected to occur?

Financial History

The financial history section of your business plan should contain three to five years of historical financial statements, a summary analysis of the firm's performance over this period, and any supporting financial documents, such as cash budgets or pro forma statements, prepared for past planning periods. The analysis of this data should include key financial ratio values; trend-values of the firm's key financial variables, such as sales, cash flow, and profits; and a narrative describing the major factors (economic, competitive, management, etc.) that have influenced or caused these trends. By documenting the numbers with explanations, you display a knowledge of the factors critical to your firm's success.

It would be to your advantage to also include related information that is not contained in financial statements in this section. In most cases, you will be required to provide the items listed on the next page.

- A detailed description of the major fixed assets, whether leased or owned, used by your firm; the description should include an asset's age, condition, remaining balance if the asset is financed or leased, and an estimate of its current market value;
- A schedule of inventory used and currently owned by the firm; the schedule should detail, by category, the description, age, value, and turnover history of these items;
- A list of major customers and a current aging schedule of the accounts receivable for these customers;
- A list of major suppliers and a current aging schedule of accounts payable for these suppliers;
- The names and addresses of creditors, the type of financing provided, and the existing amount of debt owed to each; and
- A description of any lease agreements, and any major lease-hold improvements made to leased property or equipment.

Ideally, the historical financial statements included in this section should be prepared by your accountant and accompanied by his or her other cover letter stating the validity of the financial data. If your business uses its own computerized accounting system, the type of system used should be identified and explained.

If creative accounting procedures have been employed in preparing financial statements, the financier needs to know. Often, conservative procedures, such as inventory valuation or depreciation method, are used to soften the tax bite. While ideal for tax purposes, these procedures may understate reported profit or the value of the assets contained on the balance sheet. If clearly explained, this is not a problem. On the contrary, financiers are well aware of the need to take any opportunity to legally avoid taxes and would no doubt applaud your foresight.

Again, if your business is in an embryo stage, the financial history section would not be used.

Products or Services

The products or services section should provide the financier with a clear, informative description of what your firm produces, sells, or the specific services it offers. If your firm is a manufacturing business, a description of the production process is needed. This description explains how products are produced, the labor skills required, the raw materials used, and the sourcing of these raw materials. An important part of this section is a discussion of the prices at which the products or services are offered, how these prices are determined, and the gross profit margin and/or contribution margin on each. Be careful to identify the key factors that affect pricing.

Industry and Markets

The industry and markets section meets two important objectives by describing the market arena in which your business operates and presenting your forecast for the future. The former objective can be met by providing a thumbnail sketch of your firm's industry and the specific geographical areas that constitute its markets. To the extent possible, your discussion should include an estimate of the dollar volume of industry sales; the dollar volume of sales in the firm's particular market(s); the rate at which sales have grown; the key factors that influence demand for the industry's products or service; and an estimate of the firm's share of this market. When possible, this data should be supported with hard evidence.

In the remaining discussion, include your projection for your future products and markets. Again, these projections should be substantiated with factual information obtained from acceptable sources, such as:

- State and local industrial authorities;
- State or local chambers of commerce;
- Business, industry, or trade-association periodicals;
- Research bureaus of college or university schools of business; and
- Any variety of business and economic forecasting agencies.

In cases where the cost can be justified, a professional market research firm can be hired to provide market analysis or business feasibility studies.

All too often entrepreneurs — especially those associated with new or infant firms — do not have a clear understanding of their market and competition. This is a failing that, when identified by the target financier, often prompts a rejection of the proposal. For example, when requesting help with a loan proposal for financing a new restaurant operation, a prospective business owner may be asked why he wishes to do go into this business, and the answer most often may be "I have always liked to cook." A fascination with culinary delights may be the reason for an enjoyable hobby; it is not the reason for going into the restaurant business. A successful restaurant is one that can fill an identified market niche and can profitably capitalize on some aspect of product, service, or price differentiation.

The answer a prospective financier wants to hear in response to this type of question is something along these lines:

"My research efforts, which are substantiated with the following data, have convinced me there is an unfulfilled need for this business. The market and profit potential is more than sufficient to provide a fair rate of return on all invested capital."

Remember, the purpose of any financing is to make money for both parties. A hard-nosed financier is not going to put funds at risk on the basis of wishful thinking. He or she has long since met the quota for these type of ventures.

Competition

The competition section describes your firm's direct competition and the products or services with which it must compete. This discussion should include an estimate of the dollar sales volume the competing products or firms are generating or the percentage share of the market they hold, or both. If your product or service is unique or holds a specific advantage over competition, such as quality, price, service, or location, you should describe and explain it. Likewise, if there is no immediate competition, explain the reasons why this is the case.

As indicated above, many small business people lack a clear understanding of their firm's competition and market. Without this understanding, it is impossible to have a firm grasp of the key factors that determine the success or failure of a business. When this void exists, the financier's rejection of the proposal usually follows.

Marketing

Detail your firm's marketing and promotion efforts in the next section of your business plan. This includes a description of your target customer or customer group; the channel(s) of distribution used to reach this target; and actual or planned promotion and advertising vehicles. Where possible, demonstrate how the effectiveness of the dollars spent for advertising and promotion is measured.

Employees

Your business plan should also include an overview of your work force: its size, skill level, employee turnover rate, and an assessment of the available pool of potential employees in the area. If critical skill employees are required, a plan indicating how they are found and trained should be provided.

Major Suppliers or Subcontractors

If your firm's products or services rely on unique or specialized sourcing or the services of a critical subcontractor, include this information in the plan. Any financier will be concerned about the contingency plans you have made in the event product sourcing or subcontractor relations are disturbed. If such conditions do not apply, a simple listing of major suppliers or vendors is sufficient.

Property, Facilities, and Equipment

Since your firm's assets are a source of potential collateral that may be required to support financing, identify your firm's real property, facilities, and equipment. If fixed assets are leased, a description of the asset and the conditions of the lease should be provided. With regards to real property, list essential information, such as:

- The location; square footage, adequacy of the property and facilities;
- The financing involved and unpaid balances;
- The names and addresses of creditors; and
- A reasonable estimate of current market or liquidation value.

With regards to equipment and other fixed assets, discuss these items:

- The age and quality of the asset;
- The estimated remaining useful life;

- The estimated resale or liquidation value; and
- The description of any special purpose equipment that may be difficult to obtain or subsequently sell.

Your business needs to also describe any intangible assets that create value. For example, your firm may have a patent on its product, a desirable location, or a highly talented research staff that distinguishes your firm from its competition or provides a unique profit advantage.

Unique Features or Intangible Assets

Another section of your plan should describe your firm's top management, directors if any, and key personnel. Any financier will view this group as the lifeblood of the organization. In the final analysis, creditor's and owner's funds are entrusted to the firm's management, and it is management that has the ultimate responsibility to generate a compensatory return on those funds. Financiers are aware of the validity of the old business adage: "Even a poorly managed firm can make money when times are good, but it is good management that keeps the firm afloat when times are bad."

Management and Key Personnel

To present the education, training, experience in the field, and overall administrative experience of the individuals deemed vital to your firm, organize the information in resumé form. These resumés should describe each individual's duties and responsibilities and where relevant, the special talents or skills he or she brings to the firm.

The heart of your business plan is the section on your intended future for the business. This material should describe your short- and long-range objectives and the particular strategies and programs of action necessary to implement and achieve them. Clearly document all forecasts and plans with supporting evidence. Without plausible supporting evidence, financiers view forecasts and plans as nothing more than wishful thinking. Here are some examples of what to use as supporting evidence:

Management's Intended Future for the Business

- A discussion of your firm's most recent growth trend in sales, assets, cash flows, and profits, including an explanation of the reasons for the existence of these trends and why they can be expected to continue;
- Research efforts that support market potential or growth estimates; for example, the documentation may cite recent studies by reputable sources such as a relevant state agency, the local industrial or planning authority, a noted economic forecasting agency, a relevant trade journal, or business and economic periodicals. This data would take such forms as GNP estimates, percentage sales-growth rates, market potential in dollar volume, or changing consumer demographics;
- The results of a marketing research effort conducted by a professional research firm;
- The results of your analysis of your industry and market;
- Recent sales orders or contracts for products or services; and

- Written statements from prospective customers regarding intended purchases.

In short, this section on your firm's intended future ought to convey the picture of a management that has identified the steps required to provide a solid foundation for the firm's future.

Cash Flow and Financial Projections

From a financier's perspective, the section on cash flow and financial projections is as critical to the business plan as the plan itself. No business plan, regardless of its merit, is practical unless it is financially feasible. Your analysis and discussion in this section of your business plan should clearly validate:

- The financial feasibility of your plans;
- The amount of needed financing;
- Your firm's ability of the firm to meet the obligations associated with the proposed financing; and
- Your firm's ability to produce a compensatory return on the investment of the proposed financing.

Focus your narrative on a tabular presentation of the key values from the projected statements used to make the cash flow estimates. For example, such period-by-period values as sales, net cash flow, required financing, profit margins, and selected ratio values can be displayed in a summary table.

As with other forecast and planning data, your financial projections should be accompanied by an explanation of the underlying assumptions and documented with supporting evidence. For example, sales estimates can be substantiated with the firm's most recent growth trend; primary or secondary market research data indicating industry or market growth potential, customer orders; or statements of intention to buy. Or, estimates of balance sheet asset values can be validated by combining historical percentage-of-sales relationships with projected sales.

For new businesses, income statement and balance sheet values can be estimated and supported using percent-of-sales relationships based on ratio data for the average firm in the same industry. There are several sources that publish ratio data by industry category and firm size. The two most prominent among these are *Annual Statement Studies* published by Robert Morris and Associates and *The Almanac of Business and Industrial Financial Ratios* published by Prentice-Hall. One or both sources are usually available in college and university libraries or public libraries with a large business literature collection.

An experienced financier is well aware that financial projections can range from the realistic to pure fantasy. Since there is no method for determining which is the case until after the fact, your forecast's validity will be measured by the quality of the data presented and your subsequent assumptions. If projections cannot be substantiated, the financier will see them as fabrications or as the result of incompetence.

The pro forma documents used to produce financial projections should be included in this section. These documents would normally consist of a month-by-month cash-flow forecast for the next year, and annual pro forma financial statements for the time period of the proposed financing. The firm's financing needs, repayment expectations, and overall financial performance should be clearly indicated in the projections and summarized in the accompanying narrative. The cash budget and pro forma statement formats discussed in Chapter 4 are ideal for these purposes.

A Final Word on the Business Plan

Preparation of a business plan requires time and effort, and these are usually scarce commodities for the typical small firm manager. Yet, the effort will produce bottom-line returns for the firm. For help with your business plan, see *The Successful Business Plan: Secrets & Strategies*. It gives worksheets for your financials, plus tips from bankers and venture capitalists. The book is available through The Oasis Press, (800) 228-2275.

Planning is what you should and are expected to do regardless of whether or not a financing proposal is being prepared. Sound planning is the only tool available to you for influencing your firm's uncertain future. If you do not establish the plans and strategies that will direct your business and make advance preparation for likely contingencies, the business is rendered victim to random circumstances that will usually be beyond your control.

The Financing Proposal

The financing proposal is simply a selective summary of the business plan. The amount of detail included in this proposal and the decision whether to include it as a separate document accompanying the business plan depends on the type of financing sought and the strength of the relationship between your business and the financier. If there is an established association between the two, as is often true of a small business and its commercial bank, the presentation package may be limited to an embellished loan proposal. In this case, the essential elements of the business plan would be summarized in the loan proposal. At the other extreme, a proposal to an unfamiliar lender or one designed to raise venture capital would require both a complete business plan and a financing proposal. There is no formula for deciding the issue. It is a matter of judgment, and the key to making this judgment is knowing the target financier.

Since debt is the most often used type of external financing by small businesses, the financing request usually takes the form of a loan proposal. To avoid needless repetition of business plan material, the following discussion of a loan proposal assumes an ongoing bank/business relationship. In this situation, the bank would be familiar with the descriptive material normally contained in the business plan, and the loan package would be limited to the proposal, the required financial and legal exhibits, and a cover letter. Appropriate information from the business plan would be summarized in the body of the loan application.

Keep in mind that even though a complete business plan is not included in the example, preparation of the loan proposal assumes its existence. Without a supporting plan, the financing request is without merit.

Essential Components of the Loan Proposal

When the bank is familiar with your business, many of the descriptive sections of the business plan should be excluded from the loan proposal unless there has been a fundamental change in the business or its operation. For example, discussions of the business, its history, explanations of its operations, and its management are not necessary. There is, however, certain essential information that should be contained in the proposal regardless of whether the business plan is included. These essentials are discussed below. The exact format for presenting this information and the amount of detail included are, however, a matter of personal preference and perceived need.

The Cover Letter

A cover letter, or letter of transmittal, is simply the formal introduction for the loan proposal and serves as a concise summary of the nature and purpose of the proposal. An example of a typical cover letter is shown on page 163.

This particular letter should:

- Be succinct. The loan officer is no doubt busy and not interested in reading needless dialogue.
- Remind the loan officer of what has been tentatively decided to this point. Loan officers are not only busy but human; they do forget details.
- Summarize the key elements of the supporting loan proposal. It literally tells the loan officer what is forthcoming.
- Be positive, but not presumptuous.

Recent Financial History

At a minimum, the financial history should cover the period from the last time the bank reviewed your firm's financial data to the date of the current loan application. If the trend of a data series, which is important to the loan request extends beyond this time frame, it should be included as well.

A table of key financial values by period, and a narrative summarizing the performance of each should be included in this section. In addition to the essential variables such as sales, cash flow, and profits, those specific financial values known to be important to the loan officer should be included. For example, if the loan request is made for a retail firm, the loan officer will be interested in particulars on inventory level, age, and turnover rate. Knowing the lender's concerns and addressing them before being asked enhances both the loan proposal and your status.

Example Cover Letter for a Financing Proposal

Current Date

Ms. Kindred Spirit, Loan Officer

The Friendly Bank

Valdosta, GA

Dear Ms. Spirit:

As agreed in our recent conversation, I am presenting on behalf of my firm, The Ideal Leverage Company, a formal loan proposal for your consideration. As discussed in the body of this document, the loan request is in the amount of $XXX,XXX. The following repayment schedule of this amount is proposed.

[Insert Proposed Repayment Schedule]

The proceeds of the loan will be used for the following application(s).

[Insert Intended Application(s)]

In support of this request, the following documents and exhibits are enclosed:

[Insert a List of Enclosures]

It is my understanding that a variable interest rate equivalent to X percentage points above the prime rate would apply to the approved loan.

Thank you for your consideration. I eagerly await your reply.

Sincerely,

Joe Entrepreneur, President

The Ideal Leverage Company

Valdosta, GA

The Loan Request and Justification

A financing proposal needs a section on the loan request and should indicate why the request is justified. Begin this section with a statement of the precise amount of financing requested, and a clear, detailed description of how the proceeds will be used. It is not advisable to use a range of figures for the amount requested. Doing so suggests that you may be uncertain about what is actually needed. This may lead a loan officer to the conclusion that the loan request is based on inadequate analysis and planning.

For the same reason, avoid generalities when describing how the loan proceeds will be used. Rather, state specific amounts for specific applications. For example, instead of indicating the loan will be used to support working capital, identify the amount of each component of working capital (inventory, accounts receivable, payroll, etc.) to be financed. In the case of expenditures for fixed assets, provide a detailed description of the asset, its cost, the vendor, and any legal documentation required to support the acquisition.

To justify the loan request, attach an appropriate summary of your planned activities that is detailed in your business plan. Again, the amount of the business plan to be summarized is dictated by by the circumstances. In general, the more tenuous the loan request, the greater the need for documented planning detail to support it.

Cash Flow and Financial Projections

The cash flow and financial projections in your financing proposal must convince the loan officer the business plan is financially sound, the loan request is valid, and operations will produce the cash flows necessary to repay the loan. Your narrative summarizing the financial projections should be accompanied by a tabular presentation of the key values from the projected statements. For example, the period-by-period net cash flow, required financing, and excess cash figures from the cash budget should be shown along with selected balance sheet and income statement items. It is often helpful to calculate and include on the summary table key ratio values such as liquidity and profitability measures for the pro forma statement data. These data will highlight the firm's expected financial performance for the intended loan period.

A useful document to incorporate in this section of the proposal is a cash flow projection of the anticipated loan-repayment schedule. Detailing the expected timing of a repayment plan provides the loan officer with strong evidence that management understands the bank's overriding concern about ability to service the loan.

Personal Financial Statements

More often than not, a lender will require a personal guarantee from a firm's owner(s) for a small business loan. This personal endorsement of a loan gives the lender an additional measure of security: the personal assets of the endorser.

The information for the personal financial section of the proposal should include personal balance sheets and tax returns for the past one to three years. Attach these documents to the loan proposal as separate exhibits with reference to their existence made in the proposal. They should be accompanied by a written summary of the key information contained on each statement. For example, such items as income level, total payments on debt obligations, and personal net worth can be summarized in tabular form accompanied by a brief description.

Intangible Factors in the Search for Financing

Assuming the important criteria is met, paying attention to the smaller details discussed below may help you receive your requested financing. This is especially true if your request is viewed as 50/50 by the financier.

Be Professional

To make a good impression, your package should be typed and well-written. Typing errors, misspellings, incorrect grammar, or sloppiness of any kind is usually interpreted as a reflection of the way the business is run. Make another good impression in your personal appearance. Dress professionally and be on time for appointments with the loan officer.

Be Honest

While your proposal should present the business in its best possible light, don't bend the truth or misrepresent facts or events in the attempt to do so. Lies will almost certainly be discovered, and the discovery will spell immediate rejection. If misrepresentations are not discovered until after the financing is granted, the financier has the grounds for legal action. Any financial arrangement is built on some degree of faith, and no financier wants to do business with someone that cannot be trusted.

Portray Confidence

You are placed at a distinct disadvantage if an impression of uncertainty, insecurity, or desperation is conveyed to the financier. Remember, a financing arrangement is a business deal and both parties must have confidence that the other will perform as promised. If a sound proposal reflecting analysis, planning, and management competence, has been prepared, there is every reason for you to convey confidence to the financier. If this background effort has not been made, there should be no financing proposal in the first place.

Know Your Target

As with any human endeavor, financing arrangements cannot be reduced to an exact science. The type of proposal written, the amount and type of detail included, and the exact manner in which it is presented is a result of the circumstances and personalities involved. The safest approach is to investigate the prospective financier and follow a time-honored rule for authors: Know your audience and write for them. There is, however, one constant in this process. Factual data presented in a positive, professional manner will go a long way toward convincing the financier that your firm is worthy of consideration.

Do the Necessary Groundwork

A major theme of this chapter has been the need to provide the financier with sufficient information to understand the business and to convince him or her that it is run by capable management. As suggested in Chapter 7, this is best accomplished if the target financier knows the firm and its management beforehand.

Maintain the Relationship

Given the limited number of external financing sources available to small firms, it is imperative that you work hard to maintain the banking relationship once financing has been obtained. First and foremost, meet the spirit and letter of the loan agreement. Second, communicate with the financier. If problems develop, discuss them openly so that a mutually acceptable solution can be developed. The worst thing you can do when a problem develops is to hide from the financier or to violate the terms of the loan without explanation. Above all, be honest in your relationship. This quality is as important after the financing has been received as when it was sought.

Financing for the Rapidly Growing Firm

Chapter 9:
Venture Capital Financing

Chapter 10:
Financing Through a Public Offering

Chapter 9

Venture Capital Financing

Even for those fortunate businesses poised on the brink of the rapid growth stage of their life cycle, one stubborn fact of small business life remains unchanged: Adequate financing is difficult to obtain. Since the financial needs of growth firms are incompatible with the policies or interests of traditional institutional lenders, you are forced to look outside these sources for any needed capital. Unfortunately, few such opportunities exist beyond a public stock offering. Unless your business is qualified for this large undertaking, venture capital financing is virtually the only available alternative source of either equity capital or long-term debt financing.

Venture capital is the financing made available for investment in promising firms but with a risk exposure greater than what is acceptable to the traditional institutional lender. Financing for these situations is often supplied by sophisticated investors seeking investments that hold the prospects for significant capital gains.

Such investors are referred to as venture capitalists, and they fall into two basic groups: 1) privately owned firms licensed and regulated by the U.S. Small Business Administration; and 2) nonregulated firms. The former group is known as Small Business Investment Companies (SBICs). SBICs provide financing in the form of equity capital, debt financing with an equity sweetener, and in some cases, straight long-term loans. The nonregulated firms, which specialize in equity financing, are commonly referred to as Venture Capital Companies (VCCs).

The Venture Capital Company

Because VCCs have differing philosophies and a wide range of investment interests, it is difficult to generalize an acceptable definition. VCCs do, however, share a common trait: they are professional investors, who for the most part, are attracted to those high-risk opportunities offering potentially large returns. To obtain returns sufficient to compensate both for the inevitable losses associated with high-risk investment, and for the extended time period that the financing is committed, a VCC must share in the earnings success of a highly promising firm through an equity interest. Investments that meet this rigid requirement are rare. Available evidence indicates that only between one and five percent of the proposals presented to VCCs are found to be acceptable candidates for financing.

For those firms with the good fortune to attract VCC interest, the financing will often have these type of characteristics:

- The financing will be the first equity financing for a firm outside that of the original owners. While the VCC financing will cost a firm a substantial share of its common stock, the amount will usually be less than 50% of a firm's ownership.

- The financing often represents intermediate or gap financing that fills a firm's needs until the intended public offering of common stock takes place.

- The financing provides management assistance to the target firm in those areas of identified administrative weakness. Through this assistance and its share of a firm's ownership, the VCC will have an active voice in the firm's policy- and decision-making processes. Although the VCC's relationship to a firm is technically that of investor, the VCC is in reality a working partner.

- The financing expects to earn large returns. Depending on the financing stage at which funds are provided, the typical VCC limits investments to opportunities that provide expected returns from 25% to better than 50% per annum on invested funds.

- The financing expects a lengthy investment period. Successful venture capital investments often take five to seven years to come to fruition.

- The financing has an agreement specifying a clearly defined opportunity for the VCC to exit the target firm. Contrary to the common misconception that the VCC wishes to takeover the target company, the goal is to liquidate the investment. VCCs finance businesses with the expectation of a return that compensates for the risk involved, they do not wish to own them. The liquidation can take place through an agreement to repurchase the VCC shares at a specified date, to go public with a common stock offering, or to seek a suitable merger partner interested in buying the target firm.

In theory, a VCC may become involved at any of the four major financing stages of your firm's life cycle. In practice, however, some stages are more appealing than others.

When Will a VCC Become Involved?

A start-up firm is in the embryo stage of its life cycle and involved with fundamental activities, such as developing the prototype product or service, structuring the organization, and creating channels of distribution. Financing at this stage, which is referred to as seed capital, involves the highest degree of risk exposure for both you and the VCC. To compensate for this level of risk, a typical VCC would have to be convinced of an opportunity for returns of 50% per annum or better. While most VCCs claim to give investment consideration to start ups, evidence indicates that less than 10% of total VCC financing goes to these types of firms.

The Embryo Stage

A formative stage business is established, operating, and has evidenced the potential for significant growth, but it is not yet profitable. While slightly less perilous than the start-up case, formative-stage financing also entails significant risk exposure. To compensate for this level of risk, an acceptable project must promise returns of between 40% and 50% per annum for the VCC. In practice, the VCC rejection rate for first-stage proposals is only slightly lower than start-up proposals.

The Formative Stage

The third growth stage is for businesses which have reached the growth phase of their life cycle. There is demonstrated market acceptance for a firm's product or service, an acceptable level of profit, and the prospect for continued rapid growth. A typical rapid growth firm is no longer capable of financing its needs with internally generated funds and has used its available debt capacity. It must look to risk capital to support continued growth. To attract such capital, the VCC would expect returns of between 30% and 40% per annum.

The Rapid Growth Stage

In the maturity stage, a business is at the threshold of going public. VCC financing is used to bridge the gap between current needs and the funds made available through the stock offering. While maturity-stage opportunities entail the least amount of investment risk for the VCC, returns of approximately 25% per annum are still expected.

The Maturity Stage

Because of a VCC's need to focus on high-return opportunities, some investments are often eliminated from consideration at the outset. These fall into two broad categories: firms with limited market potential and firms requiring a large, initial investment in fixed assets. Since a VCC is seeking significant returns, firms operating in single markets, such as the typical retail, wholesale, or service business, are not appealing. While the returns from these businesses may be adequate for the entrepreneur, there is either too much competition or too little potential volume to generate the returns required by a VCC. Also, start-up or young firms requiring

Investment Opportunities for the VCC

large investments in fixed assets do not make attractive venture capital investments. A heavy investment in specialized assets compounds the risk exposure of an already risky investment.

Which investment characteristics are attractive to the typical VCC? In general, the closer the proposed venture is to having the attributes listed below, the more attractive its prospects:

- **Large potential.** A VCC must be convinced that a firm has the opportunity and is capable of exploiting a clearly defined market niche, or has an unequivocal advantage over competitors. A firm, therefore, needs to have a product or service with large-scale marketability and profit potential. In general, attractive products or services fall into the following categories:

  - Innovative, which represent new or revolutionary ideas, such as the Walkman® or diet soda;

  - Evolutionary, which represent the next version in a series, such as anti-lock disc brakes or color television; and

  - Substitutes, which represent better or lower cost replacements, such as the temporary office-help service, or a technologically improved method of production.

- **Low cost.** A firm should have a product or service with low output or production cost. Such opportunities are usually consistent with low fixed-asset investment and low risk. For example, a commercially marketable genetic-engineering application is a more attractive venture than the opportunity to invest in the manufacture of equipment required to produce an untried product.

- **Large margins.** A firm's product or service needs to have a healthy profit margin. Slim profit margins require considerable sales volume to produce sizable returns. On the other hand, large profit margins are usually associated with enthusiastic market acceptance or the absence of significant competition.

- **Competent management.** A firm ought to have an experienced, capable, trustworthy management team.

- **Clear-cut exit.** This is an opportunity which, when successful, offers a VCC a clearly defined opportunity to withdraw from a firm and liquidate the investment.

When a VCC Makes a Decision

In general, a VCC's decision to make an investment will depend on the quality of information provided by your firm's proposal and what is gleaned from meetings with you. Certainly, the most important information source is the proposal. To be effective, your proposal must be a complete, well-documented, clearly articulated presentation of all the essential facts and figures relevant to your business and its situation. This includes information on the firm's principals, product or service, human and physical assets, markets, competition, financial condition and projections, and a defined exit opportunity for the VCC. In short, the VCC wants a comprehensive business plan. Table 9.1 is an outline for such a

Table 9.1 – Outline of a Business Plan's Key Points

I. Overview of the Business
 1. Introduction and description of the company and its history.
 2. Description of the firm's product or service.
 3. Description of the firm's industry and markets.

II. The Management
 1. Organizational structure.
 2. Duties, responsibilities, and skills of key personnel.
 3. Background resumés of key personnel.
 4. Evaluation of management strengths and weaknesses.

III. The Market and Marketing Plan
 1. Background and analysis of the firm's industry and markets.
 2. Analysis and comparison of competitive firms and products or services.
 3. Market goals such as sales growth, market penetration, or share of the market.
 4. Marketing philosophy.
 5. Sales, pricing, promotion, and advertising strategies.
 6. Evaluation of marketing strengths and weaknesses.

IV. The Production Plan (if applicable)
 1. Description of manufacturing process.
 2. Description of manufacturing facilities and needs.
 3. Development programs and requirements.
 4. Schedule of development programs by stage.
 5. Evaluation of production strengths and weaknesses.

V. The Financial History and Plan
 1. Historical financial statements.
 2. Projected financial statements.
 3. Evaluation of financial strengths, weaknesses, and risk exposure.

VI. The Investment Proposal
 1. The financing plan:
   a) amount required
   b) timing of financing required
   c) scheduled use of funds
 2. Proposed terms of the financing agreement.

VII. The Exit Opportunity
 1. Terms of the stock repurchase (if applicable).
 2. Intended public offering date.
 3. Available collateral (if applicable).

For more information on creating a business plan, plus tips from bankers, venture capitalists, and business leaders, see *The Successful Business Plan: Secrets & Strategies*, by Rhonda M. Abrams, from The Oasis Press® (800) 228-2275.

plan. The outline is an enhanced version of the document discussed in Chapter 8.

A VCC will focus on the key items discussed below during the first stage of evaluation.

Detailed Numbers

A VCC will have extensive financial expertise, and finance people are known to live by numbers. An accurate presentation of past sales and financial performance and well-documented projections for a three- to five-year future is an absolute must for your proposal. Equally as important, you must understand these numbers and be capable of explaining all the whys and wherefores behind the projections, regardless of whether they were prepared personally, by your accountant, or by a hired consultant.

Potential Returns

To provide a rate of return commensurate with the degree of risk encountered, your business has to represent a unique opportunity. To make this determination, a VCC will require an answer to one basic question: What speciality does your firm bring to the marketplace? This feature can take a number of forms, such as a patent, a proprietary process, a new product or service, or a cost-saving technological development. In each case, however, the evidence must indicate that the special feature has the potential for large-scale market acceptance.

Quality of Management

You and your management team are responsible for planning, organizing, and controlling your firm's operation, and the VCC will look for evidence of the following characteristics in you and your team:

- Experience in your business industry;
- Demonstrated business and personal achievements;
- Motivation and a high-energy level;
- Honesty and integrity; and
- Compatibility of all concerned parties.

While venture capital financing is technically an investment for the VCC, it is also a close-knit partnership. Success is dependent on a good fit between your firm's principals and those of the VCC.

An Exit

In addition to a compensatory return, a clearly defined opportunity to liquidate the investment is critical to the VCC. Without it, the investment will not be of interest. There are only three ways the VCC can recoup its investment.

- Your firm will eventually go public with a common stock issue.
- Your firm is purchased by another company (preferably one whose stock is publicly traded).
- Your firm repurchases the shares held by the VCC.

When to Seek Venture Capital Financing

Proper timing of a VCC investment proposal is important. Approaching a VCC before your business is ready to do so may weaken your chances of obtaining future consideration. Conversely, by waiting too long, the window of opportunity may be closed. At what point, then, should you consider proposing venture capital financing? While there is no precise formula for making this calculation, there is one strong indicator.

Assuming your firm meets the basic requirements of an attractive opportunity as suggested above, the proper timing of the venture capital request is dictated by the business plan. When your plan can be completed to the extent suggested in Table 9.1 and discussed in Chapter 8, you will have the necessary information to identify a clearly defined need and the profit potential. Approach a VCC at this time. The inability to provide any of the essential information on which the VCC bases an investment decision is the best indicator that your venture capital request is premature.

How to Market the Venture Capital Proposal

The typical venture capitalist is inundated with investment proposals and the rejection rate is high. If your proposal is to standout from the crowd, it first must contain the necessary ingredients; and second, the ingredients must be packaged and presented in a manner that will attract attention. The guidelines listed below will help you accomplish this task.

Be Selective

Approach only VCCs with mutual interests. Not all VCCs have the same investment goals nor are their preferences, policies, outlook, and ability to provide management services identical; therefore, find a VCC whose interests are compatible with your needs.

The search process should not take the form of a blanket mailing or telephone campaign. A shotgun approach is a waste of time and effort, and risks giving the impression that you are pitting one VCC against another. Rather, your search should be used to narrow the likely prospects to a manageable number and only these firms should be contacted. Contacting a small number of likely candidates offers these benefits:

- Several reactions to the proposal by interested VCCs provides a strong indication of its validity;
- Different VCCs may offer different financing terms; and
- Financing from more than one VCC may be necessary or advisable.

An address list of venture capital firms may be obtained from:

The National Venture Capital Association
1655 North Fort Myer Drive, Suite 700
Arlington, Virginia 22209
(703) 528-4370

Your VCC contacting should be by mail, and the package should contain the items discussed below.

Have a Good Summary

Prepare and include as an early part of your package a concise summary of your business plan. The summary should be no longer than three pages, and it should emphasize only the plan's key elements. A well-prepared, succinct summary will attract the venture capitalist's attention and provide the incentive to study the entire business plan and proposal. Realize that a typical venture capitalists may get as many as 20 to 25 investment proposals per day. They are not going take the time to read each of these, so the summary is used to weed out unattractive ventures.

Include a Cover Letter

Introduce your package with a brief cover letter. For an example of how to structure an effective cover letter, as well as a comprehensive business plan, see *The Successful Business Plan: Secrets & Strategies,* by Rhonda M. Abrams, available from The Oasis Press, (800) 228-2275.

Attach a Sound Business Plan

After the summary, the next most important piece of information contained in the proposal is your business plan. While this statement may seem unnecessarily repetitive, it cannot be over emphasized. Your business plan is pivotal to a VCC's entire evaluation and decision process, and it should be comprehensive, well-documented, and clearly articulated. In short, if the presentation is to be successful, your business plan must be impressive.

To accomplish this end, when necessary do not hesitate to seek qualified assistance with its preparation. The document itself should be well-written, free from grammatical, spelling, and typing errors, and neatly packaged. The numbers and projections must be logically consistent, well-documented with underlying assumptions and supporting evidence, and defensible. While the thought of incurring the cost of hiring professional assistance may seem excessive, it is money well spent. If the venture is truly an attractive investment opportunity, this cost is insignificant compared to the potential benefits.

Critique the Business

In the business plan, include a careful analysis and thorough discussion of the problem areas faced by your business and its strengths and weaknesses. Again, be open and honest here. Don't hide any particular facts from the venture capitalist. He or she recognizes all small firms have problems and weaknesses.

Borrowing from a Small Business Investment Company

A Small Business Investment Company (SBIC) is a venture capital firm licensed by the U.S. Small Business Administration (SBA) to provide either long-term debt or equity financing to qualified small businesses. Much of the financing made available by SBICs is borrowed from the SBA at attractive rates. SBICs fall into two broad categories:

- Captive firms whose management and operating policies are dictated by a parent organization, which is often a bank or insurance company; and
- Privately owned and operated noncaptive firms.

As is true with venture capitalists in general, SBICs have divergent philosophies and operating policies. Some specialize in equity financing while others provide debt financing in several different forms. This latter group of SBICs is the richest source of debt financing for small businesses outside commercial banks, and they are the focus of the subsequent discussion.

SBIC Debt Financing

SBICs, which offer debt financing, make either straight, long-term loans or hybrid loans that have an equity participation feature. An SBIC specializing in straight debt financing is content to earn the differential between its borrowing costs from the SBA and the interest rate charged the target small firm. SBICs seeking more growth-oriented opportunities expect to share in a target firm's future through equity-participation loans. There are three forms of debt financing which SBICs offer: straight loans, loans with warrants, and convertible bonds.

Straight Loans

Borrowing in the form of a straight loan — conventional loan — from an SBIC can be an attractive proposition. The SBIC can offer a larger amount of financing and longer loan maturities than traditional institutional lenders, such as a bank. These advantages, however, are offset to some extent by higher interest rates. This differential is necessary to compensate the SBIC for its own borrowing cost, greater risk exposure, and lengthened maturities.

The SBIC will also insist on collateral, a personal guarantee of the loan, and restrictive provisions in the loan agreement. These provisions are designed to protect unnecessary erosion of your firm's asset base and its liquidity position. Violations of any loan covenants allow the SBIC to assume a predetermined, minority ownership position in your firm or to demand the immediate repayment of the remaining principal and interest on the loan, or both.

Loans with Warrants

By using a loan-with-warrants financing arrangement and the convertible bond alternative described below, an SBIC can share in your growth through an ownership interest. An equity participation loan provides the target firm with needed debt financing, but it also allows the SBIC an opportunity, referred to as a sweetener, to obtain a designated number of shares of your firm's common stock. This feature produces a tradeoff between a lower interest rate for you, the borrowing firm, and the value of the potential equity interest your business surrenders.

Under the loan-with-warrants arrangement, an SBIC obtains a contractual option, the warrants, to purchase a specified number of shares of your firm's common stock during a designated time period. The purchase price on the warrant(s) is usually low and favors the lender. Thus, you obtain financing with the legal obligation to meet all provisions of the debt contract, but you also face the possibility of surrendering a share of your ownership at some future date. Benefits gained by your small business in exchange for this possible proportionate loss existing equity are:

- Needed financing that may not be possible if only a straight loan were considered;
- Lower interest costs than would be possible if only a straight loan were considered; this feature may be especially attractive to the cash-starved growth firm;
- A cash inflow, if and when the SBIC exercises the warrants — i.e., buys the agreed upon shares of stock; and
- The sacrifice of only a minority interest in your business, if the SBIC exercises the warrant. An SBIC is prohibited by SBA regulation from owning a majority interest in a target firm.

Convertible Bonds

Convertible bonds also offer the SBIC an equity sweetener. It differs, however, from the loan with warrants in two important areas: the nature of the equity option and the status of the loan obligation.

A convertible bond is simply a long-term promissory note governed by an underlying contract known as an indenture. The indenture specifies the provisions you, the borrower, agree to honor. In addition to the standard provisions, such as interest rate, payment dates, and collateral requirements, the indenture also specifies that the bondholder — the SBIC in this case — can convert the bond into a specified number of shares of your firm's common stock at any time during the life of the bond.

If the conversion option is exercised by the bondholder, the bond along with its interest and principal obligation literally disappear. The bond and its repayment obligations are replaced in the owner's equity section of the balance sheet by the number of shares of common stock specified in the indenture. Contrary to the loan-with-warrants arrangement, you do not enjoy a cash inflow from a conversion of the bond into common stock. This disadvantage is usually more than offset by the elimination of the obligation to repay the principal amount of the bond.

Management Assistance

Many SBICs offer management assistance, both technical and administrative, as a supplement to the provided financing. Since virtually every small business has some identifiable management weakness, especially if the firm is in the rapid growth stage of its life cycle, it is in the SBIC's best interest to provide administrative help. Repayment of the loan or the value of the equity participation depend on the success of the target business. On the other hand, SBICs which concentrate only on providing well-secured loans to businesses with acceptable risk exposure usually do not offer management assistance.

Who Qualifies for SBIC Financing?

In general, SBICs do not confine their financing to specific industries or business types. Rather, they tend to focus on investment opportunities that are consistent with their investment policies. Those SBICs specializing in equity or equity participation financing lean toward small firms with large growth potential, while those specializing in debt financing favor stable firms with a history of profitability.

To qualify for SBIC consideration, your business must meet the SBA's rigid definition of a small business as outlined in Chapter 6. Beyond meeting these standards, the individual SBIC has total discretion over whether financing is extended and the specific features of the financing agreement. An SBIC is restricted by the SBA only from investing more than 20% of its capital in any one firm and from holding more than 49% of any one firm's common stock.

Tips for Finding and Selecting an SBIC

Start with the SBA

The following guidelines should help you in your quest for SBIC debt financing.

Begin the search process by contacting the nearest regional SBA office for information on SBICs operating in your area. Although the SBA representatives cannot recommend a specific SBIC, they can provide information on the industries and types of investments in which SBICs in your area are interested. A free directory of SBICs can be obtained by contacting the:

National Association of SBICs
1156 15th Street, Suite 1101
Washington, DC 20005
(202) 833-8230

Shop Around

Limit your contacts to SBICs whose interests are compatible with your firm's capabilities and needs. Identify a sample of SBICs who specialize in your preferred type of financing; are capable of providing additional financing in the future if needed; and have the expertise to provide the specific management assistance required. The goal for both parties should be a good fit.

Once a representative sample of SBICs is established, contact all of the listed SBICs. There is a great deal of variation in SBIC lending policy, and it pays to shop around.

Prepare a Quality Proposal

A proposal for SBIC financing serves the same purpose as that presented to a nonlicensed venture capitalist. Again, the basis for this proposal is a well-prepared, thoroughly documented, comprehensive business plan. Regardless of how attractive your business may be as a financing candidate, this fact must be made known in the accepted manner. As previously indicated, your package should contain as separate items a cover letter and a concise summary of the critical elements of the business plan.

Negotiate from Strength

Do not be timid about negotiating specific features of the loan agreement with an interested SBIC. SBIC lending terms are not predetermined. Aside from the specifics of SBIC lending that are mandated by existing law or regulation, particulars such as interest rate, maturity, equity participation, and collateral requirements can be negotiated. In general, the more attractive your firm as a financing opportunity — that is, the stronger the business plan — the more negotiating leverage you possess. For further instruction and advice on creating a strong business plan, refer to *The Successful Business Plan: Secrets & Strategies,* by Rhonda M. Abrams, available at your local bookstore or through The Oasis Press, (800) 228-2275.

Chapter 10

Financing Through a Public Offering

For some small businesses, the public sale of its securities is the only acceptable means of obtaining the financing needed to accommodate accelerated growth. These businesses have usually reached the limit of their debt capacity, and venture capital financing may be an inadequate or undesirable alternative. For other businesses, the prestige of being the chief executive officer (CEO) and major stockholder in a publicly traded firm means the fulfillment of an entrepreneur's dream.

Regardless of the reason, the potential price the small business must pay for this decision is high. If the public offering is unsuccessful, the cost of unrecouped expenses and the expenditure of management's time, effort, and emotional energy will have a long-term impact on the firm's resources. Even when the offering proves successful, the cost to the firm is significant, and the personality and character of the firm will be changed forever.

The decision to go public, therefore, represents a major milestone in your small firm's life, and its far-reaching consequences should give you considerable pause for reflection.

The discussion outlined in this chapter provides you with a general overview of the many intricacies and issues involved in going public. Before making any decision to go public, consult with an attorney or professional adviser using this information as a foundation for raising questions and concerns.

What Is a Public Offering?

Legal precision aside, a public offering is described as the procedures associated with selling the securities of a privately held corporation to the public in order to raise needed financing. The securities to be sold can be common stock, preferred stock, straight bonds, or convertible bonds. While each of these choices is technically possible for any small business, common stock is typically the only realistic alternative. The public sale of straight or convertible bonds or preferred stock often takes a level of market acceptance beyond that of the small, first-time issuer.

If the common shares being sold belong to you, the existing owner, the offering is referred to as a secondary distribution. While a secondary distribution is technically possible, the more common situation for a first-time issuer is the sale of additional shares of a firm's authorized stock.

Often, a secondary distribution is more difficult to market than an offering of additional new shares, because there is a feeling among many financiers and investors that management may have inside information about a possible dismal future for the firm and is, in effect, using the secondary distribution to bail out of a losing situation.

Before either a public offering or secondary distribution is seriously considered, however, be certain that these four essential conditions are met:

- **Your firm must be well suited to a public offering.** This means the business, its earning capacity, and its future must be attractive to potential investors.
- **You have to be fully committed to the effort.** A public offering process is demanding and costly. A successful offering requires you to be intimately familiar and involved with the entire process. Be ready and able to devote a great deal of your time and resources to the effort.
- **Use qualified assistance.** The offering process is complex and no place for the uninformed. You will need the assistance of experienced professionals in the area of finance, accounting, law, and investment banking (underwriting) at each step of the way.
- **The time must be right.** To maximize the likelihood of a successful offering, the offering should be made when general stock market conditions are strong, and your firm's industry is not out of favor with investors.

The decision to go public is not easy, even if your business is ideally positioned to do so. To help you better understand the complicated process of a public offering, read the following discussion which briefly outlines the two major phases of the public offering process: 1) the pre-underwriting or preparatory phase; and 2) the underwriting and distribution phase.

The Public Offering Process: Pre-Underwriting Phase

A first-time public offering is a complex process, and the tasks that must be performed during the pre-underwriting or preparatory phase as well as the underwriting and distribution phase (discussed later) must be carefully planned and executed. Because of this complexity, you will require the assistance of a battery of professionals.

During the pre-underwriting or preparatory phase, you will require the assistance of financial, accounting, and legal specialists. During the second phase, the actual registration, sale, and distribution of the offering is handled by a specialized financial institution known as an investment banker or underwriter. The investment banker or underwriter assumes responsibility for the following factors:

- Registering the issue with the Securities and Exchange Commission (SEC) and the proper state agencies through required statements (See page 190);
- Underwriting the issue by contracting to buy it from your firm on a designated offering date at a predetermined, contractual price; this price is the sale price of the stock minus the underwriter's expenses and fees. These combined costs to the firm are known as the underwriter's discount or spread;
- Selling or, as it is often called, distributing, the issue; and
- Maintaining an "after market" for the stock; maintaining or "making" a market means the underwriter actively seeks to buy or sell the stock from its inventory. This important function helps to sustain public interest in the stock after the initial offering by ensuring that there is an active market through which it can be traded.

All these factors are outlined in a contractual agreement known as the underwriting agreement.

Meeting the Prerequisites of Going Public

Before a public offering can be seriously considered and the search for an investment banker started in earnest, you must be reasonably certain your business is a viable candidate for such an undertaking. Unfortunately, it is not always clear when this stage of the business' development has been reached or when investors will be receptive to a new issue of this type. Security markets are subject to price swings, mood swings, and fads. This makes it difficult to pin down precise rules for timing an issue. There are instances during strong markets when "hot prospect" companies with no demonstrated earnings have been successfully sold to the public. In other cases, firms with solid credentials have been rejected by investment bankers for underwriting, or the issue failed to gain market acceptance because the time was not right.

Despite these interferences, the criteria discussed below provides broad standards for judging whether your business is realistically positioned for a public offering.

An Appealing Product or Service

A product or service with a favorable public image, an identifiable edge over competition, and the potential for solid growth are primary considerations for a successful public offering. These attributes are the foundation for sales and earnings growth and, therefore, market acceptance. It is virtually impossible to attract widespread investor interest without them.

An Acceptable Earnings Record

An established earnings record as evidenced by the amount, stability, and expected growth trend of net income and cash flow are also essential to meeting acceptance standards for going public. While there is no clear-cut minimum, acceptable earnings level and growth rate, net income of less than approximately $300,000 to $500,000 and a growth rate, which does not exceed the average for your firm's industry, would generally be considered inadequate even by a regional investment banker. Few, if any, investors buy the small business stock for dividends. Unless there is the promise of rapid growth and price appreciation, the stock issue will attract little, if any, attention.

Quality Management

Given the widespread impression that small businesses often lack capable management or management depth, prospective underwriters and investors consider the quality of management a critical component of market acceptance. Quality refers to management's:

- Experience in the industry or a related field and in an administrative capability;
- Track record for performance and integrity;
- Depth in all functional areas of the business; and
- Capacity to work effectively under close public scrutiny.

Of particular concern to an investment banker is your capacity for dealing with a meddlesome public. When your business is privately held, you have free reign to make decisions without question; however, once your firm goes public, you will be bombarded with queries from stockholders, security analysts, and former underwriters. Many small business managers cannot, or are not willing to, adjust to these demands.

Sufficient Size

Your business and the common stock offering have to be sufficiently large enough in both monetary value and the number of shares to justify an underwriting. Because of the large amount of fixed cost associated with a public offering, a small issue is not economically feasible and often beyond the reach of small businesses. Of greater importance to the investment banker or underwriter is the number of shares to be issued. After the issue, the investment banker will support the market for the stock by buying and selling shares from its own inventory. Without a sufficient number of shares outstanding, there will be no active trading in the stock and the investment banker cannot justify involvement with the issue.

An important part of the public offering is the required filing of a registration statement with the SEC and the dissemination of a prospectus. Both of these documents require detailed disclosure on the firm and its operations for the SEC and potential investors. In a case where particulars such as sales levels, profit margins, and share of the market must be protected for competitive survival, full disclosure can mean disaster for a small business.

Public Disclosure Must Not Be Damaging

Establishing an appropriate selling price for a new issue is one of the most difficult decisions in this preparatory phase. The price must be satisfactory to you, the underwriter(s), and the investing public. If your issuing business does not receive a compensatory price for the stock, it is denied cash flow and you suffer a loss of equity value. An offering price that is too low will also result in losses for the underwriter because of insufficient profit margin or the cost of carrying unsold shares, or both. On the other hand, if the offering price is too high, the stock will not sell.

An Acceptable Price for the Issue

Closely related to the pricing problem in both importance and difficulty is the matter of choosing the appropriate time to market the issue. If stock market prices are generally strong, if the industry in which your business operates is not out of favor with investors, and if public offerings of small businesses have been well received, the new issue will have little trouble gaining market acceptance. Conversely, if stock prices are weak or if investors have taken losses on small issues or on other stocks of firms in the same industry, a new-issue offering would be disastrous. While a knowledgeable, experienced investment banker can reduce the risk of poor timing, solving this problem to the satisfaction of all parties concerned is often as much a matter of luck as skill.

Good Timing

One of your first responsibilities in the preparatory phase of the public offering process is to conduct a thorough investigation of your firm's capacity and readiness for the undertaking. Your goal is twofold: 1) to gain sufficient information to make an educated judgment on whether going public is in the best interest of all parties involved; and 2) if so decided, to prepare for the second phase (underwriting and distribution) of the offering process.

Gathering and Evaluating Information

To make a sound decision, you will need to become familiar with the requirements of the offering process by enlisting the help of qualified professionals and by answering the following questions:

- What amount of financing is needed; what maturities are needed; and how urgent are these needs?
- How will these funds be used; what are the growth prospects for sales and earnings if the funds are used in the indicated manner?

- Is a public stock offering the only realistic alternative for raising the required financing?
- Is this the proper time for a public offering?
- Why is an investment banker or underwriter needed?
- How do you find a qualified investment banker?
- What steps and procedures are followed for a new-issue public offering?
- What are the costs of the preparatory, underwriting, registration, and distribution phases of the process likely to be?
- What principles apply in establishing the offering price of the stock and the amount of the underwriting discount?
- How long will the process take?
- What are the risks of a public offering to the firm, and to its officers and directors?
- Do you have enough information on the rigors of the public offering process to determine if you are willing to make the required commitment?

Financial Information

A qualified financial adviser can provide you with a clear picture of your firm's current financial position, the amount and maturity of all required financing, and the future prospects for sales and earnings. Your financial adviser assists you with evaluating the pros and cons of going public, and if required, directs the preparation of the firm's business plan. If the offering is decided, he or she can prepare the projections required for the SEC's registration statement and assist you with negotiating the offering price and underwriter's discount. A sample of requirements for the SEC registration statement is provided on page 190.

Legal Information

An attorney experienced with public offerings can educate you on the legalities and legal costs of the process; and if preparatory work is undertaken, he or she can review all corporate records, agreements, leases, and contracts for possible legal defects. This legal review step is critical since all parties connected with the underwriting, including the firm's officers and directors, are liable for any misrepresentations and omissions in the registration statement and prospectus.

Accounting Information

An accountant familiar with the rigors of a public offering will advise you on the nature and cost of the accounting work needed to satisfy registration statement requirements. If the offering is undertaken, the accountant, working in conjunction with your firm's investment banker, can review and audit all of your accounting records and prepare the audited statements and other required accounting documents.

Underwriting Information

A primary function of the investment banker or underwriter in the preparatory phase is to provide you with a general overview of the requirements, steps, and problems associated with a first-time public offering. In order for the investment banker to gain an impression of your business and its potential for going public from this preliminary interview, be prepared to supply extensive information about your business. The appropriate source for this information is your business plan and business plan summary. The summary should contain sufficient information to allow the investment banker to offer tentative responses to four key concerns.

- The market's receptiveness to the issue;
- The probable price range and underwriter's discount or profit margin on the issue;
- The estimated total issue cost to the firm; and
- The extent of the investment banker's interest in pursuing a possible underwriting.

After learning of the probable cost of going public and recovering from the resulting sticker shock, you may ask yourself: "Is it necessary to pay an investment banker to do something that the firm with its many contacts can do for itself?" The answer is almost always yes; the investment banker is needed. The experience of small businesses attempting the do-it-yourself route to selling their own initial stock offering can be dismal.

Searching for an Underwriter

Finding and selecting the ideal investment banker to underwrite a small business issue is not an easy task. An underwriting firm should have that special blend of technical capability, experience with small, first-time issues, familiarity with a firm's industry, and the capability to distribute the issue in a geographic pattern that closely follows the geography of interest in the stock. Often, bankers, financial advisers, lawyers, or accountants experienced with public offerings can recommend suitable investment bankers or underwriters for the preliminary interview.

Understand that investment banking firms are not monolithic organizations with uniform business philosophies. Rather, they are personalized firms with differing interests, expertise, and capabilities. When beginning your search for an underwriter, limit your selection of underwriters to several candidates with credentials that are consistent with your firm's needs. While it is necessary to interview enough underwriters to ensure that offers are competitive, it is also wise to avoid widespread shopping. Investment bankers are not receptive to firms that give the impression of pitting one underwriter against another.

The search process should provide you with sufficient information to decide whether more serious underwriting negotiations are advisable. Come away from the preliminary interview(s) with answers to these key questions:

- Is the investment banker experienced with underwritings of comparable size?
- Does the investment banker have sound credentials and a reputation for integrity?

- Is the investment banker sufficiently familiar with your firm's business and industry to communicate effectively with potential buyers of the security?
- Does your business meet the necessary prerequisites to attract a public following of investors?
- Has the investment banker indicated a strong interest in the security and its prospects for market acceptance?
- Has the investment banker indicated willingness to support an after market in the stock?

This last question regarding an after market is critical to the long-run success of the stock issue and should be given substantial weight in the selection of an underwriting firm. When an investment banker maintains an active market after the public issue, their firm not only provides liquidity for investors, but it also maintains a closer relationship with your business.

The Public Offering Process: Underwriting and Distribution Phase

The underwriting and distribution phase begins with the investment banker's letter of intent, which is issued after the preliminary interview. This letter indicates the investment banker's interest in the offering, the basic terms of the underwriting, and the intention to further investigate its feasibility. This investigation is conducted by the investment banker's buying department and takes the form of an extensive analysis of every aspect of your firm and its operation. If the analysis requires the services of an outside professional, such as an engineer's evaluation of your firm's assets, you pay for these services.

The Underwriting Agreement

Assuming the outcome of the investigation is favorable, the buying department prepares a proposal to underwrite the issue. This proposal specifies the amount and type of securities the investment banker is willing to underwrite and a tentative date for the offering. If the proposal is acceptable to your firm and the investment banker, both parties enter into what is referred to as an informal agreement. This document is simply an agreement to enter into an underwriting agreement (a binding contract) at a later date, if the registration process is successfully completed and a mutually acceptable price and discount for the issue can be decided upon.

If the size or risk of the issue warrants additional assistance, the investment banker will invite other underwriters to share in the offering. This group is known as a syndicate and is headed by the original investment banker, who is known as the syndicate manager or originating house. The investment banker, will delay negotiating the binding underwriting agreement until shortly before the registration statement is to become effective in order to minimize the risk associated with an expected major change in stock market conditions. Negotiation of the underwriting agreement will focus on the price at which the stock will be issued to the public and the price the underwriter will pay you. The difference between these two values is the underwriter's discount or spread, and its size is determined by the issue's perceived degree of price risk. The spread is literally the underwriter's profit margin. If the underwriting is to be profitable, the spread must compensate for all costs incurred by the syndicate, and the risk of adverse price changes in the stock market.

Registering and Offering the Stock

Acceptance of the underwriter's informal agreement initiates the tedious process of preparing and filing the SEC and any appropriate state registration statements. To provide a perspective on the detail and technical complexity associated with a typical first-time public offering, Table 10.1 (on the following page) lists the general information requirements for a SEC registration statement, and Table 10.2 indicates the major responsibilities and functions of the underwriter. Some of these functions are performed solely by the underwriter, and others are handled in conjunction with your management, lawyers, accountants, and any needed outside specialists. Note again that you are responsible for all costs of registration and issue, regardless of success or failure.

After filing the registration statement, a preliminary prospectus is prepared and distributed by the underwriter to interested buyers of the issue. A prospectus outlines the general features of the issue and contains key information from the registration statement. It is used by the underwriter(s) to advertise the stock to prospective investors. Since, at this point, the registration statement has not been approved by the SEC, the preliminary prospectus, known as a red herring, will not indicate the date and price of the issue. Also, all sales commitments obtained at this time by the underwriter or syndicate are not final until the registration has been approved.

The registration statement will not be approved until all inconsistencies or shortcomings discovered in the statement by the SEC have been corrected. Any such problems are identified for you through correspondence known as a deficiency letter. When all deficiencies have been remedied to the satisfaction of the supervising SEC staff, all that remains to be done is the filing of the pricing amendment. This document is added to the registration statement and provides information on the issue price to the public, the underwriting discount, and the net proceeds to the business. Depending on the complexity and problems involved, approval of a registration statement for an initial issue can take as much as two months to attain.

When the registration statement is approved, a final prospectus will be issued. This document will reflect any amendments to the preliminary prospectus demanded by the SEC, along with an indication of the price and offering date of the issue. On the specified date of sale, the issuing firm is paid the agreed price by the underwriting syndicate.

Distributing the Stock

The sale or distribution phase of the public offering process is possibly the point at which the investment banker's or syndicate's expertise is

Table 10.1 – Information Requirements for the SEC Registration Statement

I. Notification

1. Significant Parties

   List names, business and residential addresses for "a," and names and business addresses of "b – j" below.

   a. directors, officers, and general partners

   b. record owners of 10 percent or more of any class of the securities, or any other person who has the right to vote or direct the voting of the securities

   c. promoters of the issue

   d. predecessors of the issue

   e. affiliates of the issue

   f. counsel to the issues in connection with the offering

   g. each managing underwriter

   h. the underwriter's directors, officers, general partners, and counsel

II. Offering Circular

1. Cover Page

   a. name of issuer

   b. address of principal executive offices

   c. date of the offering circular

   d. description and amount of securities offered

   e. statement required by Rule 259

   f. tables depicting distribution spread (Item 2 below)

   g. the name of the underwriter or underwriters

   h. any materials required by the law of any state in which the securities are to be offered

   i. if applicable, identification of material risks in connection with the purchase of the securities

   j. approximate date of commencement of proposed public sale

2. Distribution Spread

3. Summary Information, Risk Factors and Dilution

4. Plan of Distribution

5. Use of Proceeds to Issuer

6. Description of Business and Property

7. Directors, Executive Officers, and Significant Employees

8. Remuneration of Directors and Officers

9. Security Ownership of Management and Certain Security Holders

10. Interest of Management and Others in Certain Transactions

11. Securities Being Offered

12. Financial Statements

III. Exhibits

1. Underwriting Agreement

2. Charter, Bylaws, and Voting Trust Agreement

3. Instruments Defining the Rights of Security Holders

4. Material Contracts and Material Foreign Patents

5. Statement Concerning Issuer's Financing

6. Plan of Acquisition, Reorganization, Arrangement, etc.

7. Escrow Agreements

8. Consent by Experts and Underwriters

Table 10.2 – Selected Steps in an Underwriter's Preparation of a New Issue

1. Review with management the steps, procedures, and cost estimates of a public offering.

2. Review with management the SEC and state rules and regulations for a public offering.

3. Evaluate proposed issue and prepare informal agreement.

4. Issue letters of invitation, if necessary, to prospective syndicate members.

5. Meet with interested syndicate members and determine the make-up of the group.

6. Prepare underwriting agreement or purchase contract.

7. Prepare agreement among underwriters.

8. Arrange "due diligence" meetings with management and syndicate members.

9. Meet with outside accountant and underwriter's accountants to decide the financial data requirements for the registration statement.

10. Meet with printers to decide the form of the stock certificate, the number of copies of the certificate, and the preliminary prospectus to be printed.

11. Prepare registration statement.

12. Prepare prospectus.

13. Obtain indemnity insurance policy.

14. Clear proposed "comfort letter" with firm's auditors.

15. File the registration statement with the SEC.

16. Prepare preliminary state blue sky law (or state securities laws) memorandum.

17. Determine where and how the offering will be advertised.

18. Establish selling efforts and responsibilities with syndicate members.

19. Hire registrar and transfer agent for the issue.

20. Prepare published announcements and schedule of publications and tentative dates.

21. Compile summary report of distribution of the red herring and amendments thereto.

22. File red herring list with the SEC.

23. Clear deficiencies with the SEC and make required revisions, amendments, and corrections.

24. Prepare final prospectus.

25. Make arrangements with printer for the number of copies of the final prospectus to be printed.

26. Send copies of final prospectus to syndicate members, dealers, and financial services.

27. Direct and supervise the selling effort for the issue.

28. Take the necessary steps to get the issue quoted in newspapers and listed in stock guides.

29. Meet with National Association of Security Dealers representatives to make arrangement for listing the stock for over-the-counter trading.

30. Advise company on its responsibilities after the offering.

most crucial. One of the important services brought to a public offering by the underwriter is the breadth of its sales network along with the ability to effectively promote the issue within this network. Without these two vital ingredients, your time, energy, and money spent to this point will be for naught. Fortunately for you, this is at least one step in the offering process that does not require your active involvement.

An integral part of the sale or distribution phase is the after-issue market. The success of a first-time stock issue is measured not only by its initial reception, but by continued investor trading in the issue. By maintaining an after-market and an active promotion effort, the investment banker helps make this possible. Whether it becomes a long-standing reality, however, depends on the continued earnings success of your business.

After reading about the public offering process, the following sections can give you some ideas as to the advantages and disadvantages of going public. Keep these factors in mind when working with your financial and professional advisers.

Advantages of Going Public

Business Advantages

The advantages produced by a public offering serve as a powerful incentive if your business is properly positioned. Through a successful public offering, your business can satisfy its need for working capital, and you can realize a variety of personal benefits. Among the many possible reasons for going public, the following represent the most important:

- **Meet current financial requirements.** The most fundamental reason for going public is to obtain needed financing. Growth firms require large amounts of funds for the expansion of working capital and fixed assets or to meet the needs of researching, developing, and marketing products. This financing is usually not available from traditional lenders in the amounts needed because of the inherent risk. Moreover, venture capital financing may not be a viable option because the measure of control conceded in such an arrangement may be unacceptable.

- **Gain financial stability.** A successful public offering not only provides needed long-term financing in a single undertaking, it simultaneously enhances your firm's present and future financial position. The large influx of equity capital expands its equity base, strengthens its capital structure (debt-to-total capital ratio), and reduces the current level of financial-risk exposure. Also, because equity as opposed to debt financing is used, your business is not burdened with interest and principal payments. This means that future cash flows are protected from debt service requirements.

- **Facilitate future financing.** By improving the equity base, your business increases its debt capacity and makes it possible to raise additional debt financing in the future. Equally as important, if your business continues to enjoy success and the price of the stock performs well, market acceptance increases. This lays the foundation for any needed future stock issue.

- **Maintain owner control.** Stock held by a backer, investment group, or venture capitalist is usually accompanied by a provision granting majority control, if your business does not meet prescribed performance standards. On the other hand, a large block of stock that is widely distributed among public stockholders allows you to maintain majority control of your business. When your business performs well, the matter of who owns the stock may not be an issue, but if things go badly — and they sometimes do even for those small businesses that ultimately succeed — voting control is a serious consideration.

- **Provide incentives for key employees.** Having its stock publicly traded allows your firm to offer a more enticing incentive package to key employees or to qualified personnel you are attempting to attract. These incentives can take the form of stock options or other company supported stock purchase plans. Opportunities to share in the ownership of the firm can be a strong inducement for employees to remain on board and increase productivity.

- **Create public relations.** The very act of going public tends to advertise a firm and create a favorable image in the minds of its customers, suppliers, and creditors. This advantage is magnified if a firm's stock performs well shortly after the public issue.

Personal Advantages

As owner of a publicly held business, you gain a number of personal advantages. You can:

- **Facilitate estate planning.** Stock with a public market eliminates the difficulty of establishing an acceptable market value for estate taxes and may offer advantages for passing the shares to heirs through the owner's estate.

- **Facilitate the diversification of your personal fortune.** By having a stock that is publicly traded, you are in position to sell portions of your holdings and reinvest in other assets.

- **Provide better collateral for obtaining personal credit.** Publicly traded stock is usually more acceptable as collateral for personal loans than stock in a privately held firm.

- **Facilitate future mergers or acquisitions.** Common stock that has a tested market value is more valuable in a merger negotiation than that of a privately held firm. Most shareholders of a firm being merged or acquired are simply not interested in trading their privately held stock for the securities of another privately held firm.

- **Provide psychic income.** Control over a publicly traded corporation may be the overriding reason you went into business, and achieving this goal may provide you with that ultimate satisfaction.

Disadvantages of Going Public

Although the lure of a public offering is strong, you must also weigh the possible disadvantages to this decision. The opinions of those who have gone public are strong testimony to the costly tradeoff to the inherent advantages and disadvantages; many small business owners indicate they would not have done so had they been aware of the problems and changes a public offering creates.

High Cost

The cost of going public can be prohibitively high, and for this reason alone your small business may be discouraged from doing so. The costs associated with a public offering fall into two distinct categories: 1) the costs of preparing the firm for the undertaking; and 2) the costs of the undertaking itself. Preparatory costs include your time, effort, and emotional energy and the out-of-pocket outlay for professional services, such as financial, accounting, and legal consultants. Depending on the volume and complexity of the preparatory work to be done, the out-of-pocket costs can amount to several hundreds of thousands of dollars.

The major costs associated with the underwriting and registration of a public offering include:

- Underwriter's fees, plus warrants to buy stock in the firm at a bargain price;
- Underwriter's expenses;
- Legal and accounting fees;
- Printing costs;
- Federal registration and issuing costs and transfer taxes;
- State registration and issuing costs;
- Registrar and transfer agent fees; and
- Indemnity insurance costs.

For small offerings, the underwriting and registration costs can reach as much as 25% of the amount of funds raised. This means that with a successful $10 million offering, your firm would surrender $10 million of equity value to new stockholders, but receive only $7.5 million in return. Obviously, there should be no consideration of a public offering if the funds can be obtained more readily and economically from other sources.

Management Commitment

The preparation and actual public offering will require a major commitment from you and your management team. The thought process and preliminary effort may begin as much as two years before the eventual offering and the registration and issue process can require up to six months of your time. Because of limited staff and administrative resources, this factor can present a major obstacle. Your business must also continue to operate, and a superhuman effort is necessary to juggle these two major responsibilities for an extended period of time.

After the offering, the character and personality of your firm will undergo noticeable changes. The most significant of these changes will occur in the area of management decision making. Preoffering decisions were made privately, whereas many post-offering decisions will be made under close public scrutiny, or only with the consent of stockholders. Publicly traded firms are also subject to stringent financial reporting requirements to stockholders, the Securities and Exchange Commission (SEC) and any security exchange on which the stock is listed. While a public offering may not significantly change your firm's size for several years, the business will no longer be run in the personal manner of a small, privately held company.

Change

When your business becomes a public entity, the liability of officers and the board of directors will increase. This risk exposure is insurable, but the cost of the coverage is expensive.

Liability

Final Thoughts on Going Public

An initial public offering is a tedious, demanding process, and there is no easy path through the maize of legal, financial, and regulatory requirements. For a typical small business, the decision to pursue a public stock offering has more serious and widespread ramifications than any original decision to start the business. Regardless of the success or failure of the offering, the consequences of the effort will have a long-term impact on the business.

Given these realities, a public offering should only be considered as an avenue of last resort for raising funds. First, exhaust all other possibilities, including the alternative of purposely slowing the firm's rate of growth to reduce financing needs. Equally as important, be thoroughly convinced that you are in position to make the demanding commitment to go public.

Conclusion

Having finished *Financing Your Small Business*, you now have a better understanding of how to evaluate your business' financing needs and alternatives. You can see how debt financing can work both for and against you, and you know how to avoid the danger of taking out more debt than you could repay if something went wrong.

Strong, well-implemented techniques for planning, acquiring, and managing your small business' debt financing are the keys to avoiding potential dangers. *Financing Your Small Business* has outlined the basic financial management skills and techniques it will take for you to accomplish a successful debt financing endeavor. Regardless of your business' life cycle stage, however, the assistance of your professional advisers is always recommended.

One final thought to take with you: Without an adequate supply of cash flow from operations (CFFO), other sources of funds will not be available. Creditors will not loan money without assurances of repayment, and investors will not buy equity interests without the expectation of a compensatory return on invested capital. Also, if your business is able to generate increasing supplies of CFFO, you will need less external debt financing. Therefore, make it a high priority to maintain adequate CFFO in your small business.

Index

Accruals, 85, 90, 111

Accumulated depreciation, 2–3

Add-on interest method, 42

Add-on method, 122

Additional external financing required (AFR), 74, 76–77

Advance factoring, 104–105, 111

After-tax cost, 34–35, 119

Amortization, 115–116

Annual effective rate (AER), 88–89, 91–94, 96, 105–107, 110, 119

Annual percentage rate (APR), 36, 42–43, 114, 122–123

Asset-based loans, 123

Asset lending, 83

Assets, 2–4, 7–10, 12–13, 15, 19–23, 25–27, 29–31, 35–36, 45–46, 48, 55, 60, 69, 72–75, 77, 82–84, 90, 98–99, 101, 106, 112, 113–114, 118, 121, 123–125, 127–131, 144, 149, 153, 156, 158–159, 164, 171–172, 188, 192–193

Authorized stock, 182

Availability, 34–35, 83, 85, 94, 96, 103, 110, 118–119

Average collection period (ACP) ratio, 11–13, 17–18

Average daily cash expenditures (ADE), 17–18

Average payment period (APP) ratio, 13, 17

Balance sheet, 1–2, 4, 7, 10–13, 15, 28, 48, 72–73, 75–77, 82, 85, 90, 125, 156, 160, 164, 178

Balloon payment, 121

Bank, 1, 4, 37, 46, 73, 82–83, 85, 88, 90–97, 99–100, 102–103, 108, 110, 116, 126, 128–131, 134–135, 139–149, 152–153, 161–164, 177

Bank credit, 94, 96–97, 143

Bank loan, 1, 82–83, 85, 90, 93, 130–131, 134, 152

Bank regulation, 141

Banker, 72, 83, 97, 122, 139–143, 145–150, 151, 183–189, 192

Banking relationship, 96–97, 139–140, 145–146, 148, 166

Binding contract, 118, 125, 188

Blanket lien, 108

Blue sky, 191

Bonded warehouse receipt, 108

Budget, 55, 59–72, 75, 78, 95, 134, 153, 161, 164

Burden coverage ratio, 14–15, 49, 51–53

Burden coverage results, 53

Business development officer, 146

Business plan, 78, 136, 150, 151, 153–155, 157–165, 172–173, 175–176, 180, 186–187

Business risk, 33–34, 45–46, 57, 84

Capital lease, 125

Capital structure, 25–26, 28, 30, 32, 35, 45, 50–51, 53–56, 58, 119, 192

Captive financing subsidiary, 130

Cash before delivery (C.B.D.), 87

Cash budget, 55, 60–63, 65–72, 75, 78, 95, 153, 161, 164

Cash conversion cycle (CCC), 16–18

Cash disbursements, 60, 69

Cash flow, 7–10, 13–15, 19–20, 23–27, 33–35, 46–50, 52–58, 61–62, 66, 69–71, 76, 81–82, 90, 112, 117–120, 123, 130, 153, 155, 160, 162, 164, 184–185

Cash-flow analysis, 48, 54

Cash flow from operations (CFFO), 7, 9, 14, 25–26, 49–54, 76–77, 153

Cash-flow lending, 83

Cash-flow statement, 1, 7–9, 14–15

Cash inflows, 54–55, 60, 65–66, 69–70, 82, 107, 142

Cash on delivery (C.O.D.), 87

Cash outflows, 54–55, 60–61, 68–70, 116

Cash receipts, 60–61, 65–67, 69

Charter, 141–142, 190

Clear-cut exit, 172

Collateral, 22–23, 82–83, 98–103, 107–108, 110, 113–114, 120, 123, 130, 135, 146, 153, 158, 173, 177–178, 180, 193

Collection pattern, 61–66

Commercial banks, 83, 85, 90, 94, 100–101, 111, 123, 128–131, 140–141, 177

Commitment fee, 84, 95–96, 111, 121

Common stock, 4, 21, 121, 131, 135, 170, 174, 178–179, 182, 184, 193

Compensating balance requirement (CBR), 84, 93–95

Competent management, 136, 153, 172

Competition section, 157

Conditional sales contract, 130

Convertible bonds, 177–178, 182

Cost, 2, 5–7, 12–13, 17–18, 20, 23–25, 27–32, 34–38, 43, 51, 56, 60, 68, 71, 74, 83–84, 86, 88–92, 94–100, 102–112, 113–114, 118–131, 136, 142–144, 147, 153, 157, 164, 170, 172, 176–177, 181, 184–187, 191, 194–195

Cost of sales, 5–7, 12–13, 17–18, 24–25, 74, 142

Cover letter, 156, 162–163, 176, 180

Coverage ratios, 47–48, 52–53

Credit sales, 4, 9, 11, 56, 63–66, 101, 143, 153

Credit terms, 11–12, 16–17, 46, 68, 85–89, 102, 143

Current assets, 2–3, 72, 74–75, 82, 98–99, 113

Current liabilities, 3–4, 74, 82

Current liability, 82, 85, 90

Debt agreement, 20–21, 23, 135

Debt and coverage ratios, 48

Debt, 1, 4, 10–16, 18, 19–23, 25–36, 43, 45–58, 59–60, 71, 77, 81–86, 94, 97–98, 104, 113, 116, 119–121, 123, 125–127, 131, 135, 140, 149, 151, 156, 161, 165, 169, 171, 177–179, 181, 192

Debt financing, 1, 14–15, 20–23, 25–36, 43, 45–55, 57–58, 59–60, 82, 119–120, 125, 131, 151, 169, 177–179, 192

Debt ratio, 13–14, 26–27, 35, 48–49

Debt ratios, 48, 119

Default risk, 90, 98, 100, 102, 104, 134, 142

Deficiency letter, 189

Deposits, 100, 104–105, 141–142, 145, 148

Description, 99, 109, 127, 154–156, 158–159, 164–165, 173, 190

Detailed Numbers, 174

Discounted interest, 38–40, 42, 91, 93

Discounted-interest method, 38, 91

Discretionary cash flow, 25–26

Distribution phase, 182–183, 188–189, 192

Due diligence, 191

Earnings before interest expense and taxes (EBIT), 50–52

Effective rate of interest, 36–39, 42, 91, 93

Embryo stage, 46, 155–156, 171

Equipment, 2–3, 56, 66, 69, 71–73, 113, 116, 121, 123, 125–130, 134, 140, 156, 158–159, 172

Equipment manufacturers, 128, 130

Equity, 3–4, 9, 11, 13, 15, 19–21, 23, 25–36, 45–46, 48, 50–51, 53, 57–58, 74, 77, 119–121, 124–125, 128, 131, 135, 169–170, 177–180, 185, 192, 194

Equity capital, 3, 20–21, 30, 34, 45–46, 48, 58, 74, 119–120, 169, 192

Equity kicker, 131

Equity participation loan, 177

Equity sweetener, 121, 131, 135, 169, 178

Estimating sales, 62

Estimating the receivables collection pttern, 63

Exit opportunity, 172–173

Extended-term financing, 23, 34, 40, 46, 82, 84, 100, 113–115, 117–121, 123, 125, 127–131, 133, 135–137

External financing, 7, 19–20, 71, 74, 76–77, 81, 161, 166

Factor, 103–107, 111, 119, 136, 139, 194

Factoring, 100–101, 103–107, 111

Factoring agreement, 104

Favorable financial leverage, 16, 29–30

Federal Deposit Insurance Corporation (FDIC), 141

Field warehouse, 109

Financial adviser, 186

Financial burden coverage ratio, 14–15

Financial cushion, 57

Financial flexibility, 22, 57, 120, 140

Financial history, 155–156, 162, 173

Financial lease, 125–127, 130

Financial leverage, 16, 27–31, 48, 50–51

Financial leverage ratios, 48

Financial ratio analysis, 10

Financial risk, 14, 26–27, 33–35, 45–54, 57, 120

Financing decision, 32–34, 84, 118–120, 136

Financing mix, 45–49, 51, 53, 55–57

Financing proposal, 48, 136, 151–155, 157, 159, 161, 163–165

Financing section, 9, 69, 71

First-time public offering, 183, 186, 189

Fixed assets, 2–3, 8–10, 22, 35, 55, 60, 69, 72, 74, 82, 84, 114, 118, 121, 127, 153, 156, 158, 164, 171–172, 192

Fixed cash costs, 68

Flexibility, 22, 57, 83–86, 97, 103, 110, 118, 120–125, 140

Floating lien, 108–109, 111

Floating-rate method, 91

Floor planning loans, 109

Formative stage, 46, 171

Free cash flow, 25–26, 56–57

Full-amortization method, 40, 42

Full-amount method, 122

Gap financing, 170

General lien arrangement, 101

General partner, 21

Gross profit margin, 5, 11, 156

Hidden factors, 118–119

History, 83, 102–103, 148, 154–156, 162, 173, 179

Honesty, 101, 148, 174

Hot prospect companies, 183

Hybrid loans, 177

Ideal Leverage Company, The, (Ideal), 2–15, 23–25, 35, 37–40, 42, 50, 62–67, 91–95, 102–106, 108, 110, 115–119, 126, 156, 161, 163, 187

Income statement, 1–2, 4–5, 7, 10–15, 17, 22–24, 28, 30, 49, 68–69, 72–73, 75–76, 160, 164

Indenture, 178

Independent leasing companies, 128, 130

Index number, 10

Industrial leasing companies, 130

Industrial revenue bonds (IRB), 128

Informal agreement, 188–189, 191

Installment loans, 129

Insurance company, 131, 177

Intangible asset, 148

Intangible assets, 159

Intended future, 155, 159–160

Interest earned ratio, 49–50

Interest, 5–6, 14, 20–42, 46–53, 55–56, 60, 81, 83–86, 88–100, 102–111, 113–126, 128–131, 133–135, 142–144, 147, 149, 163, 170, 174, 177–180, 183–185, 187–188, 190, 192

Interest on the unpaid balance, 40

Internal financing, 7, 19–20

Inventory financing, 107–108, 110, 123

Inventory turnover ratio, 12, 17

Investment banker, 183–189, 192

Issue, 47, 54, 123, 128, 146, 161, 174, 183–185, 187–194

Large margins, 172

Large potential, 172

Lease financing, 125–127, 130

Leasing, 14, 22, 124–131

Lender's standards, 47

Letter of intent, 188

Leverage ratios, 48–50, 54

Liabilities, 3–4, 9, 13, 15, 48, 72–74, 77, 82, 90, 141, 143

Life cycle, 45–46, 154, 169, 171, 179

Life insurance companies, 128, 131

Line of credit, 90, 93–94, 121, 146

Liquid balances, 71

Loan-with-warrants, 177–178

Long-term liabilities, 3–4, 9, 73–74

Mandatory repayment, 21

Maturity factoring, 104–105, 107

Maturity stage, 46, 171

Maturity, 118, 127

Milestones, 155

Mortgage lending, 123

Mortgage loan, 9, 73, 77

Muni, 128

National banks, 141

Net lease, 126

Net period, 86, 88–89

Nonregulated firms, 169

Operating expenses, 5–7, 14, 18, 23–25, 54, 56, 68, 74

Operating lease, 125–127

Opportunity cost, 71, 88, 106, 111, 120

Ordinary-interest method, 91–92

Originating house, 188

Outline, 172–175

Owner control, 118, 193

Owner's equity, 3–4, 11, 15, 27, 51, 74, 77, 178

Ownership interest, 20, 23, 46, 120, 128, 144, 177

Participating loans, 134

Partnership interest, 21, 34

Payments pattern approach, 63

Percent-of-sales method, 68, 73

Percent of sales, 5, 10, 69, 75–76

Percentage advance, 98–99, 102, 109

Permanent component of working capital, 118, 121

Perplexed Company, 27–28, 30–32, 50–53, 55–56

Planning horizons, 72

Pledging arrangement, 101

Pledging, 98, 100–101, 103, 107, 123

Potential returns, 22, 174

Preferred stock, 23, 182

Preparatory phase, 182–183, 185–186

Pricing amendment, 189

Pro forma statements, 72–73, 78, 155

Products or services section, 156

Property, 113, 121, 123–125, 134, 156, 158, 190

Prospectus, 185–186, 189, 191

Public offering, 170, 173, 181–189, 191–195

Purchase contract, 191

Rapid growth stage, 46, 169, 171, 179

Ratio analysis, 10

Recapture clause, 121

Receivables collection pattern, 63–64

Red herring, 189, 191

Registration statement, 185–186, 188–191

Reliability, 83–84, 97

Restrictions, 20, 22, 35, 83–84, 99, 115, 120, 124–126, 141

Restrictive covenants, 22, 35, 84, 114, 119–120, 126–127

Retail banks, 145

Retained earnings, 3–7, 74, 76–77

Return on investment ratio (ROI), 15–16, 30–31, 51, 89, 106

Return on owner's equity ratio (ROE), 15–16, 27–32, 51

Revolving credit loan, 121

Risk, 13–15, 20–23, 26–27, 32–35, 45–54, 57–58, 59, 61, 84, 86–87, 90–91, 97–104, 108–109, 113–114, 118–121, 124–125, 127, 130–132, 134, 136, 140–145, 147, 151, 157, 169–174, 177, 179, 185, 188–190, 192, 195

Savings & Loan (S&L), 113–114, 116–121, 124–137

Sale-and-leaseback financing (SAL), 124–125

Secondary distribution, 182

Secured credit, 83

Securities and Exchange Commission (SEC), 183, 185–86, 189–191, 195

Security agreement, 99

Security devices, 108

Security interest, 22, 83, 98–99, 103, 123

Seed capital, 171

Selective receivables financing, 101–102

Self-liquidating loans, 90

Service lease, 126

Short-term credit sources, 82

Short-term debt, 23, 81–82, 97–98

Short-term financing, 9, 37–38, 59–60, 71, 76, 81–85, 90, 94, 96–100, 107, 111–112, 114, 123

Simple-interest method, 37–38, 40–41

Small Business Investment Companies (SBICs), 132–133, 135, 169, 177–179

Sources of financial information, 1

Spontaneous liabilities, 74, 77

Spread, 183, 189–190

Start-up firm, 135, 171

Stop-gap funding, 82

Straight loan, 177–178

Subcontractor, 158

Supplier, 17, 59, 68, 84–86, 88, 90, 111, 140, 151

Syndicate, 188–189, 191

Tax-exempt municipal bond, 128

Tax shield, 24–25, 29, 116, 118–119, 127

Term loan, 121, 123, 126–127, 130

Term-loan financing, 121, 123

Terminal warehouse, 109

Times interest earned (TIE), 48–53

Trade credit, 4, 13, 72, 83, 85–86, 88, 90, 97, 111, 143

Transaction loan, 90, 94, 111

True cost, 23, 34–37, 43, 91, 95

Trust receipt, 108–109

U.S. Comptroller of the Currency, 141

U.S. Small Business Administration (SBA), 100, 132–135, 169, 177–179

Underwriter, 183–187, 189–192, 194

Underwriting agreement, 183, 188–191

Underwriting discount, 186, 189

Underwriting, 182–191, 194

Unpaid balance method, 122

Unsecured credit, 82–83

Venture capital companies (VCCs), 169–171, 174–176

Venture capital, 91, 135, 161, 169–177, 179, 181, 192

Venture capital proposal, 175

Venture capitalist, 135, 175–176, 180, 193

Wholesale banks, 145

Working capital loan, 16

Working capital needs, 13, 16–18, 46, 71, 82–83, 91, 95, 97, 130

Notes

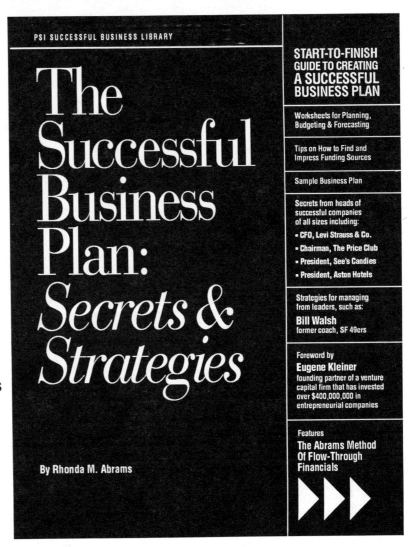

Related Resources from PSI Successful Business Library

Acquiring Outside Capital

Financing Your Small Business
Book

Essential techniques to successfully identify, approach, attract, and manage sources of financing. Shows how to gain the full benefits of debt financing while minimizing its risks. Outlines all types of financing and walks you step by step through the process, from evaluating short-term credit options, through negotiating a long-term loan, to deciding whether to go public.

The Loan Package
Book

Preparatory package for a business loan proposal. Worksheets help analyze cash needs and articulate business focus. Includes sample forms for balance sheets, income statements, projections, and budget reports. Screening sheets rank potential lenders to shorten the time involved in getting the loan.

Venture Capital Proposal Package
Book

Structures a proposal to secure venture capital. Checklists gather material for required sections: market analyses, income projections, financial statements, management team, strategic marketing plan, etc. Gives tips on understanding, finding, and screening potential investors.

Financial Templates
Software for IBM-PC & Macintosh

Software speeds business calculations including those in PSI's workbooks, *The Loan Package, Venture Capital Proposal Package, Negotiating the Purchase or Sale of a Business, The Successful Business Plan: Secrets & Strategies.* Includes 40 financial templates including various projections, statements, ratios, histories, amortizations, and cash flows. *Requires Lotus 1-2-3, Microsoft Excel 2.0 or higher, Supercalc 5, or Lotus compatible spreadsheet and 512 RAM plus hard disk or two floppy drives.*

Managing Employees

A Company Policy and Personnel Workbook
Book

Saves costly consultant or staff hours in creating company personnel policies. Provides model policies on topics such as employee safety, leave of absence, flextime, smoking, substance abuse, sexual harassment, performance improvement, grievance procedure. For each subject, practical and legal ramifications are explained, then a choice of alternate policies presented.

A Company Policy and Personnel Workbook
Software for IBM-PC & compatibles and Macintosh

The policies in *A Company Policy and Personnel Workbook* are on disk so the company's name, specific information, and any desired changes or rewrites can be incorporated using your own word processor to tailor the model policies to suit your company's specific needs before printing out a complete manual for distribution to employees. *Requires a word processor and hard disk and floppy drive.*

People Investment: How to Make Your Hiring Decisions Pay Off for Everyone
Book — available July 1992

Makes the hiring process easier for small business owners. Clarifies the processes of determining personnel needs; establishing job descriptions that satisfy legal requirements; and advertising for, selecting, and keeping good people. Over 40 worksheets help forecast staffing needs, define each job, recruit employees, and train staff.

Managing People: A Practical Guide
Book

Focuses on developing the art of working with people to maximize the productivity and satisfaction of both manager and employees. Discussions, exercises, and self-tests boost skills in communicating, delegating, motivating, developing teams, goal-setting, adapting to change, and coping with stress.

Safety Law Compliance Manual for California Businesses
Book

Now every California employer must have an Injury and Illness Prevention Program that meets the specific requirements of Senate Bill 198. Already thousands of citations have been issued to companies who did not comply with all seven components of the complicated new law. Avoid fines by using this guide to set up a program that will meet Cal/OSHA standards. Includes forms.

Also available — Company Illness and Injury Prevention Program Binder — Pre-organized and ready-to-use with forms, tabs, logs and sample documents. Saves your company time, work, and worry.

Mail Order

Mail Order Legal Manual
Book

For companies that use the mail to market their products or services, as well as for mail order businesses, this book clarifies complex regulations so penalties can be avoided. Gives state-by-state legal requirements, plus information on Federal Trade Commission guidelines and rules covering delivery dates, advertising, sales taxes, unfair trade practices, and consumer protection.

To order these tools, use the convenient order form at the back of this book or call us toll-free at: 800-228-2275

Marketing & Public Relations

Marketing Your Products and Services Successfully
Book

Helps small businesses understand marketing concepts, then plan and follow through with the actions that will result in increased sales. Covers all aspects from identifying the target market, through market research, establishing pricing, creating a marketing plan, evaluating media alternatives, to launching a campaign. Discusses customer maintenance techniques and international marketing.

Customer Profile and Retrieval (CPR)
Software for IBM-PC & compatibles

Stores details of past activities plus future reminders on customers, clients, contacts, vendors, and employees, then gives instant access to that information when needed. "Tickler" fields keep reminders of dates for recontacts. "Type" fields categorize names for sorting as the user defines. "Other data" fields store information such as purchase and credit history, telephone call records, or interests.

Massive storage capabilities. Holds up to 255 lines of comments for each name, plus unlimited time and date stamped notes. Features perpetual calendar, and automatic telephone dialing. Built-in word processing and merge gives the ability to pull in the information already keyed into the fields into form or individual letters. Prints mail labels, rotary file cards, and phone directories. *Requires a hard disk, 640K RAM and 80 column display. (Autodial feature requires modem.)*

Publicity and Public Relations Guide for Businesses
Book

Overview of how to promote a business by using advertising, publicity, and public relations. Especially for business owners and managers who choose to have promotional activities carried out by in-house staff rather than outside specialists. Includes worksheets for a public relations plan, news releases, editorial article, and a communications schedule.

Cost-Effective Market Analysis
Book

Workbook explains how a small business can conduct its own market research. Shows how to set objectives, determine which techniques to use, create a schedule, and then monitor expenses. Encompasses primary research (trade shows, telephone interviews, mail surveys), plus secondary research (using available information in print).

EXECARDS®
Communication Tools

EXECARDS, the original business-to-business message cards, help build and maintain personal business relationships with customers and prospects. Distinctive in size and quality, EXECARDS get through even when other mail is tossed. An effective alternative to telephone tag. Time-saving, EXECARDS come in a variety of handsome styles and messages. Excellent for thanking clients, following up between orders, prospecting, and announcing new products, services, or special offers. *Please call for complete catalog.*

How To Develop & Market Creative Business Ideas
Paperback Book

Step-by-step manual guides the inventor through all stages of new product development. Discusses patenting your invention, trademarks, copyrights, and how to construct your prototype. Gives information on financing, distribution, test marketing, and finding licensees. Plus, lists many useful sources for prototype resources, trade shows, funding, and more.

International Business

Export Now
Book

Prepares a business to enter the export market. Clearly explains the basics, then articulates specific requirements for export licensing, preparation of documents, payment methods, packaging, and shipping. Includes advice on evaluating foreign representatives, planning international marketing strategies, and discovering official U.S. policy for various countries and regions. Lists sources.

To order these tools, use the convenient order form at the back of this book or call us toll-free at: 800-228-2275

1/1/92

Related Resources from PSI Successful Business Library

Business Communications

Proposal Development: How to Respond and Win the Bid
Book

Orchestrates a successful proposal from preliminary planning to clinching the deal. Shows by explanation and example how to: determine what to include; create text, illustrations, tables, exhibits, and appendices; how to format (using either traditional methods or desktop publishing); meet the special requirements of government proposals; set up and follow a schedule.

Write Your Own Business Contracts
Book

Explains the "do's"and "don'ts" of contract writing so any person in business can do the preparatory work in drafting contracts before hiring an attorney for final review. Gives a working knowledge of the various types of business agreements, plus tips on how to prepare for the unexpected.

Complete Book of Business Forms
Book

Over 200 reproducible forms for all types of business needs: personnel, employment, finance, production flow, operations, sales, marketing, order entry, and general administration. Time-saving, uniform, coordinated way to record and locate important business information.

EXECARDS®
Communication Tools

EXECARDS, business-to-business message cards, are an effective vehicle for maintaining personal contacts in this era of rushed, highly-technical communications. A card takes only seconds and a few cents to send, but can memorably tell customers, clients, prospects, or co-workers that their relationship is valued. Many styles and messages to choose from for thanking, acknowledging, inviting, reminding, prospecting, following up, etc. *Please call for complete catalog.*

PlanningTools™
Paper pads, 3-hole punched

Handsome PlanningTools help organize thoughts and record notes, actions, plans, and deadlines, so important information and responsibilities do not get lost or forgotten. Specific PlanningTools organize different needs, such as Calendar Notes, Progress/Activity Record, Project Plan/Record, Week's Priority Planner, Make-A-Month Calendar, and Milestone Chart. *Please call for catalog.*

Customer Profile & Retrieval (CPR)
Software for IBM-PC & compatibles

Easy computer database management program streamlines the process of communicating with clients, customers, vendors, contacts, and employees. While talking to your contact on the phone (or at any time), all notes of past activities and conversations can be viewed instantly, and new notes can be added at that time. *Please see description under "Marketing & Public Relations" section on previous page.*

Business Relocation

Company Relocation Handbook: Making the Right Move
Book

Comprehensive guide to moving a business. Begins with defining objectives for moving and evaluating whether relocating will actually solve more problems than it creates. Worksheets compare prospective locations, using rating scales for physical plant, equipment, personnel, and geographic considerations. Sets up a schedule for dealing with logistics.

Retirement Planning

Retirement & Estate Planning Handbook
Book

Do-it-yourself workbook for setting up a retirement plan that can easily be maintained and followed. Covers establishing net worth, retirement goals, budgets, and a plan for asset acquisition, preservation, and growth. Discusses realistic expectations for Social Security, Medicare, and health care alternatives. Features special sections for business owners.

Career Recordkeeping

Career Builder
Book

This workbook collects all of an individual's career-related data in one place for quick access. From educational details, through work history, health records, reference lists, correspondence awards, passports, etc., to personal insurance policies, real estate, securities and bank accounts, this manual keeps it all organized. Gives tips on successful resumés.

To order these tools, use the convenient order form at the back of this book or call us toll-free at: 800-228-2275

Financial Management

Financial Management Techniques for Small Business
Book

Clearly reveals the essential ingredients of sound financial management in detail. By monitoring trends in your financial activities, you will be able to uncover potential problems before they become crises. You'll understand why you can be making a profit and still not have the cash to meet expenses, and you'll learn the steps to change your business' cash behavior to get more return for your effort.

Risk Analysis: How to Reduce Insurance Costs
Book

Straightforward advice on shopping for insurance, understanding types of coverage, comparing proposals and premium rates. Worksheets help identify and weigh the risks a particular business is likely to face, then determine if any of those might be safely self-insured or eliminated. Request for proposal form helps businesses avoid over-paying for protection.

Debt Collection: Strategies for the Small Business
Book

Practical tips on how to turn receivables into cash. Worksheets and checklists help businesses establish credit policies, track accounts, and flag when it is necessary to bring in a collection agency, attorney, or go to court. This book advises how to deal with disputes, negotiate settlements, win in small claims court, and collect on judgments. Gives examples of telephone collection techniques and collection letters.

Negotiating the Purchase or Sale of a Business
Book

Prepares a business buyer or seller for negotiations that will achieve win-win results. Shows how to determine the real worth of a business, including intangible assets such as "goodwill." Over 36 checklists and worksheets on topics such as tax impact on buyers and sellers, escrow checklist, cash flow projections, evaluating potential buyers, financing options, and many others.

Financial Accounting Guide for Small Business
Book

Makes understanding the economics of business simple. Explains the basic accounting principles that relate to any business. Step-by-step instructions for generating accounting statements and interpreting them, spotting errors, and recognizing warning signs. Discusses how banks and other creditors view financial statements.

Controlling Your Company's Freight Costs
Book

Shows how to increase company profits by trimming freight costs. Provides tips for comparing alternative methods and shippers, then negotiating contracts to receive the most favorable discounts. Tells how to package shipments for safe transport. Discusses freight insurance and dealing with claims for loss or damage. Appendices include directory of U.S. ports, shipper's guide, and sample bill of lading.

Accounting Software Analysis
Book

Presents successful step-by-step procedure for choosing the most appropriate software to handle the accounting for your business. Evaluation forms and worksheets create a custom software "shopping list" to match against features of various products, so facts, not sales hype, can determine the best fit for your company.

Financial Templates
Software for IBM-PC & Macintosh

Calculates and graphs many business "what-if" scenarios and financial reports. Forty financial templates such as income statements, cash flow, and balance sheet comparisons, break-even analyses, product contribution comparisons, market share, net present value, sales model, *pro formas*, loan payment projections, etc. *Requires 512K RAM hard disk or two floppy drives, plus Lotus 1-2-3 or compatible spreadsheet program.*

Related Resources from PSI Successful Business Library

Business Formation and Planning

The Successful Business Plan: Secrets & Strategies
Book

Start-to-finish guide to creating a successful business plan. Includes tips from venture capitalists, bankers, and successful CEOs. Features worksheets for ease in planning and budgeting with the Abrams Method of Flow-Through Financials. Gives a sample business plan, plus specialized help for retailers, service companies, manufacturers, and in-house corporate plans. Also tells how to find funding sources.

Starting and Operating a Business in... series
Book available for each state in the United States, plus District of Columbia

One-stop resource to current federal and state laws and regulations that affect businesses. Clear "human language" explanations of complex issues, plus samples of government forms, and sources for additional help or information. Helps seasoned business owners keep up with changing legislation, and guides new entrepreneurs step-by-step to start and run the business. Includes many checklists and worksheets to organize ideas, create action plans, and project financial scenarios.

Starting and Operating a Business: U.S. Edition
Set of eleven binders

The complete encyclopedia of how to do business in the U.S. Describes laws and regulations for each state, plus Washington, D.C., as well as the federal government. Includes lists of sources of help, plus post cards for requesting materials from government agencies. This set is valuable for businesses with locations or marketing activities in several states, plus franchisors, attorneys, and other consultants.

The Essential Corporation Handbook
Book

This comprehensive reference for small business corporations in all 50 states and Washington, D.C. explains the legal requirements for maintaining a corporation in good standing. Features many sample corporate documents which are annotated by the author to show what to look for and what to look out for. Tells how to avoid personal liability as an officer, director, or shareholder.

Surviving and Prospering in a Business Partnership
Book

From evaluation of potential partners, through the drafting of agreements, to day-to-day management of working relationships, this book helps avoid classic partnership catastrophes. Discusses how to set up the partnership to reduce the financial and emotional consequences of unanticipated disputes, dishonesty, divorce, disability, or death of a partner.

California Corporation Formation Package and Minute Book
Book and software for IBM-PC,

Provides forms required for incorporating and maintaining closely held corporations, including: articles of incorporation; bylaws; stock certificates, stock transfer record sheets, bill of sale agreement; minutes form; plus many others. Addresses questions on fees, timing, notices, regulations, election of directors and other critical factors. Software has minutes, bylaws, and articles of incorporation already for you to edit and customize (using your own word processor).

Franchise Bible: A Comprehensive Guide
Book

Complete guide to franchising for prospective franchisees or for business owners considering franchising their business. Includes actual sample documents, such as a complete offering circular, plus worksheets for evaluating franchise companies, locations, and organizing information before seeing an attorney. This book is helpful for lawyers as well as their clients.

How To Develop & Market Creative Business Ideas
Paperback Book

Step-by-step manual guides the inventor through all stages of new product development. Discusses patenting your invention, trademarks, copyrights, and how to construct your prototype. Gives information on financing, distribution, test marketing, and finding licensees. Plus, lists many useful sources for prototype resources, trade shows, funding, and more.

The Small Business Expert
Software for IBM-PC & compatibles

Generates comprehensive custom checklist of the state and federal laws and regulations based on your type and size of business. Allows comparison of doing business in each of the 50 states. Built-in worksheets create outlines for personnel policies, marketing feasibility studies, and a business plan draft. *Requires 256K RAM and hard disk.*

To order these tools, use the convenient order form at the back of this book or call us toll-free at: 800-228-2275

BOOKS - Please check the edition (binder or paper) of your choice.

TITLE	BINDER	PAPERBACK	QUANTITY	COST
Accounting Software Analysis	☐ $ 39.95			
California Corporation Formation Package and Minute Book	☐ $ 39.95	☐ $ 24.95		
Career Builder	☐ $ 34.95	☐ $ 12.95		
A Company Policy and Personnel Workbook	☐ $ 49.95	☐ $ 29.95		
Company Relocation Handbook	☐ $ 49.95	☐ $ 19.95		
Complete Book of Business Forms	☐ $ 49.95	☐ $ 19.95		
Controlling Your Company's Freight Costs	☐ $ 39.95			
Cost-Effective Market Analysis	☐ $ 39.95			
Debt Collection: Strategies for the Small Business	☐ $ 39.95	☐ $ 17.95		
The Essential Corporation Handbook		☐ $ 19.95		
Export Now	☐ $ 39.95	☐ $ 19.95		
Financial Accounting Guide For Small Business	☐ $ 39.95			
Financial Management Techniques For Small Business	☐ $ 39.95	☐ $ 19.95		
Financing Your Small Business		☐ $ 19.95		
Franchise Bible: A Comprehensive Guide	☐ $ 49.95	☐ $ 19.95		
How to Develop & Market Creative Business Ideas		☐ $ 14.95		
The Loan Package	☐ $ 39.95			
Mail Order Legal Manual	☐ $ 45.00			
Managing People: A Practical Guide	☐ $ 49.95	☐ $ 19.95		
Marketing Your Products and Services Successfully	☐ $ 39.95	☐ $ 18.95		
Negotiating the Purchase or Sale of a Business	☐ $ 39.95	☐ $ 18.95		
People Investment: How to Make Your Hiring Decisions Pay Off for Everyone	☐ $ 49.95	☐ $ 19.95		
Proposal Development: How to Respond and Win the Bid (hardback book)	☐ $ 39.95			
Publicity & Public Relations Guide For Businesses	☐ $ 39.95			
Retirement & Estate Planning Handbook	☐ $ 49.95	☐ $ 19.95		
Risk Analysis: How To Reduce Insurance Costs	☐ $ 39.95	☐ $ 18.95		
Safety Law Compliance Manual for California Businesses		☐ $ 24.95		
Company Illness & Injury Prevention Program Binder	☐ $ 34.95			
Starting and Operating A Business in... BOOK INCLUDES FEDERAL SECTION PLUS ONE STATE SECTION –	☐ $ 29.95	☐ $ 21.95		
SPECIFY STATES:				
STATE SECTION ONLY (BINDER NOT INCLUDED) – SPECIFY STATES:	☐ $ 8.95			
U.S. EDITION (FEDERAL SECTION – 50 STATES AND WASHINGTON, D.C. IN 11-BINDER SET)	☐ $295.00			
Successful Business Plan: Secrets & Strategies	☐ $ 49.95	☐ $ 21.95		
Surviving and Prospering in a Business Partnership	☐ $ 39.95	☐ $ 19.95		
Venture Capital Proposal Package	☐ $ 39.95			
Write Your Own Business Contracts (hardback book)	☐ $ 39.95	☐ $ 19.95		

BOOK TOTAL (Please enter on other side also for grand total)

SOFTWARE - Please check whether you use Macintosh or 5-1/4" or 3-1/2"Disk for IBM-PC & Compatibles

TITLE	5-1/4" IBM Disk	3-1/2" IBM Disk	MAC	PRICE	QUANTITY	COST
California Corporation Formation Package Software	☐	☐		☐ $ 69.95		
★ California Corporation Formation Binderbook & Software	☐	☐		☐ $ 89.95		
Company Policy & Personnel Software	☐	☐	☐	☐ $ 99.95		
★ Company Policy Binderbook & Software	☐	☐	☐	☐ $129.95		
Customer Profile & Retrieval: Professional	☐	☐		☐ $149.95		
Financial Templates	☐	☐	☐	☐ $ 69.95		
The Small Business Expert	☐	☐		☐ $ 59.95		

SOFTWARE TOTAL (Please enter on other side also for grand total)

Please add above totals on other side to complete your order.

PSI Successful Business Library / Tools for Business Success Order Form (see other side also)
Call, Mail or Fax to: PSI Research, 300 North Valley Drive, Grants Pass, OR 97526 USA
Order Phone USA (800) 228-2275   Inquiries and International Orders (503) 479-9464   FAX (503) 476-1479

Sold to: PLEASE GIVE STREET ADDRESS NOT P.O. BOX FOR SHIPPING

Name _____

Title _____

Company _____

Street Address _____

City/State/Zip _____

Daytime Telephone _____

Ship to: (if different)   **PLEASE GIVE STREET ADDRESS NOT P.O. BOX FOR SHIPPING**

Name _____

Title _____

Company _____

Street Address _____

City/State/Zip _____

Daytime Telephone _____

Payment Information:

☐ Check enclosed payable to PSI Research (When you enclose a check, UPS ground shipping is free within the Continental U.S.A.)

Charge - ☐ VISA ☐ MASTERCARD ☐ AMEX ☐ DISCOVER Card Number: _____ Expires _____

Signature: _____   Name on card: _____

EXECARDS

ITEM	PRICE EACH	QUANTITY	COST
EXECARDS Thank You Assortment (12 assorted thank you cards)	$ 12.95		
EXECARDS Recognition Assortment (12 assorted appreciation cards)	$ 12.95		
EXECARDS Marketing Assortment (12 assorted marketing cards)	$ 12.95		
EXECARDS TOTAL (Please enter below also for grand total)			$

Many additional options available. Please request complete catalog.

PLANNING TOOLS

ITEM		NUMBER OF PADS
Calendar Note Pad	☐ **1992**	
	☐ **92/93**	
	☐ **1993**	
☐ **Progress/Activity**		
☐ **Make-A-Month**		
☐ **Milestone Chart**		
☐ **Project Plan/Record**		
☐ **Week's Priority Planner**		
Total number of pads		
Multiply by unit price:	x	
PLANNING TOOLS TOTAL	$	

UNIT PRICE FOR ANY COMBINATION OF PLANNING TOOLS

1-9 pads $3.95 each
10-49 pads $3.49 each
50 or more pads $2.98 each

GRAND TOTAL

BOOK TOTAL (from other side) $ _____

SOFTWARE TOTAL (from other side) $ _____

EXECARDS TOTAL $ _____

PLANNING TOOLS TOTAL $ _____

TOTAL ORDER $ _____

Rush service is available. Please call us for details.

Please send:

_____ **Successful Business Library Book Catalog**

_____ **EXECARDS Catalog**

_____ **PSI Software Information**

FYSB 3/9/92

Use this form to register for advance notification of updates, new books and software releases, plus special customer discounts!

Please answer these questions to let us know how our products are working for you, and what we could do to serve you better.

Title of book or software purchased from us:_____

It is a:
- ☐ Binder book
- ☐ Paperback book
- ☐ Book/software combination
- ☐ Software only

Rate this product's overall quality of information:
- ☐ Excellent
- ☐ Good
- ☐ Fair
- ☐ Poor

Rate the quality of printed materials:
- ☐ Excellent
- ☐ Good
- ☐ Fair
- ☐ Poor

Rate the format:
- ☐ Excellent
- ☐ Good
- ☐ Fair
- ☐ Poor

Did the product provide what you needed?
- ☐ Yes ☐ No

If not, what should be added?_____
_____
_____
_____
_____

This product is:
- ☐ Clear and easy to follow
- ☐ Too complicated
- ☐ Too elementary

Were the worksheets (if any) easy to use?
- ☐ Yes ☐ No ☐ N/A

Should we include:
- ☐ More worksheets
- ☐ Fewer worksheets
- ☐ No worksheets

How do you feel about the price?
- ☐ Lower than expected
- ☐ About right
- ☐ Too expensive

How many employees are in your company?
- ☐ Under 10 employees
- ☐ 10 – 50 employees
- ☐ 51 – 99 employees
- ☐ 100 – 250 employees
- ☐ Over 250 employees

How many people in the city your company is in?
- ☐ 50,000 – 100,000
- ☐ 100,000 – 500,000
- ☐ 500,000 – 1,000,000
- ☐ Over 1,000,000
- ☐ Rural (under 50,000)

What is your type of business?
- ☐ Retail
- ☐ Service
- ☐ Government
- ☐ Manufacturing
- ☐ Distributor
- ☐ Education

What types of products or services do you sell?
_____
_____
_____

What is your position in the company?
(please check one)
- ☐ Owner
- ☐ Administration
- ☐ Sales/marketing
- ☐ Finance
- ☐ Human resources
- ☐ Production
- ☐ Operations
- ☐ Computer/MIS

How did you learn about this product?
- ☐ Recommended by a friend
- ☐ Used in a seminar or class
- ☐ Have used other PSI products
- ☐ Received a mailing
- ☐ Saw in bookstore
- ☐ Saw in library
- ☐ Saw review in:
  - ☐ Newspaper
  - ☐ Magazine
  - ☐ TV/Radio

Where did you buy this product?
- ☐ Catalog
- ☐ Bookstore
- ☐ Office supply
- ☐ Consultant
- ☐ Other_____

Would you purchase other business tools from us?
- ☐ Yes ☐ No

If so, which products interest you?
- ☐ EXECARDS® Communication Tools
- ☐ Books for business
- ☐ Software

Would you recommend this product to a friend?
- ☐ Yes ☐ No

If you'd like us to send associates or friends a catalog, just list names and addresses on back.

Do you use a personal computer for business?
- ☐ Yes ☐ No

If yes, which?
- ☐ IBM/compatible
- ☐ Macintosh

Check all the ways you use computers:
- ☐ Word processing
- ☐ Accounting
- ☐ Spreadsheet
- ☐ Inventory
- ☐ Order processing
- ☐ Design/graphics
- ☐ General data base
- ☐ Customer information
- ☐ Scheduling

May we call you to follow up on your comments?
- ☐ Yes ☐ No

May we add your name to our mailing list?
- ☐ Yes ☐ No

If there is anything you think we should do to improve this product, please describe:_____
_____
_____
_____

Thank you for your patience in answering the above questions.
Just fill in your name and address here, fold (see back) and mail.

Name_____
Title_____
Company_____
Phone_____
Address_____
City/State/Zip_____

PSI Research creates this family of fine products to help you more easily and effectively manage your business activities:
The Oasis Press®   PSI Successful Business Software
PSI Successful Business Library   EXECARDS® Communication Tools

FYSB 2/10/92

416030

If you have friends or associates who might appreciate receiving our catalogs, please list here. Thanks!

Name_____   Name_____

Title_____   Title_____

Company_____   Company_____

Phone_____   Phone_____

Address_____   Address_____

City/State/Zip_____   City/State/Zip_____

FOLD HERE FIRST

‖‖‖

NO POSTAGE
NECESSARY
IF MAILED
IN THE
UNITED STATES

BUSINESS REPLY MAIL

FIRST CLASS MAIL PERMIT NO. 002 MERLIN, OREGON

POSTAGE WILL BE PAID BY ADDRESSEE

PSI Research
PO BOX 1414
Merlin OR 97532-9900

‖‖.‖..‖...‖.‖.‖..‖‖...‖.‖‖.‖.‖.‖..‖‖...‖‖...‖‖.‖

FOLD HERE SECOND, THEN TAPE TOGETHER

✂

Please cut
along this
vertical line,
fold twice,
tape together
and mail.
Thanks!